The Mystery Shopping Cart

ESSAYS ON POETRY AND CULTURE

The Mystery Shopping Cart

ESSAYS ON POETRY AND CULTURE

Anita Lahey

Palimpsest Press
5 King St. Kingsville, Ontario. N9Y 1H9
www.palimpsestpress.ca

Book and cover design by Dawn Kresan. Typeset in Adobe Garamond Pro and Always Regular, and printed offset on Rolland Zephyr Laid at Coach House Printing in Ontario, Canada. Edited by Carmine Starnino.

Palimpsest Press would like to thank the Canada Council for the Arts, and the Ontario Arts Council for their support of our publishing program. We also acknowledge the assistance of the Government of Ontario through the Ontario Book Publishing Tax Credit.

Canada Council for the Arts Conseil des Arts du Canada
ONTARIO ARTS COUNCIL
CONSEIL DES ARTS DE L'ONTARIO
Ontario
Ontario Media Development Corporation

MIX
Paper from responsible sources
FSC® C004071
FSC www.fsc.org
ANCIENT FOREST™ FRIENDLY

LIBRARY AND ARCHIVES CANADA CATALOGUING IN PUBLICATION

Lahey, Anita, author
The mystery shopping cart : essays on poetry and culture / Anita Lahey.

Includes bibliographical references.
ISBN 978-1-926794-17-4 (PBK.)

I. TITLE.

PS8623.A393M97 2013 C814'.6 C2013-905971-7

For my parents, who gave me books and the world they come from

CONTENTS

A little nibble before writing:
Reviews, 2001-2006

Short Reviews and Notes from Arc Poetry Magazine

The real ones are more expensive: Personal Essays

Introduction: On Reading and Reviewing

When I was editing poetry reviews for *Arc Poetry Magazine*, I had my radar tuned for pieces that were mean-spirited, careless or just plain blind. These sins, however, were rare, and when caught (usually) easily addressed. What troubled me more was reticence, reserve—any smokescreen cloaking the reviewer's true feelings. I believe a review should offer some indication of what it was like to be at the author's mercy for however many pages the experience lasted. But more often than I expected, I found myself trying to extract a reluctant confession. What did the reviewer *really* feel about the book? Would he or she recommend it if asked? If our contributor remained coy, we were left with a noncommittal description of poems that "evoke," "provoke," "reflect," or "interlace" this with that—to what effect we were left to guess—the kind of report that gives credit neither to the book's author nor its potential readers; prose as boring to read as it must have been to write.

In a reader's life, turning the cover on a new book is a moment fat with anticipation. I sometimes pause with the book in my lap, cover pressed back for the first time, and look around the room. Something is about to happen and I have no idea what, so I hold off before delving into that first line. If the line is good, and if those that follow are rich, assured and compelling, I'll disappear from the room for a time and sink down into the environment of the book. When I resurface, the room might feel or look different to me. *I* might feel or look different to me.

Where a book will take me, and what will happen along the way, in the text and in me, matters to me. I don't want to know this ahead of time, at least not all of it. But if I read a review of a book before cracking its spine, my main concern is the whether the reviewer found it worthwhile being led along by this author, and why. Honesty doesn't seem like an extraordinary thing to ask, but I've been surprised to learn that it's often the very thing a critic avoids. A reviewer should absolutely do her best to anchor a book in its time and place, and peer inside its craft. But reviews can become crowded with context: how such-and-such a book fits into an author's career, where it lies on the continuum of books attempting a similar thing. Is it new? Is it gutsy? Is it metaphysical, political? Is it genre-busting? As a reader, I accept such information appreciatively. Meanwhile, there are two questions in the back of my mind, rising more and more insistently the longer the review fails to address them: Okay, great, thanks, but did you *like* it? It is any good?

Answering those questions, even asking them, is more controversial than I ever would have imagined before I served as editor of *Arc*. In what has become a years-long CanLit debate—at times an almost vicious undercurrent—two sides have, it appears, become firmly entrenched. One side argues that there is no legitimate defence for wasting precious print real estate explaining why we don't like a book. We have no luxury for negative reviews. It's our job to steer the public toward books we'd encourage them to read. The opposite extreme calls for a concerted effort to root out dreck—to expose and dismiss the books (or, more pointedly, their authors) hogging attention better deserved by others. I sympathize with both of these impulses; indeed they might be diametrically opposed means toward the same end. We have no shortage of books, and few strategies for matching the books that most deserve them with hungry, discerning readers. Prizes catch some, but many fine, even great books slip through with barely a whisper.

I can't help feeling that the parameters of this debate miss something essential: the connection between writer and reader, which gives literature its purpose and its pulse. The reviewer is an appointed messenger between the two, the one who makes the introduction. (It's up to the reader to decide whether he or she wants to hang out with the writer.) In this one task lies our integrity. A colleague once told me that when he reads a poetry review, he doesn't want the reviewer's opinion so much as to learn about the work of the poet in question, some context that will broaden his skills as a reader and his reading landscape. I want this too. But is it too much to ask for both the lesson *and* the frank response? I like what Heather Jessup says on her website about reviews being complex pieces of literature in their own right, built on "listening" to a writer and endeavouring to "find genuine delight in the texture and impulse of the words" and to "write about the experience of reading in a way that is as complex as reading it itself." I agree that our overriding impulse should be generous, curious, open. We must be willing to be drawn into a writer's project even, or especially, when it throws us. But I also think that the piece of literature we call a review should be plain-spoken and forthright about the ways a book did or didn't work on the reviewer, trusting its reader to know that their own experience with a book may be quite different. If the reviewer skips over her own relationship with the book in question, she's engaging in subterfuge. She's abandoning her post. Doesn't the crux of any literary adventure rest on who we are inside the world of that book and what follows us out? I am one reader, and you another. If I can't tell you what I'm truly thinking while sitting at my desk, considering the lingering effects of the volume of poems I just closed, then what is the point of talking to you at all?

In Wisława Szymborska's collection of short essays, *Nonrequired Reading*, she confesses that she attempted to review books, mainly overlooked titles on the newspaper's books received list, and found that she could not: "Basically I am and wish to remain a reader, an amateur, and a fan, unburdened by the weight of ceaseless evaluation." Despite her claim to eschew evaluation—she even threatens to cast displeasure against anyone insisting on calling her pieces "reviews"—Szymborska offers her honest response in these brief, marvellous pieces. It's not evaluation in the grander sense, not by setting an author's work against or beside that of his peers and forerunners, but in the sense of assessing her own encounter with a book. In her summations and reflections, in her ruminations and arguments that sometimes stray far from the work that spurred them, and in her complaints (when they require airing, she doesn't hold back), you glean a book's impact on her. What's more, you are allowed a glimpse of who she is, what kind of reader, what sort of mind she has, what sense of humour and wit, what nature of cares and concerns. When this happens, a review offers a triangular meeting of minds, which is so much more than an impassive description, a gratuitous dismissal or even a recommendation.

I grew up, career-wise, in the world of journalism, mainly as a magazine writer and editor. I was trained by those who kept and promoted the highest standards and ideals for the trade. In that milieu, when something you write is lacking in any way, you are told, sometimes in impressively emphatic ways by multiple editors, all on a single draft of your story. You are pushed constantly to improve: your reporting, your clarity, your brevity, your ability to synthesize facts and judge their relevance, your skill at drawing a reader in. Your entire effort, in fact, is toward the reader. To inform, enlighten, engage. And every such effort is, in part, an exercise in learning where you come up short and how to do better next time. I'm not suggesting our literature would be better off if there were hard-nosed editors breathing down the necks of our reviewers, but I confess I've imagined how such a scenario would play out. How would a reviewer respond if "Huh?" and "English, please!" were scrawled in red all over her piece and all her obfuscating literary jargon unceremoniously crossed out? How would she fill the gaps? What would she say? Obviously, expectations for news reporting are different than those for poetry, for good reason: poets take facts and observations and assemble them for different purposes than journalists do, and those who review such works are rightly mindful of that. But our consideration for that creative intent can clam us up or lead us into an exclusive, poet-to-poet conversation that entirely disregards the reader. If you've read *Journey with No Maps*, Sandra Djwa's biography of P.K. Page, you know that the violinist Isaac Stern's declaration that communication with his audience was the artist's "main task" once angered Page enough to cause her to throw a glass of red wine over her shoulder and out the window. Well, I stand in awe of Page the poet. But on the question of the importance of communicating with people when we write—no matter what we are writing—I'm with Stern.

The reviews collected here are all on collections of poetry (save one collection of prose written by a poet), and originally appeared in *Arc*, *The Malahat Review* or *Canadian Notes & Queries*. When piecing them together, I noticed for the first time that every review I've written over twelve years, save one, has been on a collection by a woman. I was surprised, given the general dearth of reviews on work by women and the persistent shortage of female reviewers, an issue that has been raised in the U.S. and in Canada, here by the recently formed CWILA, Canadian Women in the Literary Arts. My focus on women poets has not been intentional: I'm not that organized. Nor do I read primarily female poets; some of my favourite authors are men. But it's clearly the work of women I've most often been compelled to analyze, to mull in a broader context and to discuss publicly. Has there been something subconscious at play here? An instinctive attempt to help even the field? Or—this is a little more troubling—a sense that I have permission to engage with fellow women writers in this way, whereas I'd be reticent to dissect and "judge" a collection by a man? I don't know for sure, but these personal stats give me pause.

Regardless of who has written it—first-time author, veteran, icon—when reading a collection for review, I note my thoughts and reactions in the margins so that I can track and revisit my evolving response. I immerse myself in the voice and world of the book and, as best I can, figure out what the author is up to. I try to look at previous collections if I'm unfamiliar with the writer, as well as read past reviews. I seek those idiosyncrasies that make every book and every newly encountered writer's voice uncharted territory. Never far from my mind is the possibility that I am missing the boat. The late poet Diana Brebner, a mentor and friend whose voice informs this collection, once wrote a biting response, in poetic form, to a reviewer who had done exactly that with her work. The poem, which appears in *The Ishtar Gate* (McGill-Queen's University Press, 2005), is called "For the Poet Who Told Me to Think Less and Feel More", and it begins with the couplet: "I will not assume that you/ are an expert about feeling." The implication: that the reviewer had based his or her reading of Diana's work on assumptions about her, the poet. Assumptions (and presumptions) have a way of creeping in; I try to keep my radar tuned. I hold up as a standard the work of critics I deeply admire, such as Joan Acocella, whose every piece adheres to Bert Archer's checklist for great reviewing, a list he reveals in a discussion with Zsuzsi Gartner in *The Malahat Review*'s special issue on the topic (issue 144, fall 2003). Archer tells Gartner to trust those reviewers who "on a not-so-irregular basis give you insight, not only into the book in question, but into the world, too." (He also says to trust reviewers who "who dislike more than they like," which disqualifies me!) Lastly, I pay attention to what is happening to me as I read. [1]

As a reviewer, my word on a book is not and should not be the only or final word. Yet we are all familiar with the problem of dwindling book pages in the media. If there aren't enough venues for criticism to allow other perspectives on a particular book to balance or counter or go deeper than mine, then that is what we must strive to fix. Likewise, a reviewer should not be so self-important as to think he should be organizing our entire literature into what matters and what doesn't. Nor should he believe an author's career rides on his opinion. An author's ego may be a fierce and flimsy thing, but it's not the reviewer's job to mollify or tame it. As a writer, I know that when I put my work in the world, I'm letting it go: to be taken up, interpreted, misinterpreted, enjoyed, disdained or ignored as the case may be. If a reviewer doesn't "get it," that may be my own fault. If a reviewer is not caught by my subject, or finds my treatment of it clumsy, shallow or been-there-done-that, I want to be told. Sometimes a reviewer's bluntness is a relief. This is not to condone nastiness or attacks disguised as reviews. We should never be blasé regarding someone's heartfelt endeavour: humility and common sense demand basic awareness of the difficulty inherent in creating anything. But here's the thing: I want to be challenged. By readers, by editors, by reviewers—by people who give a damn about what I've written and what I may be capable of writing and who make no bones about letting me know.

The type of tempered offerings that used to frustrate me while editing *Arc*—reviews recast as opinion-free zones—offer an insult deeper than any take-down. They presume a fragility so pervasive as to overwhelm the artistic calling itself. Does the impulse to coddle or be coddled belong in a mature, vibrant, ambitious literary culture?

You will find here, in addition to the essays and reviews on poetry: an outsider's measure of the mood in Poland the summer after Pope John Paul II died; odes to a few people I love and have loved (a remarkable poet, an embattled redhead, a cash register repairman); discussions with writers about how to turn a one-two punch into a poem, why so many poets go ga-ga in art galleries and whether it's possible to be too happy; excerpts from my editorial notes during seven years at *Arc*; and a spirited defence of the eulogy as a literary form, its strange allure and its potency.

Somehow, the essence of all this work, and the thinking and research behind it, is intertwined. I notice a quest for understanding and a willingness to be caught by a subject, by a problem, by a poet, run through them all. Journalism begets poetry begets the reading (and reviewing) of poetry by others begets intense, exploratory discussions with fellow writers. What is going on here, in this thing we call life? And why is it all so fascinating?

By nature I'm wary of judgment. I'm also constantly casting it; on politicians, neighbours, strangers in the news and, clearly, on the work of my fellow writers. But all writing is predicated on judgment calls: only so many pieces can be written. Only so much can be said.

These pieces, whatever weaknesses they may exhibit, were all built on the solid foundation of something that, at the moment of writing, I found mattered enough to me to be put into words. Some feel odd to reread. I suspect at least a handful, chiefly among the reviews, might be quite different were I to write them today. Would the impetus even be the same? Have I been guilty, at times, of the very hedging I complain about here? I'm certainly not immune to resorting to that trusty reviewer boilerplate: evoke, reflect, provoke. The italicized notes following most of these articles are perspectives I offer now, looking back.

I was first offered the chance to review a poetry collection by John Barton, then co-editor of *Arc*, in 2000. I took home a few slim volumes to consider and felt myself drawn to Shawna Lemay's *All the God-Sized Fruit*, which delves into art history. I'd had my first poem published the previous year, a piece on a photograph by André Kertèsz, and Lemay was poking about in a world that intrigued me. That didn't mean I would like the book. In fact, it might have made me a more demanding reader than one with no inherent interest in the subject. I confessed to a colleague that I was worried about the task of reviewing: what right did I have to say what I thought? I was no scholar; there were so many famous, canonized poets whose work I'd barely dipped into; there were contexts or references I might miss. She said, yes, maybe. But you're a reader. You care.

END NOTES

[1] A friend asks whether this very attention might alter the experiment: would the result be different were I just reading for the sake of reading, rather than for the purpose of reviewing? My answer: I don't know. But it's a question all reviewers would do well to keep in mind.

Diana and the Mystery Shopping Cart

There was a shopping cart on our front lawn. Not just on it, but perfectly centered, as though it had been placed very carefully. It faced north.

It was a weekday morning in spring. Tulips bloomed in front of our house. But as I passed through the living room, my eyes had caught something through the window that was definitely not a flower.

My first thought was: *What a coincidence.* I had, the previous week, written a poem about a shopping cart called "The Silver Buggy Handbook." I was proud. Diana Brebner, my writing teacher—and never one to be careless with praise—had written on it: "Definitely for the 'to send for publication' file."

I have to call her and tell her about this, I thought. *A shopping cart on my front lawn! She won't believe it.* But I just stood there, staring. The cart was mangled and twisted. And yet it gleamed. I felt that some higher power was at play.

It would not be an exaggeration to say I'd been feeling that way since meeting Diana five months before, when she allowed me into her already-full creative-writing workshop. "Something about the sound of my voice" had told her she should, even though I'd called only to find out just how much the course would focus on poetry. I was not a poet, I'd told her; I wanted to study fiction. Diana had said, in a tone I would get to know well, "Let's just see what happens."

I had chosen Diana's course from three possible workshops after seeking out the author-teachers' books in the library and deciding that hers were the most intriguing and most polished. I based this on instinct more than anything, as I didn't yet know how to read poetry, particularly not anything as crafted, subtle and powerful as Diana's. Little did I know that library visit would bring me into the path of a formidable and generous mentor and friend who would, with an amazingly light touch, irrevocably shift my intentions as a writer.

Two weeks of studying with Diana and I suddenly remembered all those wee hours I'd spent as an adolescent, compulsively writing wretched verse in my dark, messy, suburban bedroom. All at once I was stealing space in my workdays to develop this skill that soon mattered more to me than anything I'd attempted to master before. By the time I stood facing the shopping cart I knew, without a doubt, that a poet lurked inside of me.

My first piece of "homework" emerged from me in the form of a rough twelve-line poem called "The Black Cat Swimming Hole", black cats being the assigned topic. It was more like a messy list than a poem. In her methodic script, Diana wrote some encouraging and pointed comments in the margins. But she clearly realized more dramatic measures were called for. She also *retyped* the poem—keeping most of the language intact—in the bottom, right-hand corner of the page. This "new" poem had proper punctuation and a shape in the form of four three-line stanzas. Next to it, she had written, "My revised version. What do you think?"

What I thought was, wow. She hadn't changed the meaning of my words. She'd given that meaning somewhere to be, a place to live. Something clicked. Poetry is no accident, I realized. It's no game, no stream-of-consciousness la-di-da. It's a job, and girl, you've got a lot to learn.

Soon I was writing poems about topics of my own choosing: billboards, clotheslines and, well, shopping carts. I was mining my obsessions, learning that such rigorous "play" was not only allowed but called for. With Diana's skillful guidance I began to understand the thrill of labouring over language, line breaks, sound and meaning. I also began to recognize the not-so-subtle clues offered when, in Diana's opinion, a piece showed little promise: "I wouldn't tinker with this one," she'd say. "You just take what you learned from it and move on." I resisted, more than once, the urge to ask her what I ought to have learned, a timidity I now regret.

For Diana did not just teach the craft. She tried, in her oh-so-Diana way, to teach courage. She gave us glue sticks and scissors and ordered us to cut up magazines and make collages. This sounded like a benign activity. In Diana's class, however, collage-making was "dangerous." She warned us that people would frighten themselves by the images they'd snip out distractedly or the words they would place next to each other. This wasn't soft, feel-good creativity. Diana's plan was to scare the good writing out of us—the writing that doesn't shrink from pain, but writes through it, elevates it to something awful and beautiful.

Above all Diana championed precision and commitment. It was not that poetry was a higher calling but that accepting any calling demands full and careful attention. I think of her haunting and resonant Mary Pratt poems and her many other powerful "painting" poems. She did not become ponderous over a piece of art or write about how it made her feel. She would "read" the painting painstakingly, like a map, learning its landmarks, shapes, colours and codes, until she sensed the meaning of those elements, not just inside the painting but inside her. "You can explore," she told me, "a whole wilderness inside a sculpture or a painting or a piece of music. It's an adventure for the courageous and the somewhat foolhardy."

She said to me once, "I don't do easy. I only do difficult." And then she laughed. "I would make writing a poem about my teapot something complex and difficult. I have. I do." There was no pretentiousness in this. Diana was being who she was, consistently, to the gritty core. Her work ethic and compulsion to explore were not just some poetic creed; they framed her life.

One day, I spent the afternoon in the hospital with her. She hadn't eaten much recently but was determined to try. The menu items, fetched by me and another friend, included social teas, non-salted crackers, yogurt, juice and Jell-o. Most faced unceremonious rejection. For Diana, the process mattered: the laying-out of the options on the tray in a presentable fashion. The tasting, the testing, the assessment. When her doctor arrived late in the day, Diana, by then exhausted, described with a burst of energy the "experimenting" we'd done, what a success the day had been.

In illness, success often meant getting what she needed from a well-meaning but inept helper. Even these dances were orchestrated in that particular, often unsettling, "Diana" way. I was with her at her apartment one night. She was hungry, decided she could stomach a hard-boiled egg. I put one on to boil but soon realized I hadn't paid attention to the time. I was loath to admit this to her but I did. "Bring it to me," she said. "I'll do the Diana test."

I brought her the egg. "What are you going to do?" I asked, my voice awe-tinged, wondering how she could tell a hard-boiled egg from a soft one. She shook the egg lightly, next to her ear. She looked at it. Then she shrugged, cracked the egg on the bowl that contained her rice and peeled it. She ate voraciously. A good hour passed before it sunk in that the only "trick" in this scenario had been a very hungry Diana tricking *me* into giving *her* the egg, hard-boiled or not. Such is the spell she'd cast on me.

I had little inkling of her mischievous side when I stood in my living room window, considering the shopping cart, struck by its meticulous placing, which should have been my first clue. The phone rang and it was, of all people, Diana. "I thought I'd better call," she started. I had missed her class the night before and figured she was calling to fill me in. I interrupted her.

"You won't believe what I found on my front lawn."

"Oh, yes," she said, flatly—deliberately so, I would realize later. But for now I babbled: about the coincidence and who could have put it there and geez, what a coincidence, you know? Ten minutes after our conversation, I started to think it had been odd, her tone, how little she'd said … I called her back.

"Anita," she said, with some relief. "I was wondering when you would clue in." After the previous night's class, the group had stumbled on this shopping cart in a lot. Diana's reaction: "We have to bring it to Anita." When her students became nervous, she instructed them, "Anyone asks what we're doing, just say, without hesitation, 'We're artists.'"

We're artists. This was license to be, to live. On the phone that morning, after laughing at me, a springy squeak of a laugh that I miss terribly, she said, "You see? Things happen when you write poetry."

Yes, Diana, I see. They do. You try to live your life the way you hope to write: with deliberation, wonder, and guts. You write and live with a persistent voice in a cranny of your brain asking, "Is that the word you want? Is that the best choice?" Nothing arbitrary. Nothing easy. Everything—good and bad, mangled and gleaming—a gift.

'Her time on Earth':

Three Canadian Poets and Their Legacies

Dazzling Exile: The Poetry of Dorothy Roberts

When Dorothy Roberts was twenty-four years old, recently married and living in Storrs, Connecticut, she often received cheerful, newsy letters from her father, the poet, journalist and novelist Theodore Goodridge Roberts, back in Fredericton, New Brunswick. One exuberant missive, handwritten on mustard-yellow *Acadie* letterhead and dated April 17, 1930—two days after the release of the first issue of *Acadie*, the literary journal T.G.R. had just founded—reads, in part:

> Dearest Dorkie – I have your "Northern Spring" set up in the prose form; & I think it gets across that way – but the other form is very interesting too.
>
> Your two poems in No. 1 – surely you have them by now!, & if not, let me know, please – are the best things in the mag. Have you any more of these?
> … I am receiving telegrams of congratulation! – & yesterday a contribution by air mail from Vancouver.
> … Have you gone to NY for Easter? We should have sent Easter cards – but thought you would be in New York.
>
> The magazine is getting a toe-hold; & if the Government & so on come across with advertising, all will be well – & I'll be paying contributors before we know it… Hope you like No. 1. It has its bright spots, I think.
>
> Ever your loving Dad.

Note the chattiness, the dashes and ampersands, how email-like the letter is in its lack of formality. When I first read Roberts' letters in the fall of 2006, in a cluttered reading room at the University of New Brunswick Archives in Fredericton, I was struck. Except for the mention of Easter (and thus the brief allusion to Dorothy's mother, Frances Seymour Allen), the letter seems more like one written to a colleague or friend whose professional opinion is prized rather than one from father to daughter. This was no mere interlude, either. In a letter dated 1944, fourteen years later, T.G.R. wrote: "Dearest Dorkie: I liked the sample chapter of the book very much. Very! Good work. Good writing. Keep it up. I have made three starts on novels in the past year of about 15000 words each. The first was a near miss with Collier's & other places, and I struck [?] it away. The second was a dud ..." And so on.

Consider further that Charles G.D. Roberts, the so-called father of Canadian poetry, was Roberts' uncle. She once remarked that he warmly encouraged the writing of poetry by the younger generation. Bliss Carman was her father's and uncle's cousin. Her brother Goodridge, meanwhile, became a famous painter and corresponded with his sister about their respective creative endeavours, signing off each letter as "Good." In 1959, after receiving her recent chapbook, *In Star and Stalk*, he wrote to her, "Your new collection is very impressive ... It is fine to see a strong development when so many become repetitive or frantically seek to pull themselves up by the boot-straps. I often feel depressed about my own work and wonder if I will in the end have failed dismally to do what I still feel I have it in me to accomplish ... "

Clearly nothing less than a lively, cultural conversation encompassed "Dear Dorkie" in childhood and beyond.

But one might also imagine Roberts crowded by these male cultural animals, her kin. She later claimed her family was neither boon nor hindrance to her as a poet: they did not influence her so much as did the countryside surrounding Fredericton, the landscape of her childhood. Still, I wonder. On that same trip to New Brunswick in 2006, I found a copy of *Twice to Flame*, Roberts' first full collection of poetry, in a used bookstore in Moncton, signed, incidentally, "To Mother on her birthday with love from Dorkie, May 1, 1961." It cost me twenty dollars. The front of the dust jacket bears a gaudy, yellow-and-red flame motif in script lettering; on its back is a generous endorsement from Northrop Frye that concludes, "… everything she meets is shaped into a poem of interest and distinction." Yet the bio only declares her "a sister of Goodridge Roberts and a daughter of Theodore Goodridge Roberts." Nothing about her publication credits in such prestigious journals as *Hudson Review* and *Yale Review* or, in Canada, in *The Fiddlehead*, *Queen's Quarterly* and *Canadian Forum*. Roberts' years south of the border may have left her so little-known in Canada that her publisher felt highlighting the family connection was prudent. But there is also the suggestion of a shadow here; be that of a familial literary legacy, that of the male over the female, or some murky combination of the two.

Roberts was born in Fredericton on July 6, 1906. Her father had worked as a war correspondent and lived in New York, Cuba and Newfoundland. He would serve overseas in WWI, during which time his young family would find lodgings in England. They also resided in France and Toronto before settling back in Fredericton, first for two years on a farm, then in town. For a Maritime girl, Roberts enjoyed a somewhat cosmopolitan upbringing. She read poetry avidly as a teen, studied at UNB, reported for the Fredericton *Daily Mail* as a young woman, and enrolled at Connecticut State College in her twenties. There she met August R. Leisner, a Yale English scholar whom she would marry in 1929 and who, while completing his Ph.D. in Toronto during the Depression, would embark on a lifelong project: a literary criticism of the work of her uncle, Charles G.D.

In 1927, before moving to Connecticut, Roberts launched her own literary career with the publication of the chapbook *Songs for Swift Feet* under the name Gostwick Roberts. By the time she died in 1993 in State College, Pennsylvania, where she had lived since 1945, Roberts had published seven collections of poetry. Her last collection, *In the Flight of Stars*, was published by Goose Lane just two years prior to her death and described by Rhea Tregebov in the *University of Toronto Quarterly* as "a work of extraordinary lucidity and intelligence." Her obituary, printed in the *New York Times*, described her as a poet whose work was widely anthologized in Canada and the United States. Nonetheless, by this point she was fading from view—not that she had ever been front-and-centre. In *Canadian Writers, 1920-1959, Second Series*, published a few years before her death, Louis K. MacKendrick of the University of Windsor writes: "Roberts's poetry, not great in volume, has been generally overlooked except for rare but generous reviews ..." He describes the "muscular weight" of her verbs, her "subtle sound values" and a poetry of "singular delicacy and sensuousness" which is "not complex or ambiguous but thoughtful and objective. It is formal without being reserved, austere or inaccessible[.]" In 1994, in the spring following Roberts' death, Tregebov, one of a handful of Canadians to have ever reviewed her work, wrote a brief tribute in *Canadian Literature*. She laments that Roberts was: "An expatriate who never was reconciled to exile, and a poet whose great gifts were in large part ignored by her compatriots." She describes the overriding quality of Roberts' poetry simply as "grace," and lauds her "insight into the human condition" as well as her "technical mastery of prosody, syntax, and image."

What can I say? I'm with Tregebov and MacKendrick. Reading Roberts' robust and unflinching verse has been a revelation and a treat. I can't help wondering why Roberts has been left out of the club. Was it her exile? Her more-famous (male) relatives? Her two-decade break from writing? Or was it her unapologetic attention to the basics of the human condition, as opposed to fashionable issues, in her work? She was no crusader for social justice, like, say, her contemporary Dorothy Livesay, three years her junior and also a contributor to T.G.R.'s *Acadie*, who went on to become a core part of our twentieth-century canon. Or perhaps it was due to that formal voice that never really left her writing, not even in her last collection, in which she did away with punctuation almost entirely but still maintained a parlour-proper syntax and arched tone. My call to revisit Roberts is not rooted in a nostalgia for so-called "traditional" poetics. Instead, I find myself, and not for the first time, disappointed in the dogmatic nature of the literary "trend," especially since it has left us with so little of Roberts' work to carry forward.

The two poems that appeared in the first issue of *Acadie* and earned her father's high praise do not appear in Roberts' later published volumes. Written in her early twenties, they retain a studied formalism she would later veer away from, including the convention of the first cap on each line. Indeed, you can already feel her having mastered this style of poetry and wanting out. She's done away with the Romantic sensibilities espoused by older poets such as her uncle Charles. The poems contain a restlessness and cynicism and hint at a preoccupation with the strangeness of consciousness that deepened as Roberts aged and came to dominate the psychology of her poems. The mature voice, on its way to being, pokes through the lines. The first, printed alongside E.J. Pratt's "Tatterhead," was called "Monotony":

> With glare of sun, or drift of rain, or blow
> Of high blue wind, or flurry of wet snow,
> The days pass differently, with clouded sky.
> Clear sky, or frost or thaw or haze; but I
> Walk through them with no change from day to day;
> Walk at the same pace, facing the same way.
>
> Perhaps some time I'll rise a little late,
> Dawdle in dressing, sip my tea, and wait,
> Thinking strange things above my empty plate;
> Then, having talked awhile, I'll sally forth.
> Because my way lies south, I'll travel north;
> And travel far, and not come home again
> Till I am scorched by sun and drenched with rain.

Though a little more naïve and hampered by weak phrases such as "flurry of wet snow", this poem, with its gravity and its composure, makes me think of the work of poets such as Seamus Heaney, his solidity of style combined with astute psychological mining. The second *Acadie* poem is a darker, more extreme take on the need for escape. Seemingly brooding along in a state of ho-hum and gloomy inevitability, it descends swiftly, in the final half of the final line, into an irrevocable bleakness.

I Am Going Alone

I am going somewhere, where I do not know;
Not to my Love's house to tap on her window;
Not to my friend's house to knock at his door,
But somewhere where I've never been before.
I am going somewhere, why I do not know;
Not because my Love wishes me to go;
Not because my friend will bear me company,
Tell his thoughts and laugh and listen to me.
I am going alone, perhaps because of this—
There was left no sweet from my Love's last kiss;
There was nothing new left for me to hear
In all my friend could say; and I did not care.

Surprise! The journey and the potential transformation it might promise, hinted at in the early lines, vanishes. For without care there is nothing, nothing that matters. I can't help thinking, on the one hand: what a grim poem for a twenty-four-year-old to write; but, on the other: what an apt poem for a twenty-four-year-old to write! Especially a woman recently married. Both poems rhyme straightforwardly throughout, then end on a subtle off-rhyme, a "take that" to expectation. Both are angsty and youthful, and I find it interesting to imagine her father, that romantic adventure-writer, enjoying them and publishing them for all his literary cronies to see.

A couple months later, the lighthearted "To Be My Love" appeared in *Acadie.* Playfulness for Roberts is apparently difficult to espouse without resorting to silly lines like "your hair's misty mesh," but I like the mythic reach of this poem, and its bold speaker who will settle for no less than supernatural accomplishment in her lover: "You must have drawn the flood/ Of sea into your blood./ And caught the thrush's note/ Into your throat." One can't help but feel the entire bird in the throat—song, wing and claw. This is what we mean by words that come alive. The narrator is after an earthly god, but one who will submit to her desire: "You must be kissed—/ O all your face and flesh." There was nothing wishy-washy or prudish in Roberts.

But then she stopped writing poems for a good two decades, raising two children and selling magazine stories to augment the family income. Poetry returned, as she describes in the foreword to her 1976 collection *The Self of Loss*, as a "terrible need" that grew "accompanied by nightmares." With it came an intense awareness of her exile from Canada. In the foreword to *Self* she writes, "Fredericton was a town carefully outlined with what you did and did not do according to your allotted role. But outside it, surrounding, was a countryside of as much freedom as the decorum of our own upbringing would allow ... What I foraged of this countryside, in any season, was all emotional, never destructive, only the contacts that our language preserved for me in ways sensuous and relieving, some spatial music of words to go along with the action. So began my impulse to poems."

The return of that impulse led to poems such as "Dazzle," the title piece of her second chapbook, published in 1957. "Dazzle" provides a good example of how Roberts draws the natural world into her poems. Roberts does not gaze upon "nature" so much as enter its point of meeting with us, where all the questions regarding its effect on us, and ours on nature's, reside. Often this is a tense place to be. "Dazzle" starts out rather playful: "Light looks from the dazzled leaf,/ Stares like a small sun,/ Glitters, and in the breeze/ Leaps to another leaf."

She grants to light the quality of mischief. The leaf and other objects—car windshield, grass blade, squirrel, ball, the "kindled pebble under the sprinkler"—are the poems' supporting cast, objects the light toys with in order to bring us under its spell. Here we see the beginning of a thematic thrust that Roberts will pursue throughout the rest of her writing days: the forms of the things around us and how, paradoxically and mysteriously, they give us shape. In the later poem "Tentacles" she asks how, unless by such a basic act as grasping an apple, we can grasp our own reality: "Without the hard heavy apples with their rings of rot,/ Without the wood from the sawhorse falling remote/ How shall we know that our hands are the hard tentacles of our thought?"

There's a morality in this, in literally touching and accepting that which surrounds us and defines our place. Another poem from *Dazzle*, "Cold," arguably Roberts' most successful poem (and one of her few, along with "Dazzle" and the wonderful "Verandah Spinsters," that has been anthologized in this country), takes this moral to its extreme. This is a winter survival poem that contains no mention of snow, no white-washed landscape. Instead, we find the winter of the mind, the self. Here it is, in full:

My grandparents lived to a great age in the cold—
O cruel preservative, the hard day beginning
With night and zero and the firewood
Numbing the fingers. God could have been in the flame
Responsive among the birch sticks, roaring
Up through the comforting pipes, and served all day
From the frosted woodpile, the continuing flame
As the sun almost let go of the bitter world.

But for them He stayed in the cold,
In the outer absolutes of cold among the fiery orbits,
And gave them the white breath and the blood pumping
Through hard activity stringing out the muscles

Into great age. They lived in cold
And were seasoned by it and preached it
And knew that it blazed
In the burning bush of antiquity
With starry flowers.

Here we witness that strange twist in human nature: how we embrace hardship and turn it, "the white breath and the blood pumping," into pride, into spiritual substance. This is a thoroughly original winter poem in a nation blanketed by them.

Another of my favourites, "Early Morning," appears in *Twice to Flame.* Like "Dazzle," this poem enacts a working of light through objects but finds a universality more grounded in a personal philosophy of survival, as in "Cold." Though it has not achieved the anthological afterlife of "Dazzle" or "Cold," this poem makes a metaphysical leap that is both memorable and earned, and that serves as almost a credo of Roberts' unique preoccupation: "I live in these hard things and the way they look,/ I house my uncertain self in the star and the stalk."

What I like about Roberts is that she writes about this uncertainty, this mucky human condition, without becoming mucky in the use of her craft, nor emotionally mucky. Roberts is not stoic but dresses her poems in a sheen of stoicism: simple, direct language and an easy rhythm, an even tone and a measured pace, which allows them to contain the unwieldy. Here is an example from the poem "Float," which first appeared in *Hudson Review* and later in *The Self of Loss*:

Water goes in and out of the reed's cell,
in and out of the gill
but the boat is that form that floats.

Watertight, caulked it coerces the water to be with it—
"Always when I am alive you are with me,

> yet enter not and the lapping is continual."
> This is the most graceful elaboration of the communion,
> oars dip and the ripples of progress circle about it
> and the furrow behind is a form.

Roberts moves from one form to its creation of another—from the boat to its wake—an event she reenacts plainly. Before the boat so casually makes the wake, though, the bizarre quotation in the heart of the poem has already made the boat so much more than a boat. The poem contains the revelation as the water contains the boat: wholly and gently.

Roberts wrote on war, on suburban development, on car culture—both big and workaday issues. She wrote several long series, one a remarkably composed reconstruction of her husband's death called "The Great Activity of Death." But her main preoccupation was form, what Carrie MacMillan of Mount Alison University described in a review of *The Self of Loss* in the *Atlantic Provinces Book Review* in 1977 as "an increasingly familiar and characteristic imaginative world collected, shaped and ordered in patterns of landscape and objects." Roberts' most recurrent images—apple, tree, river, farm, house, stars, woods, island, boat—are clearly shaped, ordinary objects and places that assure us of our reality, our physicality, and our limitations. Roberts used them to ground the un-groundable and shape the un-shapeable.

In her final book, *In the Flight of Stars*, published in her ninety-first year, she had begun to let go of convention, replacing commas and dashes with spaces. The result: poems that feel as though they have done away with the line between the self and the things surrounding the self, a line Roberts had walked treacherously for so many years. But these late poems are so tenuous, so airy, that they seem to fall out of your grasp the moment you turn away, a phenomenon the American poet and critic Mary Kinzie described in a review of *In the Flight* in *The American Poetry Review* as an unusual "confluence of ostensible plainness with some quality of obscurity."

She speculated that Roberts might actually have been composing from "the other side of her time on earth."

I thought about this while listening to a 1980 recording of Roberts reading poems from *The Self* aloud. She was seventy-four, and her voice was a shock. She did not read in the declarative voice her work embodies; instead she wavered through an almost incantatory recitation, rising along each line, then unceremoniously falling off its edge. I imagine that Roberts, at the time of this recording, was already writing the poems that would make up her final collection. Perhaps she was already walking toward that edge, away from the forms of the things—and the poems—in which she had housed her "uncertain self" for so long.

Back in 1930, when Roberts still went by the pen-name Gostwick and her father's *Acadie* still held promise (it would not survive the year), seven of her poems were included in the anthology *Modern Canadian Poetry*, edited by Nathanial A. Benson. That year, Benson wrote to T.G.R.: "Will you tell Gostwick, or 'Dork' as CGD calls her, that after a year's voyaging my anthology of younger Canadian poets has at last been accepted for publication this autumn by Graphic Press of Ottawa. The anthology contains 20 poets, none over 35 years of age I believe, stretching from Halifax to Nanaimo ... Gostwick and Charlie Bruce ably represent the Maritimes with 14 poems of the 120 odd therein."

Bruce and Roberts, born in the same year, were emerging into the literary limelight in tandem. But it would be Bruce, with his saltier Maritime verse, who went on to earn a more lasting recognition, much like other poets of their generation. Whatever chance or critical justification lies behind this, Roberts' finest work deserves notice. She belongs to that age when modernism meant a lively engagement between the old and the new, a disciplined rebellion that Louis Dudeck, quoted in *Canadian Poetry II*, once described as necessary: "To separate the two is to destroy the balance and the tension of high acrobatics: to produce barbarism on the one hand and sterile formalism on the other." Roberts fell into neither trap. Her poetry, with its technical aplomb, emotional grace and piercing directness, achieved heights worthy of our attention. In forgetting this, we make complete and permanent the exile she fought so fiercely and lose the ideas that she so elegantly cast into tangible shape, those precise "hard tentacles of thought."

BOOKS BY DOROTHY ROBERTS

Songs for Swift Feet, as Gostwick Roberts (Toronto: Ryerson, 1927)
Dazzle (Toronto: Ryerson, 1957)
In Star and Stalk (Toronto: Emblem Books, 1959)
Twice to Flame (Toronto: Ryerson, 1961)
Extended (Fredericton: Fiddlehead Poetry Books, 1967)
The Self of Loss: New and Selected Poems (Fredericton: Fiddlehead Poetry Books, 1976)
In the Flight of Stars (Fredericton: Goose Lane, 1991)

OTHER SOURCES

A poetry reading [sound recording]. Dorothy Roberts. Toronto: League of Canadian Poets, 1980.
Conway, Abbot and Stenbaek-Lafon, Marianne eds. *Canadian Poetry II (McGill Module Poetry)*, Montreal: McGill University Press, 1978.
Canadian Writers, 1920-1959, Second Series, Dictionary of Literary Biography, "Dorothy Roberts." (Detroit: Gale, 1989)
"Dorothy Roberts 1906-1993" by Rhea Tregebov. *Canadian Literature*,

Number 140 (Spring 1994). 156-157.
"Fiddlehead Poetry" by Carrie MacMillan. *The Atlantic Provinces Book Review* (1977-1978?).
"Meaning in Place: A Moral Essay" by Mary Kinzie. *The American Poetry Review* 21.1 (Jan-Feb 1992). 7-8.
Benson, Nathaniel A. ed. *Modern Canadian Poetry.* Ottawa: Graphic Publishers, 1930.
"Poetry" by Rhea Tregebov. *University of Toronto Quarterly* 62.1 (Fall 1992). 63-78.
Sullivan, Rosemary ed. *Poetry by Canadian Women.* Toronto: Oxford University Press, 1989.
Roberts family fonds, Library and Archives Canada (Ottawa). Roberts family holdings, UNB Archives and Special Collections (Fredericton).
Atwood, Margaret ed. *The New Oxford Book of Canadian Verse in English.* Toronto: Oxford University Press Canada, 1982.

AFTERWORD

The hours I spent among Roberts' letters, copies of her father's little magazine Acadie *and other documents were gripping and heady and had me dreaming of a life pursuing archival research—of owning my own stash of pristine white gloves with which to doggedly peel back time, unearthing forgotten stories and underappreciated masterpieces. Just as the work of taking in Roberts' life would never be done, her poetry maintains its hold on me. The "cruel preservative" of "Cold" lurks when I brace myself for a frigid day: thanks to Roberts I understand that part of me revels in winter's hardship. Like the grandparents in "Cold," I've trained myself to see virtue in trudging through snow or turning to face a biting wind; in this way, breezes and sunshine become reward. Is this why God is in the cold? Working out a way for us to feel good about ourselves? There are scenes in Roberts' work that deserve to be viewed and viewed again, like paintings that yield some new pocket of colour each time you peer into them. Her stubborn grandparents toiling in winter—"the white breath and the blood pumping/ Through hard activity stringing out the muscles"—is one. Here is another: "Without the hard heavy apples with their rings of rot,/ Without the wood from the sawhorse falling remote/ How shall we know that our hands are the hard tentacles of our thought?" The apples and the hands—the hard tentacles—have stuck with me. But now, I'm struck by the sawhorse, the wood "falling remote." Suddenly there's an invisible axe in this poem; I failed to pay its swing any heed until now.*

Hide and Seek: Looking for the Real MacEwen

Gwendolyn MacEwen was born in Toronto in 1941 to a mother who spent much of her life in and out of mental health institutions and a father who died young from alcoholism. She dropped out of high school, to study on her own terms, and eventually taught herself Arabic, Hebrew and Greek. If only to appreciate the symmetry, it's worth noting that she later wound up with corresponding lovers for each language. As a young woman in the early sixties, she earned a reputation as a precocious regular at Toronto's legendary Bohemian Café, where she wowed Margaret Atwood and other early CanLit luminaries with her powerful readings—and where she also met Milton Acorn. Their brief marriage, lived out mainly in a rough little cottage on Ward's Island in Toronto Harbour, was seen by many as a "beauty and the beast" match. MacEwen visited Israel and Egypt in a time when a woman journeying alone in the Middle East was rare and when neither country was particularly tourist friendly. Throughout her life, she moved from apartment to apartment, travelled the city by bicycle, and survived on little money. Like her father before her, she struggled with alcoholism, an addiction that led to her premature death at forty-six.

Due in part to Rosemary Sullivan's 1995 biography, *Shadow Maker: The Life of Gwendolyn MacEwen*, these facts are widely known. They insistently colour the experience of reading MacEwen's work, a truth that becomes immediately apparent upon picking up *The Selected Gwendolyn MacEwen*, edited by Meaghan Strimas. This edition updates the two pocket-sized books by Guernica from the early nineties that I carried about with me for months when I first discovered MacEwen's poetry. These thorough volumes plainly confronted her difficult life, both by direct reference to its details in their introductions and by their cover portraits. *On Volume One*, the young MacEwen looks out from the half-light, bold and promising; on *Volume Two* her face, in profile, is puffy. She appears older than her years. The new *Selected* is far too fat and tall to fit in a pocket and avoids any mention of the challenges that beset MacEwen in her personal life. Nonetheless, it too must contend with the Plath-esque aura that shadows her career.

Here is a hint of what I mean. In a review of the new *Selected* in the *Globe and Mail*, Judith Fitzgerald, identified in the bio as a close friend of the poet's in her final decade, introduces MacEwen's literary accomplishments as follows: "Unimaginably wounded by grief (dolor), passion (furor), and hardship (labor), heart-broken beyond belief, inexplicably abandoned by those who called her friend, MacEwen still somehow managed to stay the writerly course ... always mindful of her place in the holy acts of destruction and creation ..." Indeed, we are told, she "sears" pages, "miraculously reshapes them after the fashion of the phoenix," and remains true to "the long charred night of the ashen soul."

Reading Fitzgerald's review brings to mind Brent Wood's essay, "From the Rising Fire to Afterworlds: The Visionary Circle in the Poetry of Gwendolyn MacEwen," published in *Canadian Poetry* in 2000. Wood, like Fitzgerald, unabashedly reads the painful circumstances of MacEwen's life between the lines of her poetry, so much so that he even describes one particular poem as her "plea to be freed of the intensity of life, a plea that probably led her to alcohol." He equates her with "psychedelic experimentalists," mystics and shamans. He calls her a "visionary-healer" who "transcends the limitations of time's arrow."

Had I read Wood's analysis before ever encountering MacEwen's poetry, I might never have picked it up. I wonder whether other potential readers have been similarly turned off. Her current status suggests as much. MacEwen, people will tell you, was never a great poet. She was "mystical" and overwrought. Recently a friend and colleague whose judgment

I respect declared that MacEwen wrote a few memorable lyrics but that our sustained interest in her has more to do with her dramatic life story than with anything of value in her work.

Such indictments lead to a fundamental question about Strimas' edition. Not merely: do we need another MacEwen selected to improve upon those we had? But: do we need one at all? Was there anything worth bringing back into the light?

To a point, current doubts about MacEwen, and the kind of cloudy, indulgent reading that triggers them, begin in the aura she herself projected and in the symbols and tropes upon which she chose to hang her exotic scarves. She performed her poetry by heart wearing long, velvety dresses, her eyes outlined in black kohl. As a youth, she avidly studied the Hebrew and Gnostic mystics and incorporated ideas from these belief systems into her writing. She had a thing for mysterious beings, such as magicians and escape artists, who turn up frequently in her poems, as do prophetic children, "cosmic" objects, alchemy, princes, gods and kings. Her lines often unearth "terrible" and "unspeakable" things. In her earlier work especially, but even in some of her very last poems, rears a high-minded pretentiousness tinged with an otherworldly air. Some of her stuff is just plain bad. A good portion of her travel poetry following her trip to Jerusalem, which appeared in her GG award-winning collection *The Shadow Maker*, reads like the worst sort of banal, earnest, "I was here, look what I saw" reportage. The solemnity and grandeur in the voice she adopts, its descent from on high, can come across as precious and even naive.

In my early twenties I ate this stuff up; now it grates. But I would say the same about a certain amount of work by her contemporary Leonard Cohen, and by Irving Layton, who served as a mentor in some fashion to them both. MacEwen and Layton carried on a correspondence that is quoted generously in Sullivan's biography. York University scholar Branko Gorjup, in the introduction to *The Last Hieroglyph*, his bilingual

Italian-English MacEwen selected published in 1997, places her squarely in the wake of Layton's neo-romantic modernist camp, along with Klein and Avison, as opposed to simply those who followed in their footsteps, notably Cohen and Ondaatje. Her use of myth, he writes, aligns her with the older set; yet her obsessive gaze into the past, along with what Tom Marshall has called an "alchemical search for the divine in the mundane," aligns with the younger.

I would link them another way too. MacEwen's "motorcycle Icarus" in her "Poem Improvised Around a First Line" is a guy who might still seduce you post-high school but not much beyond. He's "black and leathery and lean" and "cannot distinguish between sex and nicotine." His parting pick-up lines are: "O Baby, what hell to be Greek in this country/ without wings, but burning anyway." There's a bravado here that reminds me of Layton's poem that begins, "The day you came naked to Paris," a poem that also contains "a blaze of pubic hair," "my Love, my Darling" and a cheap line (above which he was well capable of rising) about people who "became the atmosphere around them." And then there's Cohen. Take "Celebration," at which a friend of mine once grimaced and exclaimed: "Oh Leonard"—not at all in the way the guy in the poem would have hoped. Shall I quote? "When you kneel below me/ and in both your hands/ hold my manhood like a sceptre." In the next stanza we encounter the sceptre's "amber jewels." Then dancing Roman girls. Before you know it, Samson is falling from the roof.

They set off the cringe-o-meter now, but these poems were all written and published in a time when they would have felt daring to write and to read. We're talking mid-century, very Catholic Quebec for the guys; in MacEwen's case, the stiffly Protestant, early-sixties Toronto, where for her to write "each cloth is slander to your skin and/ nakedness itself is silk across your rising sex" ("Poem," *Breakfast for Barbarians*) was to tear away the loin cloth well ahead of the northern migration of women's lib.

In his introduction to the 1962 anthology *Love Where the Nights are Long*, which includes both his and Cohen's poems quoted here and which came out the year before *Barbarians*, Layton seemed to call MacEwen's "Poem" into being: "I have sought mainly for those extreme statements of surrender—for that is, after all, what love is all about: when the ego forgets its strategies of protection or retreat and men and women stand naked, revealed in all their clotheless glory."

The parallels between MacEwen and Cohen in particular, once you start to notice them, pop up suddenly all over, like tulips in spring. The voices are equally brash and often confrontational. They both regularly employ repetition, an incantatory rhythm and a colloquial diction laid over a formal syntax with deliberate lineation. They plead and command, calling toward some presence or reality beyond the "I." MacEwen, in "You Cannot Do This," also from Barbarians, states: "You cannot do this to them, these are my people;/ I am not speaking of poetry, I am not speaking of art./ You cannot do this to them, these are my people./ You cannot hack away the horizon in front of their eyes." Now Cohen, in what seems like an almost uncanny prequel: "The poems don't love us anymore/ they don't want to love us/ they don't want to be poems/ Do not summon us, they say/ we cannot help you any longer."

And consider these two side-by-side. First, from MacEwen's "The Children are Laughing," one of her most hypnotic compositions, later dubbed a "fugue" in the anthology *In Fine Form: The Canadian Book of Form Poetry* (Polestar, 2005):

> It is Monday and the children are laughing
> The children are laughing; they believe they are princes
> They wear no shoes; they believe they are princes
> And their filthy kingdom heaves up behind them

Place that against the opening of Cohen's "Sky":

The great ones pass
they pass without touching
they pass without looking
each in his joy
each in his fire
Of one another
they have no need
they have the deepest need
The great ones pass
Recorded in some multiple sky
Inlaid in some endless laughter
they pass

We could do this all night. And it wouldn't be just a fun party game. It becomes tough, after awhile, not to see them as yin and yang. Is it the old sexist double-standard that has us dismissing MacEwen as way too celestial and melodramatic, while lauding Cohen as deep and daring and lusty? Or just luck, in that he lived long enough to grow up? Or should I say "old?" They shared not only tone and technique but a sort of "macro" sensibility. Kingdoms and gods and ancients populate their respective collections, as well as the close-up history that shadowed their own youths. Allow me one more comparison. In MacEwen's "The Left Hand and Hiroshima," the narrator appears "four-fingered and garbed/ in a broken gardener's glove" and declares: "only because my poems are lies do they earn the right/ to be true, like the lie of that left hand at night/ in the cockpit of a sad plane trailing God in its wake." In *Flowers for Hitler*, Cohen's alter ego similarly spreads and accepts the blame. The poem "What I'm Doing Here" begins: "I do not know if the world has lied/ I have lied" and continues apace with conspiracy and torture and hate before closing with "I wait/ for each one of you to confess."

Against the grain of the rising Canadian or North American "confessional" lyric, these two Canucks were building new myths, both of them: baldly and boldly and sometimes badly. MacEwen sets this down, still in her twenties, in her introduction to *Barbarians*:

> These poems arise out of a willful hunger, a deep involvement with self and world, a belief that to live consciously is holy, while merely to exist is sacrilege. The barbarian, living close to his original appetites, has not lost the capacity for joy … I should like to think these poems have a certain value for what I term their essential 'optimism,' as opposed to much of the terribly cynical and 'cool' poetry written today. I write to communicate joy, mystery, passion … not the joy that naively exists without knowledge of pain, but that joy which arises out of and conquers pain. I want to construct a myth.

It is hubristic and youthful and in some way wonderful that MacEwen gave us this manifesto. Its resistance to the rise of the cool ironic stance coincides with the sentiments in Latyon's *Love* intro, quoted above, and is absolutely particular to her time. I am inclined to forgive her its excess, and those I have found when revisiting her poems, in the same way we have all tended to forgive Cohen: because, like him, she meant it. She delivered. Gorjup paraphrases critic Frank Davey in the introduction to his MacEwen selected, asserting that she has, "more than any other writer, restored the value of mythology to Canadian poetry by demonstrating that it is not merely a system by which one escapes worldly events, but instead a way to better comprehend our sensual and Heraclitean world." Put more plainly, when she got it, she got it. She broke through walls. She left rubble in her wake.

Some of the most realized, most memorable, and most read-aloud-worthy poems I know remain McEwen's. At the top of the list: "Breakfast for Barbarians" ("my friends, my sweet barbarians/ there is that hunger which is not for food –/ but an eye at the navel turns the appetite/ round"); "Dark Pines Under Water" ("You dream in the green of your time,/ Your memory is a row of sinking pines."); and "The Discovery" ("I tell you her uncovering takes years,/ takes centuries, and when you find her naked/ look again"). These might well be the three lyrics my friend was referring to when he mentioned a "handful" of fine MacEwens. They're standouts, no question. But there are many he missed. I bring forward, as one example, "The Breakfast," from *The Rising Fire*, an early foray into what would become for her a fundamental instrument and metaphor: the first meal of the day. Here is the second stanza:

> a breakfast hysteria; perhaps you have felt it,
> the weight of the food you eat, the end of the meal coming
> before you lift the spoon; or eat only apples
> to improvise an eden. or forget the end takes place
> in each step of your function.

This poem, moving as it does from "hysteria" to Eden to the blessing of forgetting, followed by that sinister nothingness taking form in the solid, heavy rhythm of "each step of your function," frightened me when I first read it at age twenty-two, incidentally the same age MacEwen was when it was published. It also brought an inexpressible relief. Note the three intangibles (hysteria, Eden and forgetting) interspersed with the spoon, the apples and the steps. Myth in reality. Weight in air. The inevitable known, the daily meal, containing the inevitable unknown, our end. By embedding the scary un-graspables within the particulars of this basic morning ritual, MacEwen cuts down their power: we can touch them after all. They're simply cutlery and fruit, our own selves moving. But this sleight of hand, which she mastered young and never stopped employing, simultaneously renders our ultimate fate more sinister and insidious. No longer is it somewhere vaguely off in the future. It's here—and here and here. It might pounce into consciousness while we're reaching for a spoon.

The enigmatic boy—or, as Atwood has termed it, the "male muse"—is another vehicle MacEwen repeatedly employs for her vigorous and unsettling explorations. In "Generation Cometh," he "grows beneath your heels/ and the city for him is easy he/ knows it from below." He later becomes "The Magician," "Manzini: Escape Artist," "The Winemaker," even "Archie Belaney"—but most memorably Lawrence of Arabia in what has been described by some as MacEwen's most powerful sequence, *The T.E. Lawrence Poems.* Published as a complete volume in 1982, this collection shows MacEwen moving past her early manifesto to "construct" a myth into a project far more interesting and complex: now she's engaged in mythmaking atop deconstruction of a myth. She brings us a fictional Lawrence confronting his own fabrication and re-fabrication of himself. In the opening poem, "Water," we are immediately given a taste of the slipperiness of identity, which will prove Lawrence's bugaboo:

> ... In France it tasted
> Of Crusaders' breastplates, swords and tunnels of rings
> On ladies' fingers.
> In the springs of Lebanon water had
> No colour, and was therefore all colours,
> outside of Damascus
> It disguised itself as snow and let itself be chopped
> And spooned onto the stunned red grapes of summer.
>
> For years I have defended water, even though I am told there are other drinks.
> Water will never lie to you, even when it insinuates itself
> Into someone else's territory. Water has style.
>
> Water has no conscience and no shame; water
> thrives on water, is self-quenching.

The particulars of Lawrence's reality are informed not just by MacEwen's reading of his memoir and her trips to the Middle East, but by a lifetime of autodidactic studies in history, philosophy, poetry, religion and language, including her mastery of Arabic—all of which permeates the writing rather than bogging it down. Combined with the poems' physicality, her immersion in Lawrence's world grounds the mythologically cloaked voice, just as, all those years before in "The Breakfast," she set death down atop a spoon.

When MacEwen published *The T.E. Lawrence Poems* with Mosaic Press in 1982, we were well into the era of the primarily personal, formless Canadian lyric—the light domestic, the mildly nationalistic kitchen and garden poems so many of us grew up reading and replicating. Meanwhile, MacEwen was forging borderless, timeless poetics. She was global before "globalism." She treated the portage or the northern lake with exactly the same attention, reverence and raised eyebrow as she did the Middle East, or people and places from ancient times, or, say, the Loch Ness Monster. She stood alone in other ways too. She lived through the rise of feminism and saw her contemporaries, such as Atwood with her wicked irony, employ the pen to critique the status quo. But MacEwen had never felt compelled to meet the societal expectations placed on women and so didn't rail against them. Instead, she operated under a precociously post-feminist disregard for the battle of the sexes that remains refreshing.

Lawrence's fraught journey, though well worth taking, isn't on offer in Exile's new *Selected*. Strimas truncates her selection from the Lawrence poems to just a handful, a selection as slim as those that appear in anthologies, giving us no sense of the ambition and accomplishment of the undertaking. Strimas either missed the value in the Lawrence poems or sacrificed them to make room for the scrapbook of photos, news clippings and letters at the back. (Or the "Questions for Discussion and Essays," which, sadly, reminded me why most people leave high school fearing poetry.) But without any word from Strimas, neither foreword nor introduction nor even a tiny bio that might provide some clue to her perspective, we are left to speculate.

This lack of context is maddening. The new MacEwen seems designed as a compendium for teachers, a sampler, and is not without its merits. The book touts itself as the first chronological selection of MacEwen's work in every genre. We get her best-known lyrics; her mesmerizing "Nine Arcana of the King;" and the long, fabulous "Helen," a translation by MacEwen and her second husband Nikos Tsingos of Yannos Ritsos' famous piece, in which Helen of Troy speaks out before she dies. This poem bears revisiting now not just for its force but as an interesting contrast to Atwood's recent re-imagining of Homer's *Odyssey* in *The Penelopiad.* The book also contains many poems from MacEwen's last collection, *Afterworlds*, which read as a farewell and reckoning. In addition, there are intriguing excerpts of fiction and memoir, the latter, in particular, setting down useful context for some of her poetry, and her excellent verse play *Terror and Erebus*, about the Franklin expedition. But compiling all this stuff in the order in which it was written doesn't make the publication of this collection a "signal event in North America's cultural efflorescence," as Fitzgerald effused in her *Globe* review. The book's sections are grouped in such a way that it is not always clear which selection belongs to which original text. Where previous knowledge couldn't help me, I was forced to refer to other collections. I was dismayed to find frequent typos. Works of art and photographs, many of them depicting MacEwen, function as intriguing dividers, but none of them appear with any attribution or credit line, an omission that had me flipping pages up and down, convinced I'd missed some hidden footnotes. Regarding the fiction, it is possible that we have been mistaken in accrediting more importance to MacEwen's poetry, but the brief excerpts here are not enough to make the case. After reading the entire volume, I'm left puzzling over how exactly Strimas reads MacEwen's trajectory and what she was attempting to redress, if anything.

All of this undermines any sense of the "definitive" for which this collection might have aimed and makes for a book that is far less meticulous than the pieces of writing contained within. A reissue of those old Guernicas would have served as well, or better. What we could have used was a strong critical essay casting a contemporary eye on MacEwen, an effort to properly place her in the Canadian canon once and for all. Instead, we're treated to a brief intro by Rosemary Sullivan that is essentially a severely truncated reprise of what she's written in the past, though without any mention of MacEwen's alcoholism or family tragedies. I suspect Strimas was tackling one of the problems I've mentioned, the overshadowing of MacEwen's work by her life, but since these facts are so well known, it seems like a head-in-the-sand approach. It's too late to pretend this stuff away. Some of these choices were possibly made with the context of the classroom in mind, clearly one intended home for this book. Such prudence might make sense and MacEwen, reportedly fiercely private, might even have appreciated it. But her artistic methods, indeed her entire poetic philosophy, has always seemed to me less an attempt to escape reality than to bring it on full-force. In 1986, the year before she died, she took the post of writer-in-residence at the University of Toronto. She reportedly used to tell students that they were better off failing than treading carefully. She encouraged swagger. As Sullivan reports, MacEwen's complaint about contemporary poetry was that it "tended to be an exploration of pain, a kind of dwelling on one's wounds and scars." She also once complained in a letter to Layton: "The art of directly experiencing one's poems is unknown in this city—the art of verifying what one has had the gall to write. Introspection itself should be a passionate thing, being sponsored from the outside." She put this another way in her poem "Let Me Make This Perfectly Clear":

You suspect this is a posture or an act.
I am sorry to tell you it is not an act.

You actually think I care if this
Poem gets off the ground or not. Well
I don't care if this poem gets off the ground or not
And neither should you.
All I have ever cared about
And all you should ever care about
Is what happens when you lift your eyes from this page.

MacEwen never apologized for wielding the pen, she never belittled its importance. She wasn't afraid of words like "beautiful" and "bloody" and she generally got away with using them. She was bold enough to risk being misunderstood. Since her death in 1987, our little literary-nation-that-could has birthed truckloads of competent lyricists, some of them really fine. But revisiting MacEwen leaves me wondering whether a flatness now reigns, a middling ambition. I see all these meticulous, thoughtful, accomplished writers neatly pressing words into the page as though decorating a cake. I think of the ubiquity of that peculiar, heavily comma-spliced "poetic" syntax. Do we have more careful literary personae being composed in this age than ambitious works? Where, I ask myself, are our new MacEwens? Is any one of us prepared to trip over our own hubris and fall down hard? When MacEwen writes, "All you should ever care about/ Is what happens when you lift your eyes from this page," it is pure irony (as opposed to that safe, cool stance we've come to love). It is the voice from within the poem telling us to look up—and we do.

BOOKS REVIEWED:

The Selected Gwendolyn MacEwen, Gwendolyn MacEwen (ed. Meaghan Strimas). Toronto: Exile Editions, 2007.

AFTERWORD

Not long after we moved to Toronto's High Park neighbourhood in 2012, I realized we'd landed in MacEwen's old stomping grounds. According to Rosemary Sullivan's biography Shadow Maker: The Life of Gwendolyn MacEwen, *MacEwen, who was born in 1941, lived at 38 Keele Street as a girl, just above the northeast corner of the park. One warm evening I hopped on my bicycle and rode south on Keele from Annette, past Keele Street Public School, glancing at house numbers while dodging buses, traffic and parked cars. Number 62, 48, 44. That was it. The houses stopped. There's nothing between 44 Keele and Bloor Street but the subway track, which briefly runs above ground here, then into a tunnel cut through a hill just west of Keele. I trekked to the archives. Old city directories listed an unoccupied property at 38 Keele in 1965, then nothing a year later, when the Bloor-Danforth subway line opened. Here's how Sullivan describes the house that I'm convinced sat atop that hill, just above where the track now lies: "Thirty-eight Keele Street stood in odd isolation from the rest of the street; it was a large, three-storied, red brick structure up to which one had to climb by three staggered flights of forty-two steps from the street. Because of its elevation, the local children used to make up stories about seeing bats circling it at night and claimed that it was haunted." That busy and noisy pocket, with its brutal overpass and silver subway trains screeching past every few minutes, feels even more haunted now.*

'An intelligent search': On Three Late Collections by P. K. Page

In the title poem of *Coal and Roses*, a triple-glosa constructed around three quatrains by Russian poet Anna Akhmatova, P. K. Page writes, "Here, my wrist—its pause/ is yours for the taking, yet it is not yours." Extraordinary moments such as these, infused with paradox—reverent yet playful, gentle yet fierce—can happen when Page writes about something as common to poetry as flowers and sunsets, or as potentially bland and sentimental as the human heartbeat. Coming as it does at the end of the book—indeed, near the end of Page's life—this one line effectively underlines all that precedes it, not just in this gorgeous book of glosas, but in her extraordinarily productive six decades of publishing. Through these words, the poet seems to say: I hold out to you the very blood that pumps through me. You may "take" my pulse: read me, know me. But you'll let go, my arm will fall, the book will close, we'll go our separate ways. Does she lament this brief, doomed connection? Not Page. She's acknowledging, owning up to what is.

Coal and Roses is Page's second and final collection of glosas. *Hologram*, published by Brick in 1994, contained a foreword in which Page described her love affair with the form popular among poets of the Spanish court half a millennium ago. Using a quatrain written by another poet, four ten-line stanzas are composed, each ending on a line from the original quatrain. There are no metre restrictions but lines six and nine rhyme, as Page puts it, "with the borrowed tenth." Page found the crossword-puzzle aspect of this compelling: "I liked being controlled by these three reining rhymes—or do I mean reigning?—and gently influenced by the rhythm of the original … A curious marriage—two sensibilities intermingling." She was hooked. In *Hologram*, she worked her way through the poets with whom she'd felt the most affinity during her formative years, including Rilke, Elizabeth Bishop, Leonard Cohen and Robert Graves. She called it a project of homage, appropriate as she approached "the end of her life"—but she kept it going long enough to bring forth a whole new set of glosas fifteen years later, in which she communes with e. e. cummings, Don McKay, Gwendolyn MacEwen, John Ashbery, Dionne Brand, Wallace Stevens, Zbigniew Herbert, Roethke, Borges and yes, Akhmatova. This new collection, interspersed with short biographies and black-and-white photographs of each quoted poet, is a marvellously Page-esque literary primer, stretching across nations from the seventeeth through the twentieth century.

Yet I read with trepidation, balking at the top of each poem. The glosa is a dangerous form. How to avoid the tedious spelling out of all that speaks with more power by implication? I have read enough bloated, boring, awkward glosas to have reason for concern. The blame for these shoddy efforts lies in part with Page herself. Her introduction of the glosa to Canadian poetry, and her impressive way with it, inspired a generation of would-be glosa-ists. The situation is similar to that of the ghazal ushered unforgettably into CanLit by John Thompson, creating an instant sensation of the form, little understood but tried and tried, *ad nauseum.* Fine glosas by other poets do turn up but it remains true that to read a successful specimen, one is safest to turn to Page. In "How to Write a Poem" she plays wickedly with Ashbery's "Paradoxes and Oxymorons": "It is raining and you've decided you are going to write a poem./ What else is there to do besides phoning your mother?" She creates, or unearths, a version of herself that belongs with Gwendolyn MacEwen in a land of sand dunes and burning winds. She cracks apart the agonized healing in Thomas Gunn's "the Wound":

> and I was earthquake country, one vast shake
> and then the aftershock and then the quiet

that follows chaos. Now I would be well.
The healing had begun. I felt each cell
Working with every other cell, a truce
Throughout my kingdom, it was peaceable.
Its valleys darkened, its villages became still,

When I read any well-wrought Page glosa, I am struck by how she manages to call up thirty-six extra lines that feel essential, as if they have always been there, hidden inside that other poem, waiting to be found.

Part of what works for Page in the glosa is its backward motion: "you work towards a known," she wrote in *Hologram*. Her glosa "Infinite Regression" is a great example of this in action. Page borrows a quatrain from the seventeeth century English Aristocrat Margaret Cavendish's poem "Of Many Worlds in this World," inspired by the discovery of the atom. It's a testament to Page's dexterity that she effortlessly echoes the cadence and feel of Cavendish's 300-year-old diction while also remaining decidedly *now*:

Once in a bathroom in a rich hotel—
all mirrors—I descried myself reflected,
naked in mercury, and multiple-
recurring endlessly, each smaller me
retreating to a vast infinity.
It was as if the largest me was cloned
and then shrunk step by step. I barely saw
the final smallest me. It was too small.
That final smallest me could not be found—
Just like unto a nest of boxes round,

This poem is impossible to read without calling to mind a much older work by Page: "A Backwards Journey," which appears along with forty-nine other classic Page compositions in *The Essential P. K. Page*, part of that growing and welcome Porcupine's Quill series of compact volumes containing the best by Canada's best. Page fans will well remember her "very busy" Dutch

Cleanser woman "hidden behind her bonnet" and "holding a yellow Dutch Cleanser can// on which a smaller Dutch Cleanser woman/ was holding a smaller Dutch Cleanser can ..." and so on until:

> This was no game. The woman led me
> Backwards through the eye of the mind
> Until she was the smallest point
> My thought could hold to.

This journey towards the thing she can hardly see but which is also her best hope for clarity, for understanding, is enacted by Page repeatedly. She's dogged, and reading through *The Essential* is an exercise in taking up her cause, in donning gumboots "to place the rectangles" in the lush garden of "After Rain"; in tilting to the word "pale" in "after Reading *Albino Pheasants* by Patrick Lane," a word that can "tip the scale, make light/ this heavy planet"; in following "The Mole" down "the slow dark personal passage." One is struck by the careful, cautious attention Page pays to the experience of the body and mind, by her faithfulness to the importance of articulation, without skimping, rushing, or aiming to be clever, and by her determination to follow the clearest line of vision she can hold. Is this visionary, a persistent label she rejected, or simply dedicated? A capacity to sit down, again and again, and worry the poem, pick at the knot?

Facing Page's entire oeuvre can be daunting; it contains little apprentice work, few throwaways. *The Essential P. K. Page* is in this sense a relief. It's a reprieve to hold in one's hand a compact sixty pages featuring the most memorable, most confounding, most re-readable poems written by Page arranged alphabetically—each allowed its own space, unencumbered by time or category. Many of Page's memorable short poems are included, such as "Truce," "Winter Morning" and "The World," which reads, in its entirety, "It is like a treacle, the world./ I am caught in its golden threads,/ a fly in a honey pot." (Page had a keen affection for the small poem, and once edited a delightful anthology called *To Say the Least: Canadian Poets from A to Z.*) *The Essential* comes with a few small disappointments and puzzlements, such as the absence of "The Stenographers" and "Planet Earth," two of Page's most popular poems. I ask myself how these two pieces fail to be classified as *essential* Page, how they can possibly not belong alongside "The Evening Dance of the Grey Flies," "The Filled Pen," "Deaf-Mute in a Pear Tree," and "Arras." A foreword offering some illumination beyond its statement that Page's poetry "needs no introduction" might have explained these choices. And I question the assumption that a reader, especially one new to Page, might not benefit from its editors' insights. Page is an exceptional poet, but she's a poet one grows into. A reader must feel her way into Page's restless and relentlessly alert mind, much as she continued to grow into the voice of her character Cullen, who dove in and out of her collections, lurking between the lines, experimenting, detouring, mulling and aging in tandem with her. The Outlaw Edition chapbook, *Cullen*, brings together the five Cullen poems in one place for the first time and is a delight and marvel to read: a romp, an epic, a tragedy, a blank comedy and a flight from reality, all in one. The chapbook does contain an afterword, both thoughtful and welcome, addressing the question of who exactly Cullen is. The author's alter-ego? A fictional self-portrait? Perhaps "a fellow pilgrim through the journey of life … a process of evolution from matter to spirit," Zailig Pollock proposes.

But I also know what Lampert and Gray mean when they say Page can speak for herself and I understand their impulse to let her. In an appreciation of Page after her death, Rosemary Sullivan wrote in the *Globe and Mail* that "no poet had a more impeccable sense of timing. Somehow, when Page broke the syntax of a line, something cracked in you and opened out to the light." I would add that the remarkable agility of Page's vocabulary is second to none. No one but she could write, as in her glosa "Poor Bird," of the plight of the little bird thus: "… distracted/ by nest-building, eggs, high winds, high tides/ and too short a lifespan for him to plan/ an intelligent search—still, on he goes/ with his delicate legs and spilikin feet." Spilikin—jackstraw—the word itself moves with the legs of the bird. Page's poems abound with such incontestably perfect selections. They're weird, they're seldom used, but at Page's behest they turn natural, inevitable. They require no explanation. It's as if she plucked them out of deep, dusty storage and created their purpose anew.

BOOKS REVIEWED:

P. K. Page, *Coal and Roses: Twenty-one Glosas* (Erin: Porcupine's Quill, 2009).
Arlene Lampert and Théa Gray, Eds., *The Essential P .K. Page* (Erin: Porcupine's Quill, 2008).
P. K. Page, *Cullen: poems* (Duncan: Outlaw Editions, 2009).

AFTERWORD

I was wary of reviewing the last three volumes Page published before her death in 2010. I had on my bookshelf copies of Hologram, The Glass Air, *and* Planet Earth, *among others, but had not read them in a long while. Would revisiting her work reveal it to be convoluted, precious, obscure? The unease receded with my first tentative steps back into her realm. Why my wariness? I can't say for sure, but I can speculate that it had something to do with that instinctive fear of the homegrown accolade: Canadian readers, myself included, considered her great, but was she? A voice inside me was skeptical and I can't entirely discredit it. Let's face it: there's a fair amount of fawning in our cultural conversation. Lately, though, my inner malcontent is more likely to look sidelong at the Next Big Literary Thing, which seems too quickly and resoundingly hailed.*

Page's writing isn't quick, clever or fashionable or, as we often like to describe our poets today—and as I myself have been described—quirky. It's challenging, sophisticated, inventive, meaty: it has depth, integrity, universality and chutzpah. It endures. It hums and grinds in the minds of poets across the land: it works on them while they mull.

I took issue in this piece with the ubiquitous glosa that Page unwittingly ushered into Canlit without admitting that I too have tried the glosa and failed. Tried it time and again, with godawful results. Like John Thompson with his tantalizing ghazal, Page made the glosa look so limitless, so doable and satisfying. How appealing, to borrow four stirring lines from another poet and dig into them, determine just how they have you in thrall, and turn them down an unforeseen path. How easily such an ambition could turn ugly. The glosa is a temptation and a challenge and far more dangerous than it looks, like so much of what Page did.

While I was "reviewing" this review for inclusion in this collection, P.K. Page's last home was transported by barge from Victoria's Oak Bay "up island" to Chemainus, where it will house its new owners. A house gliding placidly up the Georgia Strait seems a fitting gesture of farewell for a poet whose every act of composition was the equivalent of picking up and trucking a form, with all the history that clings to it, to the shore and setting it afloat.

'Things we hardly feel we own':
Conversations Between Writers

Poets on the Mat: Fighting for Muscle and Metaphor

with Sharon McCartney and Kerry Ryan

Fredericton, circa 2011, Sharon McCartney was reading from her unflinching new series about weightlifting, now appearing in the collection *Hard Ass*, which sweats its way through one rock-solid metaphor after another toward jaw-dropping insight. In the audience, I was riveted, gripped with admiration and even mildly shocked as Sharon read about achieving "an ass like rock, monolith, enduring as hatred." I was struck by the parallels between our recent poetic pursuits and the impulses behind them. In my book *Spinning Side Kick*, I drew on my experiences as a novice kickboxer to create a fictional kickboxing match in eleven poems, each named after a move in the ring. Around the time of Sharon's reading, I also found Winnipeg poet Kerry Ryan's book *Vs.*, a memoir in poems about taking up boxing for real: actually stepping into the ring. I was curious about what had drawn all three of us to these traditionally male physical pursuits, and then how and why we'd turned those experiences into poetry. What had sweat and muscle fatigue done for our line breaks and metaphors? What had dancing in the ring done for our rhythms on the page? Landing punches and kicks for our sense of writerly purpose? How did grunting and lifting, in Sharon's case, translate to weighty nouns and gravity-defying verbs? I invited Sharon and Kerry to converse with me about where the gym meets the page. As boxers attempting to hook a fancy-footed opponent, as weightlifter gripping the bar and bracing to raise it off the floor, we face these questions and more, with resolve and steely-eyes but teetering with wonder and confusion, seeing stars, not entirely sure what just happened here …

ANITA LAHEY: When I was working on my kickboxing poems, I did a great deal of reading about boxing. In her book *On Boxing* Joyce Carol Oates says that opponents will thank one another with sincerity after a bout, because, win or lose, each fighter has offered the other an opportunity to test himself. I thought of this when I read Sharon's poem "Squat Rack," in which she writes about bodybuilding as "redefinition," then follows with the lines: "Achieving ever larger defeats, that paradox in the panoply/ of mirrors, how working the muscle to failure enlarges it." I can't help but read this as a metaphor for being a writer, for we pretty much fail every time we sit down to write to meet the image of the thing we were aiming for, at least I do. Does boxing, for you, Kerry, and weightlifting for you, Sharon, offer a similar kind of test—that of pushing yourself to the limit? The chance to learn from failure? And does the sheer physicality involved mean something different from the kind of push we do when writing?

SHARON MCCARTNEY: Yes, that's it, exactly. Pushing oneself beyond what you imagined or feared you were capable of, and how we grow through that process. Failure is a big part of it. I always felt that whatever lines or words I cut from a poem remained in some way as part of the process. Like failing to get a lift in the gym, the exertion is still there.

KERRY RYAN: There are lots of parallels between boxing and writing and that includes the tension between learning/ growing and teetering on the lip of failure. I remember my running interior monologue when I first started boxing: "I can't do this. I can't hold my hands up for another second. This is impossible. Why am I even trying? Hey wait, there's the bell." With writing it's often the same. A poem isn't working, I can't crack it, I want to give up. But I can't let it go. And then a shift, a word or an image, and it falls into place. Okay, that only happens some of the time. Actually, hardly ever. But when it does, the feeling of triumph or relief is the same.

It's interesting to think about failure, both as a boxer and a poet. Both are disciplines that I know I will never master, failure is the constant state. But I don't very often *feel* like I've failed. Maybe I would have a keener sense of this if I were a "real" boxer. I've only had one real fight; most of my boxing consists of training drills. I can have a terrible round or drills where I feel like I'm dragging my butt around the gym, but I can still take something from that—some learning, some satisfaction in just having done it. And with writing, the same: yes, it's frustrating when I can't translate a poem from my head to the paper but there's still something powerful in the work of it.

Now that I think about it, I'd define failure, both in boxing and writing, not so much in terms of meeting expectations but simply as quitting before the bell rings. Most of my gains, again in both, are infinitesimal: tiny improvements in technique, stamina, strength. But more important are what I gain in understanding myself, my capabilities, and learning to trust in that.

SHARON MCCARTNEY: While failure is pretty easy to define for weightlifting, it's harder for me in writing. I know when I have succeeded—that's usually getting somewhere I didn't expect to be in the poem, coming to a new realization or a new understanding *and* coming up with language and metaphor that will make that realization compelling for a reader. I like Kerry's analogy of quitting before the bell rings. I do that sometimes. Just throw up my hands and walk away, and that hurts. Why is it so much easier to accept failure in the gym than it is to accept it in writing?

ANITA LAHEY: I think the expectations when writing versus boxing/ kickboxing/ weightlifting are different. Because it seemed a bit crazy that I would take up kickboxing in the first place—me, a kickboxer?—there was so much less at stake. Trying it at all was a bonus. In writing I am determined to accomplish something, to "reach my potential," whatever that is. This is why the failure feels different, I think. Perhaps also because the answers seem clearer in the gym. With coaching, you know what to do to try to overcome your failed efforts at the gym. With writing, you can know every manner of technique and have all kinds of guidance but there is always that intangible factor that will enter the mix and lead to whether you "nail it" or not.

KERRY RYAN: For me, it's easier to accept failure at the gym because it has only been recently that I've even thought about myself in physical terms. I have always written and read and identified as a thinker. I never thought about my body at all, until I was about twenty-five and realized I was totally disconnected from my physical self. I started running and doing Pilates and it was like discovering a person who had been dormant inside my own body. Eventually, I found my way to boxing. Coming to sport as an adult, I've been able to focus on gains more than the failures.

But my expectations of myself as a writer are much higher. Writing is the thing I'm supposed to be good at. So, when the writing isn't going well or when I'm taking a break from writing, which I do from time to time, I live in a state of constant disappointment. It's funny, because if I were to ask non-writers what they think is harder: spending an hour bucketing sweat in the gym while some ripped guy with a crew cut is shouting at you, or spending an hour sitting in a chair working on a single line of a poem, I'm pretty sure they'd pick the gym. But in the gym you're following a script: you show up, you do it, you have a shower and you feel great, even if you're hurting. Writing can be so much more gruelling. There's no clear path, no model to aim for, no bell and no endorphin rush! Plus, I almost never feel like a poem is finished, so I rarely have a sense of triumph. Just those tiny, occasional victories—a nice strand of words, a clever line break, a perfect title. How I'd love to look up from a poem and think: "Pow! Nailed it!"

Going back to your original question, Anita, involving the body does make boxing very different from writing. Bodies are unreliable, especially mine, and it's easy to blame some physical flaw for poor performance. But the truth is, boxing is so much more mental (logic and creativity) than I ever could have imagined. And the brain and body are so intertwined, it's hard to separate the body's job from the brain's job, which one is in charge, whether they work together or fight one another. I tried writing about this in *Vs.*, but I've never been satisfied that I got it. That brain-body split is my never-ending round.

ANITA LAHEY: So much of what you're saying rings so true. Two of my favourite things about kickboxing class: one, I was not in charge. My only job was to do my best to follow instructions. And two, the end of class, after the endless twenty minutes of punching and kicking routines, the stretching, the sparring sessions and bag work, and finally the push-ups and crunches and full body lie-on-your-back stretch as long as you can. I would lie there with my arms above my head, staring up at the ceiling. My mind was empty. I wondered whether how I felt at that moment was how it feels after meditating or whether I'd accidentally stumbled on the secret of Buddhism, pure detachment. I don't mean to sound flip: this experience was marvellous, foreign, an awakening. And I recognize that both of these things, the letting go of responsibility and of the mind, indicate that kickboxing (i.e. the physical) served as an escape: from choosing the next move for a character; from finding the right phrasing for a section in a poem; from selecting the poems that would make it into the next issue of *Arc*; from painstakingly figuring out the structure for a magazine article; from not just thinking, but judging, assessing. Kerry, you're right that the body and the mind become so intertwined on the mat that it's difficult to separate them, but I always found that I was so physically spent by the end of a kickboxing class that without any intent or effort I'd forgotten all about the mind and its constant noise and confusion. What sweet relief.

Then I could return to my normal life of mulling everything to death, but armed with that fresh endorphin high and a sparkling clarity.

KERRY RYAN: I'm curious to know how this relates to weightlifting, Sharon, because it seems to me that the goals would be much more clear—that you're aiming to always increase numbers. Or are you?

SHARON MCCARTNEY: Yes, the goal in weightlifting is always to increase the weight. So, numbers. And failure is simply the inability to lift the weight. Which is very real. You grab the bar for a deadlift and pull up but the bar doesn't budge. Sometimes that's a matter of form; if your form isn't right, you don't have the power that you need to lift the weight. But there is also reaching one's maximum weight. At CrossFit, it's called "program max." Once you reach your maximum weight, you go to a different week-by-week routine working around the maximum weight and, eventually, maybe pushing it up a bit.

But what is really different about weightlifting is that I don't have a human opponent. What I'm pushing against is myself, my own capacity. I also like to think about working out as a way to engage with gravity. Gravity is very real in the gym. It's what we work against. And it's transcendent; it touches us all. Failure in the gym means that gravity has gotten the upper hand, but that's also what makes us stronger. I love thinking about that. How gravity tries to hold onto things but how, in doing so, it's defeating itself because we just get stronger the stronger it holds on.

And there's a direct translation to poetry for me. Gravity is depth and strength. It's what is inside us all. That's what I try to work with in my poetry. Sometimes, that's really difficult. I've written a lot about family and relationships and I've always tried to be honest and forthright. I have a thing about not letting myself off the hook, not blaming others, not making excuses. For me, that's a way of engaging with gravity through writing.

KERRY RYAN: Oh, Sharon, I totally get the idea of the self being an opponent. That's exactly my experience with boxing, even when I am in the ring with someone else. And I am so interested in your idea of gravity as an opponent. I can see how that has broader life/ writer implications too. I so often feel like I'm working against forces pulling at me: expectations, job and career stuff, time, tiredness. Many days, the couch and TV or some fat novel have much stronger gravitational pull than my notebook.

ANITA LAHEY: I never took myself seriously as a kickboxer, yet I took it seriously enough to push myself and to marvel over this new way of using my arms and legs and of gaining strength. What a thrill it is, to feel strong! I wonder how much this has to do with beating gravity, Sharon. The way you look on gravity is enlightening. There is an invisible weight you feel pressing down on your arms and legs when you're trying to push them to whack the bag one more time. It is a force pulling down on them, pulling endlessly, eternally, without ever letting up. It is constant resistance.

The resistance we struggle against when sitting down to write is constant but also more variable, I think. Sometimes it has power over me and sometimes I can sail on by, hardly noticing it's there. And yet, as with the boxing match and the weightlifting goal, even a string of small successes doesn't necessarily lead to complete success. You can land a bunch of great hits but still lose the fight. A poem built on solid line after solid line can still be killed, or fail to rise off the page, by something extraneous or off-key at its end or in its centre. You are feeling your way when you're writing, trying to find the through line, and I guess that's also what you're doing when you're fighting or even sparring, which itself is exhausting and demanding and calls up all your inner resources to respond on the fly to the blows coming at you. Will you find the responses you've been taught to use? I seldom have.

Which brings me to my third favourite thing about kickboxing: how it feels when you fit several moves together in a seamless flow. How the pivot when you duck under a punch puts you in the perfect position to pivot back and rise into a vicious uppercut. How a proper landing after a push kick, that weight on the front foot, leaves you in a great position to throw a wicked jab-cross-jab. And the momentum you get from a spin-kick to throw into your next punch or kick. The excitement I felt working on these moves was familiar. Similar to figuring out a new kind of flow in a poem. I guess these are both forms of communication, one with the body and the other with language. You want, in either case, to streamline the moves, to be decisive and clear; to not muddy the fight with too many moves or the poem with too many metaphors or ideas; to find the exact perfect response to a given situation or idea; to neither hesitate, hedge, nor hold back. Does this speak to either of you, the equation of technique—and the mastery of technique—between the work in the gym and the work on the page?

KERRY RYAN: With boxing, I know what I'm aiming for: the precise transfer of weight, tight form, the whip-snap of fist against bag. Occasionally, I feel like I'm really getting it, and how sweet that feeling is! But even though I know what I'm supposed to do, know what it feels like to do it correctly, know that I have done it before, I still can't nail that technique with every punch.

With poetry, I don't have a strong sense of the ideal. Sure, sometimes I have the same sweet feeling of really getting a piece right but I couldn't ever tell you what makes me feel that way about a poem, mine or someone else's. As a boxer I have a checklist: knees bent, heels up, shoulders rounded, chin tucked, elbows in, knuckles at the sky. I don't have that as a writer. I feel so much like I flail around every time I write a poem.

I know my weaknesses in the ring: I drop my punches, my footwork is too slow, I run out of steam. As a poet, my tells aren't so different: I fall into predictable patterns, I don't push myself hard enough. It's easier for me to evaluate what I do wrong than what I do right.

SHARON MCCARTNEY: I think about technique a lot in the gym. There are certain lifts, the "clean," for example, that I have not been able to master. And if you can't master the move, you're not going to be able to lift any significant weight. That's me and the "clean." You have to shrug your shoulders on the jump up to get the bar moving and then get underneath the bar as it falls back down, which is a tad scary. I've been working on the shrug for a year and have not gotten it. I can jump and I can shrug. But I can't jump and shrug. Hence, I find it really hard to lift anything over 65 lbs. I don't have the momentum.

The deadlift is easier. But, again, if my bum rises up too much (bad!), the bar will not come off the ground. Technique! It's important for a reason. CrossFit is good because there's always a coach there to yell at you when you're slipping on form. I get yelled at a lot. And I appreciate that because I want my form to get better. That's the only way to get stronger. And to avoid injury too.

With poetry, what's important for me, as technique, is to work on language, imagery, and metaphor as a way of connecting with the reader. Poetry is so interior and my poetry is ultimately a dialogue with myself. Or my "Self" in the Jungian sense. Yet, I expect other people to be interested in that. Making the language interesting and using imagery and metaphor is a way, I hope, to connect my own interior dialogue with that of the reader. We all have those dialogues! And if my technique isn't good, the poem isn't working and there will be no weightiness to it. It will be dead on the ground.

Going back to the "clean," for me the shrug is the hardest part. It's a way of transferring energy from your body to the bar. If I think about that in terms of poetry, the shrug would be the idea behind the poem, the revelation, the insight, the self-accusation, whatever it is that gives the poem its life. The jump is everything else. Language, imagery, metaphor. You can have all of that but if you have no shrug, there's not going to be any life in the poem and it's not going to mean anything to anyone else. That's the energy. So, the hard part is putting the jump and the shrug together. Occasionally, I think I can do that in a poem and it feels fanfuckingtastic! Now, if only I could do that in the gym. Sigh.

KERRY RYAN: I do think I've brought some of what I've learned of boxing technique to the page as a poet. So much of boxing has to do with economy, precision and making the best use of your strength. When I started boxing, and when I was writing *Vs.*, my work became more spare, focused, and confident. Boxing has made me braver as a poet. It was unconscious but somewhere along the line I realized if I could put myself out there in the ring, vulnerable, I could do that as a poet too.

ANITA LAHEY: I'm not sure I have entirely "put myself out there" in either arena. With kickboxing, I have never put myself on the line in a real match. I haven't wanted to risk getting kicked in the head, to be frank. I was thirty-four when I started boxing: hardly young and nimble. The way in which this stretched me was more by forcing me to leave my private world in the middle of the day, to get up from my desk—where I am utterly content plowing through my "life of the mind," putting all my hard-practiced skills to work—to go to a lunch-hour kickboxing class, to do something in which I feel awkward and unskilled and without natural instinct, in a room full of other people, many of them fitter, faster, younger, stronger. It was a small risk, but a real one. It drew me out of my comfort zone. It also put me in a room full of people from other walks of life: nurses, teachers, a military person or two, tech workers, and so on.

With poetry, I follow my nose and hope I'm going as far as I can into the impulse that began a poem. I don't believe that every poem should frighten the pants off you while you're writing it. And yet to write a real poem, a strong and meaty and unflinching work, you do have to hole down inwardly to god-knows-where. Have I ever really done this? Sometimes it feels like I have but I don't trust the feeling. To really plow deep down into something should feel not satisfying but uncomfortable, right? As uncomfortable as the first time we had a "friendly sparring" tournament at my dojo and I stepped into the ring with someone three inches taller than me, several years younger, lean and muscular. She wasn't supposed to kick or punch me in the face, "friendly sparring" rules, yet I had the distinct feeling she had it in her to do so and that I did not have it in me to likewise plow a fist or foot into hers. When you are looking at someone's face that in theory you're supposed to hit, you see it differently. You see the bones and the blood under the skin, how easily they might be damaged, how it would feel to mash your hand into all that living tissue. It was not pleasant to imagine this. And yet, for a writer, a useful thing to do. And natural. I wonder if my imagination kicking in so vividly is partly what would have made it so hard for me to hit her.

SHARON MCCARTNEY: I don't feel that I have a problem with bravery in poetry. I've said just about everything I've ever wanted to say. Poetry is where I do that. I can just be me. If anything, I've bared too much. And I think I've had the opposite experience from yours, Kerry. Poetry has made me braver in the gym. I know from poetry how important it is not to lie to one's self, not to try to be someone or something that I am not. If I'm lying or hedging or pretending in a poem, it's not going to go anywhere. It will totally, totally suck. Dishonesty has zero energy. Even when I have used alternate voices, in dramatic monologues, I still had to be myself and be brutally honest with that self.

What that means in the gym is not pretending that I'm anything other than what I am, which is a small, poorly-muscled, physically timid fifty-three-year-old woman with no left breast. On the street, I wear a prosthetic breast, but, in the gym, I am just me. This is very important for me. The gym, as with poetry, is where I have no false exterior. Poetry helped me with that because once you have stood in front of a group of people and read a poem about, say, giving a blow job or how much you like the smell of your husband's sweaty, post-hockey body or how much you resented your sister's terminal illness which was no fault of her own and a tragedy of personally epic proportions for her but one that fucked up your family royally, you can't have many qualms about being a little physically "off" in front of a bunch of jocks. Beloved jocks, I should add. None of whom has ever given me even a sidelong glance. They just accept me and respect me for what I'm trying to do, half-assed as it is. That matters.

And, Anita, that thing about lying flat out on the floor after the workout. Yes, I love that. Utter and complete abandon and exhaustion. That is bliss. And it's even better when you're surrounded by people who are in the same state. It's kind of like having a sexual relationship with a group. Not really, but you know what I mean. How do we get there in poetry though? Is there an equivalent of that pleasant exertion? With writing, I just get all keyed up and then I have to go somewhere and MOVE, deplete some of that energy. I wish that I could do that with writing. Maybe I haven't worked hard enough yet in writing. Maybe that's what I should take from the gym to poetry, the need to completely spend one's self. With all of the attendant risk of it being an utter failure. That's what scares me. Not revealing shit about myself, but failing. So, okay, I do have a problem with bravery in poetry and I think that I can learn something from weightlifting about how to deal with that. Which is: don't walk away, don't give up before you have given it everything you've got. Yikes. I don't know if I can do that.

ANITA LAHEY: There seems no avoiding the issue of the sexes, and sex, in these physical poems of ours. In Kerry's poems, the narrator faces a male sparring partner and I think, in the poem "Trickster," feels a little patronized by him. She also transfers her attention to the physical as learned in the gym to the bedroom, where, for example, in the lovely little poem, "Natural," she scrutinizes her partner and envies him "the cheap strength that comes naturally." And in the poem "Muscle" we see the fighter in bed with her lover, both of them discovering her new self, manifested physically.

In Sharon's poems, there is this great marriage of effort in the gym with not only relationships, but with this insatiable attraction that rears up in us whether we want it to or not. At the end of "Kettlebell Swing": "Attraction's a force that won't be reasoned away." "Reverse Fly" is a tense, sexually charged poem that begins "Gravity's the man beneath me, anchoring / me to the up-tilted bench ..." And then, "My Favourite Bodybuilder" is an ode to a fellow gym junkie that closes with this heartbreaker of a line: "Were I ever to want anyone again."

In my kickboxing poems a kind of "girl fight" is played out, complete with name-calling and gossip, grudges avenged, and moral judgment weighed against the opponent. White lies and tomboy posturing. You always hear that when male friends fight, it's physical, merciless, and quickly forgotten. When women fight it is psychologically intense and the repercussions linger. I think this is something I was wrestling with by bringing these stereotypes into the boxing ring. I just feel so oppressed by prescribed gender roles, and also troubled and fascinated by the differences I see between the genders. All this is clearly something I've been writing my way through and I suspect it is in part what attracted me to the dojo. I think of a reporter I once heard interviewed on the radio who went undercover as a man in order to try to understand what life was like for men when women weren't around. Being at the gym, learning how to throw a punch, was a little like that.

KERRY RYAN: One of the things I love most about the club I train at is the complete lack of gender-related bullshit. Which isn't at all what I expected of a boxing club. I used to work out at the Y and it had a real meat-market vibe: leering, steroided guys pacing between sets, Lululemon-ed women afraid to break a sweat. And I can't tell you how many times I've been out for a run and ended up racing male joggers who refuse to be passed by a woman.

At the boxing club, probably half of the trainers and members are women and we're pushed just as hard as the guys are. We all use the same weight of medicine balls, even the kids do! We're all expected to do full push-ups, we're all pushed to our individual breaking points. Everyone is treated as if they're training for a fight, no matter if they ever step into the ring. It's a very supportive and nurturing environment, characteristics that I think of as being quite female but which I've come to realize are also key to coaching.

So, if it seems in the poem "Trickster" that the sparring partner is being patronizing, that's my failure. What I was trying to capture is how a very skilled trainer can be exactly the opponent the novice needs him to be. A trainer can calibrate his performance so that the novice always feels challenged, is always learning, but never feels completely clobbered and demoralized. It's a real skill and something I didn't appreciate until after I stepped out of the ring and watched another dozen fighters get in after me. Sure, it dampened my pride a bit to discover the trainer had been pulling back, but it was also such a victory just to get in there with him and to land a couple of shots.

ANITA LAHEY: Yesterday I was fuming over a Margaret Wente column about the U.S. army's decision to finally officially allow women in combat roles. She wrote, "Men are better fighters because they are bigger and stronger and can endure far more physical punishment before they break down." Something about this harkens back to a time when it would have been automatically assumed that a man would make a better writer than a woman. I do still have a feeling sometimes that there is a "boys" poetry corner that I'm not exactly part of. That corner feels combative to me: it is a place where lines are drawn between this poetic philosophy and that, where allies are secured and arguments dug out like trenches. Whereas the women poets I know are mostly interested in writing deeply, writing well—hang the debates about form and style and so on. There are definitely women in the first group and men in the second, so perhaps I am being stereotypical in seeing this gender divide, in the same way Wente is being stereotypical about women in combat.

KERRY RYAN: I don't know a thing about fighting in the military sense, but what I have learned about boxing is that it's not so much about having muscle as it is about using that muscle efficiently and effectively. It's about knowing your opponent and knowing yourself. Endurance. Strength of mind. Being quick on your feet. All of those are female traits as much as male.

I do feel there's more of a male/ female divide with poetry than I find in the gym, but age gets kind of tied up in it too. In the Winnipeg writing community, there's a lingering sense of an old boys' club with a lot of older, established male poets associated with the universities and a very academic, clinical approach to their craft. It's the kind of attitude I expected to find in a boxing club: intimidating, inaccessible, an environment that would never feel comfortable to me. But, there's also a really exciting community of young poets here bringing new energy and new voices to the fore. They, I should say we, are making space for ourselves. There's a lot of support and a lot of interesting work going on. And, true, some of it falls into the gender-specific, woman-focused stereotype: motherhood, sisterhood, girlhood, but the writing is real and startling and raw.

In my own writing I don't have a particular agenda relating to gender but it does come into play because I write about what I'm interested in, about myself, about my relationships. So, it's always there, always a factor, but I never set out to write *Vs.* as any kind of manifesto. I wanted to write about boxing and, since I'm a woman, it became the experience of a woman boxing. But, just as important, it was a *poet* boxing. And, it was just as much about *doing* the sport, as woman, as poet, as *seeing* the sport.

SHARON MCCARTNEY: I'm like Kerry in that I love the lack of gender-related b.s. at the gym. The CrossFit gym that I go to is about sixty percent female. I've been in classes that were all women and in classes where I was the only woman. There was no difference. All of the coaches but one are female. And these are strong, strong women. On joining this gym, everyone is told to leave their egos at the door. I think that a lot of gender crap gets left behind too. Plus, there's no flirting or anything like that going on that I'm aware of. If people are flirting, it's not with me. :)

Poetry is another world though. I have struggled with gender issues in poetry. When I was young, I despised what I told myself was distinctly "female" poetry. Poems about birth and children and relationships. I wanted to write tough poetry about bars in Montana and fights and people getting arrested. I laugh about this now! And, inevitably, my first book, which was mostly written after I had three kids, is almost all about childbirth and kids and relationships, etc. Such a joke on myself.

Whatever we deny rules us in the end. After having kids, I was totally obsessed with childbirth and with writing about it. That was a way to grow up a bit, I see now. To own the parts of myself that I had denigrated. This came partially from growing up in a family where the boy (I had one brother and two sisters) was the important one, the one who would carry my father's name forward. I do not blame my parents for that. That gender bias was their world. What was important for me was to become aware of how I had projected that into my world. And then to jettison the projection and write about what was possessing me so that I could, eventually, become dispossessed.

Having done that, I was able to move forward into other areas in poetry. But I still find it hard to align myself with what are seen as women's issues in poetry. Isn't good poetry, poetry that sets your insides on fire, genderless?

ANITA LAHEY: I think I've had the same problem with the idea of "female" poetry. The women's poetry I first fell in love with was along the lines of Karen Solie's early work, which is very much that tough girl in a bar stuff (in a great way). And yet half of my first book was about laundry and clotheslines! And in the few reviews the book garnered it is described as female "domestic" poetry. Bleh! But how can I argue with that description? When you see the second book, which is one-third a female kickboxer, one-third poems in male voices and about men, and one-third about a woman with a combat engineer partner gone off to war—it is gender, gender, gender, all around. It troubles me that I can't get away from this stuff, but then, this stuff troubles me, and maybe it's just like you say so eloquently: I needed to become dispossessed. I'm still waiting for that to happen. I clearly have more work to do.

SHARON MCCARTNEY: Right now, I'm utterly immersed in Eliot's *Four Quartets.* These poems are speaking to me as no other poems have for decades. It's a masculine voice, of course, with a gender bias. He's talking exclusively about men. But the transcendent quality is genderless. Kind of like the transcendence that I feel in the gym when we are all sweating and working and groaning together and it doesn't matter if you have a dick or not. Or if you have all four limbs and two breasts and all of the other traditional body parts, for that matter. What counts is the effort, the wrestling with one's self. That's true for me in poetry, in my own and that of others, and in the gym.

Nothing Too Small to Say: In Conversation with M. Travis Lane

Millicent Travis Lane lives on a quiet street "up the hill" in Fredericton, New Brunswick, across the street from the campus of the University of New Brunswick, where she has been an honorary research associate since 1967. A PhD graduate of Cornell University, where she marked for Vladimir Nabokov and wrote her dissertation on agnosticism as technique in the work of Robert Frost, Lane has published fourteen volumes of poetry plus several chapbooks, and has been reviewing poetry for *The Fiddlehead* since the late sixties. She's a recipient of the Pat Lowther Memorial Award, the Atlantic Poetry Prize, the Alden Nowlan Prize for Literary Excellence, the Bliss Carman Prize and several other awards. We spoke in her living room on a mild May evening, amid her enchanting collection of art and bric-a-brac and two very sociable cats. We continued our conversation via email afterward, and parts of this further exchange have been incorporated into what we initially discussed.

ANITA LAHEY: I wanted to start by talking about home. In "King's Landing" you write about "the wilderness of worlds" that "seems like home." In "Divinations" there's a lot about wanting to get away from home or feeling like you're in someone else's home. In the new book, *Ash Steps* (Cormorant 2012) Dorothy is "always" going home, and "Bromeliad"—

M. TRAVIS LANE: That's an air plant, it's like an orchid. They'll grow on telephone lines.

ANITA LAHEY: Home in your poems is elusive!

M. TRAVIS LANE: Definitely. You see, both of my grandfathers were in the military; my father was in the military. We moved almost every year and we left the place I was born as soon as my mother got out of the hospital. I still have dreams where we have to leave a house and get into another one, and I'll think: Oh dear. I'm homeless. I have no hometown. I have no roots.

ANITA LAHEY: Do you get sentimental about any place, even though you're "homeless"?

M. TRAVIS LANE: The places I get sentimental about are places in time as well as in geography. I can't go back to them.

ANITA LAHEY: Can you find home in a poem?

M. TRAVIS LANE: I don't know whether it's finding or not finding. It follows you around. It becomes your imagination.

ANITA LAHEY: I wonder whether you think it's just part of the human condition, that we're always looking for home.

M. TRAVIS LANE: I think so. This is a strong tradition, at least in Western European and Christian culture, the idea that life is a pilgrimage, that home is elsewhere: "Swing low, sweet chariot, coming for to carry me home!" And people get very sentimental about places that are no longer home. It's roots. And it's mommy and poppy. But it's also something, to some extent, that you make. It's a very portable idea.

ANITA LAHEY: How long have you been here in Fredericton?

M. TRAVIS LANE: I came here in 1960. And in many ways it *has* become home.

ANITA LAHEY: You came here straight from Cornell. What was it like, coming from that literary community to this one?

M. TRAVIS LANE: I don't think I've ever been a member of a purely "literary community." Most of my friends from long ago I knew through political and ecological concerns, and two of the oldest and dearest are painters and sculptors, not poets. I was meeting people partly through the church, Voices of Women for Peace, and the Conservation Council. I met musicians and writers and potters and people who make rugs.

ANITA LAHEY: But you did also discover other writers here.

M. TRAVIS LANE: Living ones, yes. But when we decided we were going to take up this job I instantly started reading Canadian poetry like mad.

ANITA LAHEY: Do you remember who you started reading first?

M. TRAVIS LANE: At this point I hardly know because I was reading so greedily. All these discoveries! Miriam Waddington, I came into her work fairly soon and I thought: this is *fine.*

ANITA LAHEY: Were there any poets here in Fredericton whose poems you encountered?

M. TRAVIS LANE: Yes. Larry [Lane's husband, an English professor at UNB] made friends with his colleagues: Nowlan and Bailey and Gibbs and Cogswell. Those were the first poets in Fredericton whose poetry I knew. But I wasn't a member of Nowlan's Flat Earth Society (who were all men). Then I started doing reviews with *The Fiddlehead* and I'd find five or six good Canadian poets a year.

ANITA LAHEY: Do you find when you make friendships with other poets that you talk a lot about the poetry and the work?

M. TRAVIS LANE: Mostly no, I don't discuss. I never joined the Ice House gang. [An "historic" poetry-critiquing group in Fredericton, meeting in a former ice house at UNB.] I cannot respond intelligently to a poem that I have just heard recited to me. And I do not think other people can do that either. I have never taken any courses in how to write poetry and I never wish to give one.

ANITA LAHEY: Can you tell me anything about what Alden Nowlan was like?

M. TRAVIS LANE: I used to enjoy telling people I was the only poet in Canada who could look down at Alden Nowlan [Nowlan's house sat downhill from Lane's]. I was not one of his group but he was fond of us, sort of at a distance, the way an amiable dog might be fond of amiable cats. He and Claudine would always invite Larry and me down for their New Year's party.

ANITA LAHEY: Has Fredericton been a good place to cultivate your poetry mind?

M. TRAVIS LANE: I think it's not so much that it is a good place as much as Larry had a good job. I didn't have to go earn my living. I had a patron.

ANITA LAHEY: For me, I'm quite new here myself, your poems that feature Fredericton give me a new way of knowing the place. I wondered if writing about it gives you that too.

M. TRAVIS LANE: I don't think writing helps me know something outside the poem. It might help me know something about me. Something outside of the poem might instruct me—

ANITA LAHEY: But if you set a poem in a moment in a place, the next time you walk through there does it feel different because now it lives in the poem too?

M. TRAVIS LANE: No. I don't think so. It's the incident that heated the poem. You bring your whole past and your desires to it and it is this combination that produces the interesting effects, if you can do it.

ANITA LAHEY: Your poems are so populated with flora and fauna.

M. TRAVIS LANE: I come from a long line of people who were fascinated by flora and fauna. It was a family thing: having picnics, climbing mountains, wandering along streams, learning the names of flowers. We'd try to explore the nature of the place that we were in. In Wichita Falls, Texas, I remember we were so enchanted by the blue bonnets.

ANITA LAHEY: Do you remember what you found enchanting when you first came here?

M. TRAVIS LANE: We walked in the university woods, until all those new shopping centres cut them off. What Larry liked to do was follow the old roads. We'd get out-of-date maps and we'd go woods-whacking.

AITA LAHEY: What else do you remember about that early time in Fredericton?

M. TRAVIS LANE: One of the chaps in the English department was going to teach contemporary Canadian literature. So he made a little mimeographed anthology. There were thirty Maritime poets. One was a woman. Most of them were men he knew in the department, some of whom hadn't published books. And I wrote a long list of all the published Maritime women poets and I pasted it over the department doors. This is, you know, ancient feminist reminiscence. When the Pat Lowther prize was first being talked about, Alden Nowlan said something that was (A) very wrong and (B) very right. The Pat Lowther was intended to help bring women's poetry into prominence. Alden got up and said he couldn't see that women were being neglected. But, he said, he thought the Maritimes were. And I think he was right. I think the Maritimes still are.

ANITA LAHEY: Has any Maritime poetry in particular had an influence on you?

M. TRAVIS LANE: Nowlan's poetry helped me quite a bit in seeing how important it was to touch the heart. Of Maritime poets I'd say he's the most influential.

ANITA LAHEY: Why did you need to learn to touch the heart?

M. TRAVIS LANE: The major poets we were taught to admire, and whom I still admire, of the twentieth-century—Yeats, Pound, Frost, Eliot, Auden, Lowell, Stevens, Williams—went in for being passionate, witty, serious, philosophical, musical, etc., but tenderness was not what they did.

ANITA LAHEY: What leads you to a poet? Do you just follow your nose?

M. TRAVIS LANE: I go down to the *Fiddlehead* office and I open the books casually somewhere in the middle, and I read the lines out loud. And if they have music and aren't just buh-buh, buh-buh, buh-buh—I can't stand that. If it's just broken sentences and lists I don't care for it. The rhythms have to have something to do with the emotions.

ANITA LAHEY: Do you think all of us poets have our own natural, built-in rhythm?

M. TRAVIS LANE: The good ones do, yes. To some extent you can tell who's writing a poem almost by the sound of it.

ANITA LAHEY: Can you alter your rhythm?

M. TRAVIS LANE: You have to, according to the emotion. You might have to break it up, or question, or suddenly stop, or you might get fast or you might get slow. My poem "Keeping Afloat" is an extreme example of the flowing, as opposed to your kickboxing poems. They're two opposite kinds of music, but both music, that's the thing.

ANITA LAHEY: Where does it come from?

M. TRAVIS LANE: We used to speak of writing elegant prose, pacing, you'd make sure you didn't bore people. People would memorize lots of poetry and eloquent pieces of prose. Speeches by Lincoln, for example, or from the Revised Standard Version of the Bible. So much of our eloquence was based in the past on reciting poetry, reading poetry, and people were very proud of speaking eloquently. Now they go for content.

ANITA LAHEY: Is this loss of the sense of sound part of poetry's problem?

M. TRAVIS LANE: Oh yes. I think there's some suspicion that prettifying things is somehow false. It's a distrust of poetry. We are becoming a very sophisticated visual culture, but anybody who'd be happy with Twitter has obviously lost any joy of the complicated and gorgeous sentence.

ANITA LAHEY: In your poem "Solar Remission," you write that nothing is too small to say. I felt like that was a key to your writing and your poetry.

M. TRAVIS LANE: It's very much a key. And it's very much related to a kind of feminism I have. For example, I think it was Roethke who made fun of women poets stamping their tiny feet at God. I was writing and publishing in the fifties and sixties and there was this awful feeling that: what could women write about? They had no experience. The men poets would list all the things they did: wranglers and loggers and whalers. Heroic stuff! And, you know, I'm not a very good cook, somewhat of a gardener [laughs] and I once hand-embroidered a pillow. I also took a great dislike to a lot of the things that many of our ancestors said about The Poet with a capital P. I still run into capital P poets. So there's all this trying to put things back in proportion.

ANITA LAHEY: What is a capital P poet?

M. TRAVIS LANE: Some idea of what a Poet is: a romantic figure, the poet as wise, as sexy, as little Laytons.

ANITA LAHEY: There was another line in one of your poems that struck me as a line *about* your poetry. In "Gold Fleece": "This is no wall or country that I weave but a plain language you can't read unless you bruise your knuckles." I think in one swoop it's saying that what you're offering is unpretentious but also demanding—

M. TRAVIS LANE: Yes.

ANITA LAHEY: Straightforward but difficult—

M. TRAVIS LANE: Yes!

ANITA LAHEY: Welcoming but potentially painful.

M. TRAVIS LANE: Yes, all that, yes!

ANITA LAHEY: It felt to me like you're admitting that you're luring us in so you can then let us have it.

M. TRAVIS LANE: Oh yes.

ANITA LAHEY: The other thing is that I can feel my knuckles whacking against the letters—"you bruise your knuckles." You have a knack for these really tactile images and metaphors. Another one is actually in "Keeping Afloat." The idea of the swimmer being like the scuba diver in the fish tank, battery-operated.

M. TRAVIS LANE: I saw that scuba diver in an airport once. You get a stockpile, this tremendous attic full of trivial stuff, and then something says, woo-hoo!

ANITA LAHEY: I see your eyes light up when there's something you take delight in. I feel like some people want poetry to be serious all the time, without it being delightful or playful.

M. TRAVIS LANE: And some people seem to want it to be cheerful and extrovert all the time. They can't stand it serious. You know, it can't be all on the same level. Life isn't.

ANITA LAHEY: On that note, we should talk about *Ash Steps.* You warned me that, like some other recent work of yours, it contains much illness and death. One of the things we're always told is that death is one of the chief subjects of poetry, but did it really feel that way when you were younger, compared to now?

M. TRAVIS LANE: Well, I was born in 1934. I was an intelligent, reading person throughout the Second World War. I was in grade six or seven when the Hiroshima bomb fell and people were bringing pictures back from Auschwitz. My father was away in the theatre getting shot at. One of my first published poems was "A Welcome to Peace" in 1945 (I can't remember which of the Washington, D.C. papers it was in). But the thing is, I couldn't have been unaware of death given the life that I was living.

ANITA LAHEY: Yet it must be different now.

M. TRAVIS LANE: The major difference is statistical. I have more friends popping off than I did.

ANITA LAHEY: I really like the poem "Wishing." That's the one that ends with "a sort of lacy yearning" and "I clutch at my twig."

M. TRAVIS LANE: That's me. A little old lady who can no longer skip. [Laughs.]

ANITA LAHEY: Another is called "She Keeps Writing the Same Poem." Is that a lament or is it actually a sort of affirmation?

M. TRAVIS LANE: It's just a nasty remark about myself. [Laughs.] "For heaven's sake, haven't I been here before?"

ANITA LAHEY: Do you sometimes feel no, that you actually are writing something new?

M. TRAVIS LANE: Sometimes, yes. Lately the opera has helped. I've done quite a number of opera poems. Some of them got into *The Book of Widows* (Frog Hollow, 2010), and I have some upstairs, hunting for a home.

ANITA LAHEY: Why opera?

M. TRAVIS LANE: It's a place to go I haven't been before, so that's very nice. And the opera, no matter how silly the plots, the music always means.

ANITA LAHEY: The music always means?

M. TRAVIS LANE: Music turns up in references all the time in poetry but it doesn't necessarily translate into words. But opera, because it does have the plot, because it does have the words, it's like fairy tales, except, you know, I was using fairy tales for quite a bit …

ANITA LAHEY: And you've also used visual art and sculpture. Why are those things useful? Sculptures, opera, fairy tales?

M. TRAVIS LANE: Well I suppose, you ask yourself, why do these things mean to me? Sometimes the words can come and sometimes they can't.

ANITA LAHEY: Earlier, I was reviewing your "Reader's Deductions" at the back of *Keeping Afloat* and I wondered what made you write it.

M. TRAVIS LANE: Because all these revered poets were writing these distinguished essays about what poetry is. And I couldn't do it in prose like that. I thought maybe what I can do is write what I believe as succinctly as I can. You might call it a failed essay.

ANITA LAHEY: There's one that says: "Imagery is not necessary to a poem. Musicality is not necessary to a poem." Which is actually contrary to something we talked about today.

M. TRAVIS LANE: But: "A poem says how its words feel." That is really important. I may like imagery and music. There's a poet, Pasquale Verdicchio, he wrote little square poems and they had no music, no imagery, but they were good.

ANITA LAHEY: A poem says how its words feel. I've never heard a statement like that.

M. TRAVIS LANE: That's the one I'll stick by.

ANITA LAHEY: In other words, the poem has to know—

M. TRAVIS LANE: Its own emotion. I hate to use the word "emotion" because so many people seem to think it means only tears and screaming, but playing Scrabble, working out, those are emotions too. We're never without emotion.

ANITA LAHEY: Is it another way of saying the words in the poem have to belong?

M. TRAVIS LANE: Yeah. You need the words to get the music right. For example, getting back to *Ash Steps*, in "Confluence," in the beginning it says: "I found them dull." That is a line that *says* it finds things dull. Call that musical, but in a sense that is, because it is saying how this person feels. The words say it.

ANITA LAHEY: They embody it.

M. TRAVIS LANE: Yep. You'd be showing off if you said, "I find it totally uninteresting." That's a different kind of emotion.

ANITA LAHEY: You mentioned once that you felt *Divinations*, which won the Pat Lowther Memorial Award in 1980, was your most ambitious book. Can you talk about what you were trying to do in that marvellous, three-part title poem?

M. TRAVIS LANE: "Divinations" is a take on the *Divine Comedy* by Dante. I knew that hell, purgatory, and paradise were all in the mind, imagination or soul. I could not imagine speaking for someone who was wicked, but I could do despair—the wish to be "nothing." The scenery and characters and anecdotes from the hell section are from my own adolescence, but the suicide is patterned on the suicide of an adolescent acquaintance.

ANITA LAHEY: Why is hell in the Catskills?

M. TRAVIS LANE: I wanted a real place for hell and material that could be interpreted as good or as bad: the apple tree, the image of fruit, comfort, fertility, beauty. But the apple tree is also, deep in our poetry and in our mistranslations, the fruit of death. And consider all those potential apple diseases, like tentworms. And I was an adolescent in the Catskills—and I wanted despair not to be rooted in events or health but in an immature frame of mind.

ANITA LAHEY: I am haunted by the woman in the next section, whose husband is digging up the ancient Aboriginal cemetery. How did you decide to write on this place and these issues from her perspective?

M. TRAVIS LANE: The locale for purgatory is very much New Brunswick. Purgatory itself is a place out of which one should move: repent, grow wiser, escape. It is a sort of Middle Earth, in a Tolkien sense. I thought using the prevailing prejudices of the European re: Aboriginal communities would give her a kind of wrongness that she has to grow out of. The character begins by thinking that Red Earth is a nowhere place and that its inhabitants are ghostly and feeble. But she matures and discovers the vigorous reality of the people and sees the need to get out of her old self. To write as a well-intentioned person finding herself confused, not quite understanding what is going on, as this character does, seems to me as very much where I am much of the time.

ANITA LAHEY: You employed so many different techniques in the third section to reveal the voice and narrative—it's marvellous. Is this your idea of paradise: all that variation?

M. TRAVIS LANE: Paradise is in the mind of an artist/ believer who "sees" Paradise around her in her real life in Saint John. She very much *makes* Paradise. Her character is filched from that of James Hampton, a black male janitor who made, with aluminum foil and cardboard tubing and posters etc. in his garage, an altar to God so beautiful that it is now collected in one of the Washington, D.C. museums. He wrote and painted religious slogans and it seemed proper that I should do shaped-poetry for Pearl to write, since she is a sculptor. Just as I did not write "as an Aboriginal" in "Red Earth," so I do not write "as a black man" in "The Book of the Thrones." But I was delighted that I could do Pearl, who is clearly a saint and a visionary. The pearl is a gem that is created by pain—it's a sickness in the oyster, an irritation. Then there is Herbert, "who sweeps a room as for His sake makes that and the action fine." Saintliness isn't necessarily going to involve doing Grand Deeds. And I wanted Saint John as Paradise because downtown Saint John does not give the impression of great wealth and civic beauty, so the beauty is in the eyes of the beholder.

AFTERWORD

When I write about a place, my hold on it, or its hold on me, shifts. So I was surprised by Lane's decisive and dismissive response when I asked whether her poems set in Fredericton had altered her relationship with the city. Reading Lane's poems certainly had an impact on my own relationship to Fredericton during the short time we lived there during 2011 and 2012. In "For the Cenotaph, November 11, 1933," she writes of Fredericton, "your face,/ like china, shows its age/ but not the past," clarifying a sense I always had of something lost or hidden as I roamed the streetscapes there. Lane's verse animated the river too, which I had not been able to read myself: it was so broad and seemed to amble so indifferently through town. For Lane, though, it "tapped at its lid of ice" ("King's Landing"), it was home to a cormorant having second thoughts ("Local Suite"), and to a near-sighted moose that turns and swims the other way. She held up, like a bird on her palm, that unease I'd felt walking home through Fredericton's unsettling quiet at night: "to believe,/ for a while, in the dark, that I am 'pure eye'—/ invulnerable, invisible, and safe,/ a sort of minor spook, star, angel, shade" ("Walking Back at Night"). Lane's situation, in Divinations, *of purgatory in rural New Brunswick and paradise in Saint John, coloured and arranged my experience of the province. When fellow writer Sherry Coffey and I attended part of the Truth and Reconciliation Commission's day of hearings at Government House, the troubled woman from "Red Earth" hovered in my mind, listening too. When my husband and I drove down to Saint John to climb the steep, narrow streets lined with proud old stone and brick buildings above the harbour, our son Henry nestled in a neat pouch, I appreciated the impulse to situate paradise in this grimy, foggy port town. Indeed, Lane's Saint John ("I looked for gloves./ I found a rainbow in the wound" and "As bruised snow melts,/ as gutters run,/ our substance pours into the sea") made the whole notion of paradise, for me, more palatable.*

'All the bounty of the Lord made manifest'

Joan Thomas on the Woman Who Unearthed a Plesiosaur

Joan Thomas's novel *Curiosity* is set on the shores of Lyme Regis, where a nineteenth-century cabinet-maker's daughter named Mary Anning spent her days scouring the rock-face for fossils. Anning brought home remarkable finds that shook pre-Darwinian ideas about evolution and rendered her one of the most significant paleontologists of her time, though she was never officially recognized as such. In the interview below, conducted over email, Thomas discusses the ideas that compelled her to bring Anning back to life as a literary heroine, namely the persistent tension between religion and science in our world and the bottomless wonder of evolution. She shares snippets of letters and other archival material that offer glimpses of the real Mary Anning and she describes how she, as a writer, imagined Anning's scientific mind at work.

ANITA LAHEY: I read an article in the *Globe and Mail* this morning about a fossil a woman named Sharon Hubbard found on a beach off Hornby Island six years ago. An artist and amateur paleontologist, Hubbard knew she was looking at something extraordinary. After measuring and photographing the fossil, she showed it to Graham Beard, her companion that day, who happened to be the curator of paleontology at the Qualicum Beach Museum. He took the fossil with him. It has since led to the discovery of a new species, a kind of pterosaur, and was named Gwawinapterus beardi after Beard, in honour of his "discovery." The story explains that Hubbard would have wished it to be named Hornbyensis humbardii. Of course I thought about Mary Anning while reading this. The scenario is eerily familiar: specimen found by citizen, turned over to expert and identified with that expert in the ensuing narrative.

In *Curiosity* you portray Anning as keenly frustrated by the gentlemen's treatment of her: their disregard for her scientific expertise and instincts, and their lack of awareness that she might deserve any credit for her work. Did she see herself as a scientist not given her rightful due? Is this one of the things about her story that drew you and galvanized you? And, finally, did this lead you to think about what it means to be a true scientist, as opposed to a hobbyist or amateur, and how we think about this dichotomy in wider society? This question reminds me of something you've mentioned before: that Charles Dickens claimed geology was not a science when Mary Anning began, that she made it one. She obviously did this by more than simply scouring the shoreline, by finding things. What was it about how she approached her calling, would you say, that raised geology to the level of science?

JOAN THOMAS: Very interesting! I guess in both stories, two-hundred years apart, we see privilege reflexively granted to people who work within an establishment.

None of Mary Anning's five major finds was credited to her and numerous gentlemen made their reputations through her discoveries, but I need to clarify that Anning was not singled out for exploitation. The gentlemen of science in the nineteenth-century routinely bought their specimens from curi-men, stone quarriers and canal-diggers, and they never credited their finders. The problem was that Mary Anning became more than a finder. She was highly skilled in identifying the fossils and preparing them for display. She dissected existing species to learn to understand the anatomy of extinct forms. In the words of one of her contemporaries, "This poor, ignorant girl … professors and other clever men on the subject … all acknowledge that she understands more of the science than anyone else in this kingdom." The divide between the finders and the scientists was largely along class lines, and it was that line that proved the greatest barrier to Mary Anning. Of course there was also systemic sexism and occasionally in the writings you get a strong whiff of misogyny: "a prim, pedantic, vinegar-looking, thin female," one colleague observed when he met Mary.

Because Anning left no scientific papers, only letters, it's a little hard to assess her understanding, but I'm not sure I'd go as far as Charles Dickens did. She was not a theorizer, as far as I can see, but she was strikingly free in her thinking. "Bezoars," considered for centuries to be stones with magical properties, were often found on the beach at Lyme Regis. It was Anning who recognized them as fossilized dung and she had a method for sectioning these coprolites so that they became a great source of information about extinct species. And the anatomy of the fossil molluscs called belemnites perplexed everybody until Anning settled the question by locating their missing (and very frail) ink sacs. Then she chipped desiccated ink out of them and reconstituted it for use in specimen drawings. Fossil sepia! She had a practical, straightforward way of looking at phenomena that I loved, and in those examples we see the movement of the period to a more empirical science.

Yes, I think Mary Anning did aspire to more. At the Natural History Museum in London, you can see her hand-copy of a lengthy article by William Conybeare describing one of her finds, without ever mentioning her, of course, and there is a private note to herself: "When I write a paper, there shall not be but one preface." When I found this note, I'd never seen it mentioned in any of the writing about Mary Anning, and it shaped my view of her. It's so poignant, because we are aware of the barriers she faced, not least her lack of formal education, her notoriously bad spelling and punctuation, and of course the fact that she was shut out of the discussions at the Geological and Royal Societies by both sex and social class. She expressed her bitterness to at least one friend, who wrote in 1832, "According to [Mary] these men of learning have sucked her brains, and made a great deal by publishing works of which she furnished the contents, while she derived none of the advantages." And apparently

Mary Anning held William Buckland's knowledge of anatomy in great contempt and was very funny on the subject.

Was this one of the things that galvanized me? Well, it moved me, and I saw it as one strand in an amazing historical episode. But what really pulled me into the subject was the dilemma all natural historians faced, confronting physical evidence that the way they saw the world was fundamentally wrong. You could say that I grew up as a pre-Darwinist myself, so I relished this story.

ANITA LAHEY: The way you describe Anning's way with the fossils above, and in the novel, is mesmerizing. When I was reading *Curiosity* I felt that she seemed to draw fossils to her, to know them, to be able to look at them and really see, and to ask questions about them that matter. I'm interested, though I realize it's pretty much impossible to know, in how much gut and instinct might have been involved in Anning's scientific "talent." And also how much this might have had to do with years of focus and concentration, uninterrupted by the distractions of "society." She was not "learned" in the traditional sense and yet she saw things that learned men missed, again and again. Do you think there's a message in her experience regarding what the true path to good science, or good literature, might be versus what we habitually think it is?

JOAN THOMAS: It's true that men of science trekked to Lyme Regis with the hope of collecting with Mary Anning because they knew they'd always go home with something; she could apparently tell at a glance which stony concretion among the hundreds scattered on the shore had an ammonite inside. Where do these instincts come from? Well, I think I agree with Malcolm Gladwell's notion in *Outliers* that what we think of as instinct or giftedness is largely the result of countless hours of applying a skill. (He ventured a number actually: 10,000.) Mary Anning was an outlier in every sense of the word, and she was out on the shore honing her collecting eye almost every day for three decades.

I really wanted to find the flesh-and-blood woman in Mary Anning; I didn't want to romanticize her or portray her as some sort of nature goddess. But I thought a lot about what it must mean to spend most of your life outside, under the sky, by the sea. Many people know that wonderful shift that comes partway through a wilderness trip, when you're suddenly open to nature in a different way, and I thought that Anning's character and view of the world must have been shaped by her intimacy with nature. Near the end of *Curiosity*, I imagined Henry De la Beche anguishing over the collapse of his belief in divine creation and Mary saying without thinking, "Well, it [the world] is no less the miracle for that." That sense of the mystery of nature and its interconnected systems must be hard for scientists to sustain in a laboratory setting, especially when each person tends to be an expert in a narrower and narrower field.

Is the fossil-hunter's intuition like the writer's process in excavating a story? When I started writing fiction, the biggest surprise to me was the way voices and images seemed to come from a place that is not quite reasoned. I count on this now, almost as a technique: deliberately not staring too directly at a scene, just trying to be attentive to the things that flicker in the corner of my eye. As writers we've stocked the pool through a lifetime of experience and observation and reading (mainly reading) and when we draw from it, there is some sort of alchemy, not dissimilar to dreams, that delivers up something new. I don't want to make too much of a mystery of it but in the best moments the offerings of the imagination are things we hardly feel we own.

In early drafts of *Curiosity*, I imagined Mary Anning blurring her eyes as she walked the shore, believing she'd see more in her peripheral vision. I had her musing that what a good collector needs is a kinship with these prehistoric creatures, "a reptilian eye, to see what had never been seen or even imagined." In the end, that text hit the cutting room floor. But Mary's last big find in *Curiosity* began to embody this idea for me. It's a plesiosaur, a mammoth monster with a risibly small head, "all locomotion and no reason." Mary Anning had to be willing to countenance things that fell outside her understanding, a useful sort of courage for writers as well.

ANITA LAHEY: The beliefs that fossils might be dragons or devil's toenails—the ideas Mary and her father had before that gentleman showed up in the town square in Lyme Regis and taught Mary the word "ammonite"—are all colourful, dramatic and poetic, with narratives and plot-related cause-and-effect. Even Buckland's idea about fossils being the remains of animals drowned in the biblical flood is a narrative way to explain what exists. Once we start to get the pure science, the hard data that has nothing to do with God and the devil but everything to do with rocks changing imperceptibly over millennia, do we lose that link between science and story? Do we lose the wonder that goes with the faith the gentlemen had in their bible-based versions of evolution? You have given us a marvellous novel about this episode in scientific history, which is certainly evidence against science being dry, but I can't help being bothered by this notion: can science and its head-on facts flatten or nullify the imagination we're forced to draw on, in our ignorance, to explain the phenomena around us? In other words, I guess, is there a cultural price for this new knowledge? Or is there nothing to mourn in the loss of the dragons and the devil's toenails?

JOAN THOMAS: Childhood is an intense time of wonder, and creation stories were hatched in the childhood of human civilization. I grew up being taught that creation all happened in a week in October 4004 BC, and for a while I did my best to believe it. Let me tell you, what stays with me is not the wonder of the creation miracle, but how crazy-making it was to try to believe something so at odds with the modern mind!

You could argue that the loss of a sense of the miraculous in nature is behind our indifference to environmental degradation and species extinction. In *The Death of Adam* Marilynn Robinson suggests that we've more or less surrendered the concept of evolution to the social Darwinists, where life is a values-free struggle for existence that the cockroach will ultimately win. She writes, "It is as if we no longer sat on chairs after we learned that furniture was only space and atoms." We haven't made a good transition from childish thinking to an informed thinking that appreciates the wonders of the natural world.

Maybe we'd think more holistically if we'd retained the terms "natural history" or "natural philosophy" for what we now call "science." There is a narrative in evolution so huge it boggles the mind. The deeper we go, the more we find to marvel at. The cultural price I'm concerned about is the price of clinging to the old narratives. Thinking of ourselves as the highest expression of divine will has not been good for the planet. We haven't really grasped the wonder of the hundreds-of-millions-of-years long narrative that gave the earth creatures as disparate and marvellous as the elephant and the tree frog. If we had, we'd act differently.

ANITA LAHEY: This makes me think of something you said earlier, about how Mary Anning had to countenance things that fell beyond her understanding. It seems we all ought to attempt such bravery, paleontologists, writers or otherwise. And of course you're right that wonder needn't be forfeited when science steps in—on the contrary. Wonder seems a close cousin to, or a possible path toward, love. The novel is full of love: between Mary Anning and Henry, between Mary and the fossils themselves, even between you, the novelist, and this kind of science, this exploration into the real stories behind existence and those insatiably curious souls who try to suss them out. I remember you saying that you were not pleased by the phrase "love story" being scripted onto *Curiosity*'s cover. I'm curious as to why.

JOAN THOMAS: When a reader sees everything in the phrase that you do, I'm happy. I just worried people might expect *Curiosity* to be a bodice-ripper with a dinosaur theme!

And of course the novel is a love story in the usual sense as well. Any novelist writing about Mary Anning will end up speculating about her relationships with the scientific gentlemen, based on a couple of tantalizing comments in letters and journals of the period. I mused over this for a long time and eventually decided that any novel alluding to evolution has to acknowledge, at its core, the incredible power of the sexual impulse.

On the Probability of Happiness

with Kim Jernigan and Alice Munro

The title story in Alice Munro's collection, *Too Much Happiness*, is based on the story of the late nineteenth-century Russian mathematician and novelist, Sophia Kovalevsky. Then *TNQ* editor Kim Jernigan and I, as editor of *Arc Poetry Magazine*, met with Munro at Bailey's restaurant in Goderich, Ontario in December, 2010, to discuss her fascination with Sophia's dual gifts; how to pilfer mathematics for metaphor; where science, superstition and emotion may meet in a brilliant mind; the complications of family, romance, Russian politics and social mores in Sophia's life; and what it means to be "too happy."

ALICE MUNRO: This story happened almost by accident. I was looking through the encyclopedia for something else when I saw Sophia's name at the top of the page. It said she was both a mathematician and a novelist, and I thought, 'No! It doesn't happen.' [Laughs.] So then I began to find out everything I could about her, and it was so wonderful, so terribly interesting.

ANITA LAHEY: Did you really think it was that surprising that the two abilities could come together in the same person?

ALICE MUNRO: Yes I did. And that's probably very ill-informed on my part. But I have a brother who's a scientist and in our family it's Bill who's got brains—and then there's Alice. [Laughter.] So I was interested in the question of how she could do both. I found this wonderful book: *Little Sparrow: A Portrait of Sophia Kovalevsky*, by Don Kennedy and his wife Nina, who has an ancestral connection to Sophia; there's a note about that following my story. Most of my factual material came from there. I was just so lucky to find it. And then, I have a friend—well we've never met—but I have a friend in Russia. She was sending me cries of astonishment: 'You know Sophia? Sophia is our heroine. All the kids in school learn about her.' This would have been in the time of the Soviet Union when my friend was at school, so Sophia had gotten a lot of press. I don't know though what Russians think of my book. I call it a book because to me it almost feels that way—it was that much work.

KIM JERNIGAN: And it feels that rich.

ALICE MUNRO: Yes, the story covers a lot of ground.

ANITA LAHEY: It felt like a departure for you to be writing about an historical figure.

ALICE MUNRO: It was very exciting. I really wanted to do it. But it was harder.

KIM JERNIGAN: You begin at a juncture where there's so much promise in Sophia's life—of love, of a new career—and then everything falls apart. But as you go back in time, we see the roots of the dissolution.

ALICE MUNRO: I can remember writing that with terrific emotion because it was really what happened.

ANITA LAHEY: As you started to read about Kovalevsky, what did you discover about this coming together of the two kinds of minds?

ALICE MUNRO: At first I read about her childhood, mostly about this terrifically beautiful, self-dramatized, marvellous sister of hers who kept the household in absolute turmoil with the things she would do and the things she threatened to do. And then there was all this stuff about women not being allowed to leave Russia unless accompanied by a male relative.

KIM JERNIGAN: She couldn't even walk in the street by herself.

ALICE MUNRO: Oh no. But that would have been true of walking in the streets of London at that time too, I think, at least for a woman of a certain class. Anyway, Sophia is just a little hanger-on to the wonderful, glamorous sister until, as in the story, she picks up a book that had been left for her father to read, because he was a general, and artillery I understand is mathematical—and as soon as she saw it, she understood it. Not all, but she started putting it together. I found this so fascinating. What is the mathematical mind like? I don't really know, even now.

KIM JERNIGAN: They say that mathematical genius manifests very young.

ALICE MUNRO: Is that right?

KIM JERNIGAN: Engineers make their best discoveries in their forties and fifties, but mathematicians make their best discoveries in their late twenties, or so my husband who's an engineer tells me.

ALICE MUNRO: So maybe she didn't lose so much professionally by dying young. I think she lost possibly a lot of happiness. But the mathematics …

ANITA LAHEY: Did you come to understand any of that math?

ALICE MUNRO: As far as I needed to, yes. But I found I was veering toward the emotional side. You know, to how her professional aspirations affected her emotional life. I understood the math to a lesser degree. I did go to high school. I was doing fine in math until about three quarters of the way through grade twelve. I went away to have my appendix out, and when I came back, I'd missed something. And that was the end of it.

KIM JERNIGAN: Sophia's work has to do with differential equations. I didn't get much farther in math than you did, but I'm told they have to do with mathematically modelling the way systems change over time and distance. I think that notion is very rich metaphorically—

ALICE MUNRO: It is! Immediately—and I feel almost embarrassed by this—I was jumping into the metaphors. Which, you know, a real scientist would never do. But I think *she* might have. It was the double-framing for her that fascinated me, because she wasn't fooling around with either the writing or the math. And then I just loved the whole business about how she had to get married to this guy so she could leave Russia.

KIM JERNIGAN: And yet he kind of hung around in her life.

ALICE MUNRO: Oh yeah, he loved her.

KIM JERNIGAN: How old would she have been?

ALICE MUNRO: Oh, she might have been sixteen, seventeen. Really a little girl. He's the sacrifice. A terrible sacrifice. Because he was so bright too. He's still remembered as a paleontologist. He would have been, perhaps, with an ideal wife. You know, I was brought up, well, to be a farm wife and that's different. But when I was a young married woman, I learned that educated women wanted desperately to worship and follow and give help to a man. It was not the uneducated who wanted this. It was the girls who read Freud. I didn't know any girls like that until I went to Vancouver. When I met them, I discovered I was barking up the wrong tree entirely, that other women didn't want to do the things I wanted to do. In the writing community it was like that too. It was women who were difficult for me to deal with. They didn't approve of me because they sensed that I wanted something of my own.

I've done a bit of reading about this recently and apparently there was a great Freudian burst before the Second World War, but then women had to go and help with the war so it got all confused. But right after the war, when the heroes came home and we started having babies to get the population up again, it was very strong. I remember the men at university. I was at the University of Western Ontario for two years. I was a waitress in the cafeteria to help pay my way. At the table where the men sat, they had terrific intellectual arguments. My present husband was one of those intellectuals. You could hear them all over the cafeteria and it was so interesting. Maybe a couple of wives sat there too but they never said anything. And they were doing the right thing. I came from a small town where nobody went to university and nobody cared about these things, so I hadn't heard about Freud and I hadn't heard about what I now should be feeling as a woman. But when I got to live in the suburbs, I found out, and it was a total surprise to me, that female achievement was so out of style. I had grown up so outside any respectable society—a farm is respectable, but it's different—that I had ambitions I wouldn't have had had I been better educated.

ANITA LAHEY: I'm surprised the women would just accept Freud's—

ALICE MUNRO: One thing I've learned is that people accept fashions very readily, and intellectual women or men are not immune to this. The sixties was when I finally began to feel alive, though I was really too old.

ANITA LAHEY: Did you feel a connection to Sophia because of that, that maybe she was a little more your kind of woman?

ALICE MUNRO: Oh yes. Of course. Why does Maxsim give up on her? Why does he go home? Because she got the prize. And this really happened. And he was a very intelligent, sophisticated man.

KIM JERNIGAN: Jealousy?

ALICE MUNRO: Well, yes. Suddenly, he's not unusual. There are lots of brilliant men around. And there she is, getting the attention because, as a woman mathematician, she's a freak. And she's getting this prize. So he goes home and starts writing these sulky letters about how he's got this other woman living with him and he can't introduce Sophia. [Pause] What interested me really was that she's part of the old world, part of the wanting to be looked after, yet also wanting to be herself. I don't know if it's a problem anymore but it's something I could relate to.

KIM JERNIGAN: I think it's perennial. And it's so interestingly developed in this story. The sense of Sophia as a child having a father she could lean into. That's kind of what she's yearning towards in Maxsim too. But at the same time she wants to have an independent life, an intellectual life that's her own.

ALICE MUNRO: She wants it all.

KIM JERNIGAN: She wants somebody to take care of her so that she can pursue her work.

ALICE MUNRO: That's true too.

KIM JERNIGAN: Her professor and mentor—he was about ideas, the life of the mind, not about fame and fortune—but he had the two sisters who cared for him and allowed him to live that life. I thought maybe that was an attractive model for her.

ALICE MUNRO: Well, if she could be in his position. But also, she would want the sexual love, which was out of the picture. I thought that was fascinating. There was the great brain in the study, and there were the two sisters, who weren't dummies. Practically adept, but they also read. On Sundays, they read novels aloud. They knew about love. But not for them.

ANITA LAHEY: Yes. I loved the ritual of that.

KIM JERNIGAN: The professor makes a comparison between poetry and mathematics, the combination of intuition and rigour required for each. On the way here, we were talking about mathematics and how it might work as metaphor, differential equations as a decision-making mechanism in situations where there's conflict or uncertainty, but I'm told mathematics isn't about decision making, it's about description. It might help her understand a situation but not resolve it.

ALICE MUNRO: Actually, I didn't think very deeply about the theories. What I thought about was the woman with a gift, it could be any gift. Though some gifts are easier than others to embrace. And mathematics I thought was not an easy one. And her excitement about it, which couldn't be held back.

ANITA LAHEY: Were you able to read any of her books?

ALICE MUNRO: Yes. I read some of her fiction. I think she was very good. The fiction I really liked was about her childhood, about growing up on the farm. You know, the beauty—you get this from Russian writers, the beauty of Russia. Then I read something she'd written for political purposes and I didn't like it. I had the feeling she didn't either, but she felt obliged to write it. The story was about a man who was a political dissident being exiled to Siberia. He would get better treatment if he had a wife, so this young woman said, I will be your wife. Never mind that I don't particularly like you.

ANITA LAHEY: I remember that Sophia was more fond of the personal novel herself but she wrote this one because she felt—

ALICE MUNRO: It was a good thing to do. I think Russians in that period really did feel that kind of duty. There was a desperation to do something about their country. Maxsim did go home to Russia to teach. He was trying to form a party based on a parliamentary democracy with a king at the head, but of course nobody went for that. And Lenin did denounce him. After Lenin denounced him I don't know what happened to him. I've lost Maxsim and I haven't found anything more about him. Of course I don't know where to look. But I think that's interesting, that he could go back and it would seem to him like it was possible to work something out, that Russia could survive without suffering the horrors it did survive.

ANITA LAHEY: There's an interesting thing in the story where you get the sense that her mentor, the older professor, is flabbergasted that she would bother to write a novel.

ALICE MUNRO: Yes. Yes. Yes. He's just at sea in the whole world of fiction. That interested me.

ANITA LAHEY: Also, the idea of her letting him down. Where did that come from?

ALICE MUNRO: After she'd been his prize pupil and got her advanced degree, she puts it in her bag, she goes home, and suddenly everything is beautiful. It's summer in Petersburg and everybody's having a wonderful time and she wonders, what is this all about? And she doesn't write to him. He writes to her. He tries to keep her interested in mathematics. Sometimes she doesn't even answer. All the pleasures of coasting along in life really get to her. She does it for about four or five years. She has a baby. She wasn't having any of that earlier. And she doesn't respond to her old teacher, hardly at all. Which I found very hard—I could understand it though. I put a line in the book about that, you know, that there are lots of people who can get through life very comfortably without any major interest, without any devotion to anything. And she was just discovering this.

ANITA LAHEY: Do you think she was having a good time?

ALICE MUNRO: Yeah. All you have to do is decide it's worthwhile to have a good time and you can thrive in life. Everybody else seemed to know this but she was just learning it. But then of course the money problem got her interested again.

ANITA LAHEY: Do you think she would have gone back if not for the money?

ALICE MUNRO: I think so, but needing the money was a great impetus. They lost their money and her husband had a nervous breakdown. And even then she wrote science stuff for the newspaper, she reviewed plays. All these things to make money rather than go back and commit herself. But when she had to, she went back. And then it was as if she'd never been away.

KIM JERNIGAN: I'm interested in the structure of the story. At what point did you decide to start towards the end of her life and work backwards?

ALICE MUNRO: I think because of that picture of them in the graveyard on the first day of the year. The rest of the story came from there. She's already hoping that she can have a normal life and be a scientist.

KIM JERNIGAN: And yet the setting is so ominous! In another of the pieces in this gathering [the joint issue of *Arc* and *TNQ* where this interview first appeared], poet Matthew Tierney writes about the poem as time machine. Writers can be very free with how they move about in time. I've always been fascinated with that aspect of your work, how much the way you arrange things temporally affects the experience of the reader. The first of your stories that really made me think about this was "Miles City, Montana," from *The Progress of Love.*

ALICE MUNRO: Oh yes.

KIM JERNIGAN: I read that when my two daughters were exactly the same age as the children in the story.

ALICE MUNRO: Oh god.

KIM JERNIGAN: A young boy has drowned and there's all kinds of drama about it. And then the story leaps forward to when the family is on a road trip going from west to east through the States. It's a hot, hot summer and the kids are cranky in the back seat so they stop at a pool they spot. It's closed, but they see the lifeguard and they say, can we let the children in to swim and cool off, and he's persuaded. Then the father's going out to the car to do whatever fathers do [laughter], and the mother's walking through the park. Suddenly the boy who drowned at the beginning of the story—I had completely forgotten about him as I was drawn into the car trip—came back into my head. At that exact same moment in the story, the mother has a premonition that she has to get back to the pool. So she goes racing back and the lifeguard has a girlfriend and is flirting and not paying attention, and the youngest daughter is on the bottom of the pool. The mother calls to the father who leaps the fence. They rescue the child and there's this great rush of relief and a sense of jubilation, of the mother and father having come together. Then you add, "That was before the divorce." And oh, it was heartbreaking but brilliant. Reading Sophia's story, a true story, I was thinking a lot about the way you positioned the narrative elements.

ALICE MUNRO: The timing.

KIM JERNIGAN: Yes, the way a reader reacts emotionally to something is very affected by what—

ALICE MUNRO: By what is around it. Yes.

KIM JERNIGAN: You arrange things in a very different way from the way your characters live them.

ALICE MUNRO: Yes. That's true. In "Happiness," I sort of worked back from the new year through her life to her death, which is coming, but with lots of stops and meanders.

KIM JERNIGAN: I recently read a moving piece in the *New Yorker* by Joyce Carol Oates …

ALICE MUNRO: Oh, I read that too! It was marvellous.

KIM JERNIGAN: What resonated with me and got me thinking again about "Too Much Happiness" was something Oates said about her own marriage, which had apparently been a long and happy one: that her husband had never read any of her fiction. I was just stunned to hear that. And at one point she wondered if he could really know her, having not read her fiction.

ALICE MUNRO: But did she want him to know her? When I read that, I was very interested because my husband and I have almost the same thing. Really we have. He does read my stories. But he can only read them when I'm out of the country. Or at least at a certain geographical distance. [Laughter.]

KIM JERNIGAN: She also says they never talked at home about any of the stresses in their life. You know, if she was having trouble with a publisher or bad reviews. When I first read that they didn't talk about anything stressful I thought, well what did they talk about?

ALICE MUNRO: Yeah. What else is there?

KIM JERNIGAN: They talked about books and they talked about things in the newspaper but not about the personal stuff. A dichotomy. There's a similar dichotomy in your story, between the intellectual and the personal, the bodily. Sophia's mentor, the esteemed professor, is so excited to have a pupil he can talk to about the intricacies of mathematics, and yet you keep reminding us that these brilliant minds are attached to bodies. They get ill, they have desires, they need to eat. The professor has to eat prunes to be regular.

ANITA LAHEY: Because he has such a sedentary life.

ALICE MUNRO: I may have made that up. It's hard to remember.

ANITA LAHEY: Speaking of making things up, we were wondering about the doctor that she meets on the train, whether he—

ALICE MUNRO: It's all made up.

KIM JERNIGAN: We figured that must be an invention. But he is a fascinating character. I felt he was a malevolent presence, Anita not so much.

ALICE MUNRO: No, not malevolent. He wished her well. I felt that he could see something. I don't want to dwell on this too much because it gets all icky, you know, the idea that someone can tell what will happen to people, but I think he noticed something about her. Maybe being a doctor made a difference.

ANITA LAHEY: Do you know why he happened into the story?

ALICE MUNRO: Maybe I was thinking a bit about her poor husband, who the doctor resembled slightly. I find her husband a terribly sad character.

KIM JERNIGAN: He takes his own life at the end?

ALICE MUNRO: He did. He did. It was so awful. Was being married to an achieving woman part of his problem? Maybe it was. Does that mean that achieving women are supposed to go to a nunnery? The question never arises, does the achieving man ever present a problem?

KIM JERNIGAN: Sophia's own death is brought about by the long trip by train and boat she takes to avoid Copenhagen where the doctor has said there's a smallpox epidemic. But she can never confirm whether there's any truth to that.

ALICE MUNRO: Well actually there was. I confirmed that. But she doesn't know that. There was a big problem because, you know, Finland and Russia were always fighting and at that time there were a whole lot of refugees who were getting unloaded in Copenhagen. So, yes, there was an epidemic and it could have been blamed on the Finns and made a lot of trouble.

ANITA LAHEY: So that rerouting that she takes, which, as I was reading it, was horrifying. You just felt somehow that she was going the wrong way, going deeper into this desolation. And having to get on ferries, the suggestion there.

ALICE MUNRO: It was my invention that she would take this roundabout route, but I did study the route, so I knew what would be happening at each point. But yes, that part of the story is where I take off from the known facts. Is it correct to do that?

ANITA LAHEY: Why not?

ALICE MUNRO: You think I want somebody to do it to me? I mean, if they're writing about my real life? No.

KIM JERNIGAN: When she speaks of the doctor later, she says he was a blind man and then she corrects herself: "no, I mean a kind man." And the blind man, the English-major in me took that to mean he was a prophet of sorts.

ALICE MUNRO: I didn't think that way at all. I just thought she made that mistake. But why did it come into her head? Or into my head.

KIM JERNIGAN: As a mother I kept thinking: You're going to take a pill that a stranger's given you? Don't do it, don't do it!

ALICE MUNRO: Yeah. But she does it when she's quite far on in the trip. The difficulty of getting her baggage onto the train has just unhinged her. And of course I don't know if that's true either. As I get to the end I do make up a lot about how she was behaving. But not right at the end. The whole business of her death is true, even that Fifi came in—

KIM JERNIGAN: —and danced for her mother. She really did that?

ALICE MUNRO: No, she had danced a day or two earlier, before the children's party. And what happens to the child of the gifted woman? Because this is always the question. I mean, when she went off to woo Maxsim in the south of France, she left her kid with one of these wonderful women who had lots of children and would take another one in. And this is where we come against the great problem. She wasn't really what would be called a good mother. But she had to get something more out of her life.

KIM JERNIGAN: And that's a reproach that was brought against her.

ALICE MUNRO: And probably she could bring it against herself if she thought of it.

ANITA LAHEY: But this idea of judging the performance of mothers is so much a part of history, I mean, we're just so anxious to judge mothers.

ALICE MUNRO: I think so. Yeah. It hasn't stopped. You know, in my generation, living with poor people on a farm, there was such a limited idea of what you could do that things like this didn't arise in women's lives. And there wasn't a big thing about educating males and not females. In fact, when it came to that, in farming families, women were more likely to get an education because they would be teachers and make some money. So if they had an education, OK. But writing is different. It takes so much out of you. It's so presumptuous. It's hard, the work you do. But what can you do? When I started writing, I just took it for granted that it was hard. But I just didn't think that I wouldn't be able to do it and have my children and everything.

KIM JERNIGAN: Would you say it's still hard?

ALICE MUNRO: God it's still hard. Every time I start a story, I wonder. Nobody with a brain in their head would do it.

ANITA LAHEY: One of the things I found really interesting in the story is how often superstition rears up. At the beginning of the story they're walking through a cemetery and it's New Year's Day and Sophia says this means one of us will die this year.

ALICE MUNRO: That is true. She said it.

ANITA LAHEY: Oh really?

ALICE MUNRO: It's not true, but she actually said it. [Laughter.]

ANITA LAHEY: Do you think she believed it or—

ALICE MUNRO: Oh, she could have been just flirting with him in her usual way, trying to say something interesting.

ANITA LAHEY: But the superstition recurs in the story. Like the black cat, even the doctor having a premonition.

ALICE MUNRO: Yes.

ANITA LAHEY: I wondered if you had intentions around that.

ALICE MUNRO: It just sort of happened. I'm not particularly ... I don't think that way. But I felt that this story sort of took over. Things just started to happen. I hate saying things like that, it sounds so fey. But, yeah.

ANITA LAHEY: I thought it was an interesting contrast—the idea of her being a scientist, a mathematician, and having these superstitious things following her around.

ALICE MUNRO: I think she was, I don't want to say superstitious, but in another generation, what would have been called very female. That means that her emotions and her emotional life meant a tremendous amount to her.

ANITA LAHEY: What made you see that in her?

ALICE MUNRO: I guess finding out more about her. You know, a lot of it is true. The whole business of Maxsim coming to see her and when they fall in love, how exciting it is and how wonderful. You know, she bandages up his leg and she goes to see him and she obviously sleeps with him. Then, the blow, when she gets the prize. I guess it was that combination that really got me. The blow with the prize, which he never really recovers from.

KIM JERNIGAN: I can see why she was attracted to Maxsim though; he's like this life force.

ALICE MUNRO: Mm-hmm! And he was smart too. Oh yes.

KIM JERNIGAN: You don't feel that she had a great deal of sexual attraction towards her husband. She eventually accommodates him because it's easier. But with Maxsim you can feel the heat.

ALICE MUNRO: Oh yeah. And maybe for the first time for her, I think. But I am so sorry for that first husband. The whole part where he gets involved with these people who are crooks, really, just terribly unworthy. He was a man with abilities. Why didn't he pursue his paleontology? I don't know. Was it uninteresting to people? Maybe one should write a book about him, all from his point of view.

ANITA LAHEY: When you're reading the story you feel like Sophia has all these different men in her life and a different kind of relationship with each of them: the husband, a relationship that changes over time; her mentor; Maxsim; even her sister's husband and her nephew.

ALICE MUNRO: Yes.

ANITA LAHEY: The nephew sticks in my mind because of that conversation they have on the way to the train station, when he's so scornful of what she does.

ALICE MUNRO: I think that's true. And I found him a really fascinating character. He says: I'm going to do something useful. I'm going to call out the stations on the bus. I'm not going to fool around with—

ANITA LAHEY: Mathematics. Which in a way felt to me reading it as the way writers often feel the world is looking at *them*.

ALICE MUNRO: [Laughs.]

ANITA LAHEY: I wondered if that crossed your mind when you were working on the story. This idea of usefulness versus art, or versus the more abstract branches of mathematics?

ALICE MUNRO: Certainly that was in my upbringing. But I've often thought that if I'd come from a different background, it would have been harder. Because nobody knew what I was doing. When they found out they weren't terribly pleased, but I don't know if they ever thought that I should have done something different. No, because there never was anything different.

ANITA LAHEY: One thing I found almost a little heartbreaking, given Sophia's brilliance and the kind of life that she'd led, was the way her uncertainty around Maxsim had her weighing his affections in an almost mathematical way, playing a "he loves me, he loves me not" game. It's a kind of calculus.

ALICE MUNRO: Believe me, that is true. There was no way she was secure. And did he love her? That's what I wonder too. After the first blow, which is her fame and her ability, does he love her as much?

KIM JERNIGAN: Were you going on your own intuition here or are there documents? Did she keep a diary?

ALICE MUNRO: Not that I know of. No. No. I'd love to know more about her. Which I think Russians know. But maybe they would find it trivial, her trying to figure that out. It's a terrific story about a woman trying to have it all.

KIM JERNIGAN: The story is called "Too Much Happiness." I'm interested in that idea: can there be an excess of happiness?

ALICE MUNRO: I feel you could be almost crushed by happiness, lost in it. Maybe also something about paying for it. I am the child of Presbyterians.

KIM JERNIGAN: The story sets out a number of opposing ideals of what the good life is: is it being politically engaged, is it the life of the mind, is it finding love? And why do these things so often seem mutually exclusive? It made me want to ask, if I may, what makes you happy?

ALICE MUNRO: [Pause.] I don't know because the conflict is always there. Writing is the final thing. But. I probably couldn't do it without support from elsewhere. Which is interesting, the whole business of women writers, how they want to manage to do their best work without having a lonely life.

ANITA LAHEY: Do you think that's harder for women?

ALICE MUNRO: Oh yes. Of course it is. I think men are often with different sorts of women at different stages, depending on what they need in life. I think women want something steady. You read about these older novelists with these young wives. No, I'm being unfair. [Laughs.]

KIM JERNIGAN: At the end, under the influence of the mysterious pill she has taken and also her fever, Sophia enters this incredible state of excitement. I wonder if that isn't her happiest time, when she has this notion that her mind can't keep up with her thoughts? She's in a fever of creativity and yet she is also dying. It's a bitter irony.

ALICE MUNRO: Mm-hmm. I think that's the happiest moment. The craziest moment for any human, that kind of creative delight before you have to get down to doing any of it. And then there's the happiness of the person on the other side, making a comfortable human life for the writer to come back into? I don't really know about that. Like it was with Weierstrass's sisters?

KIM JERNIGAN: Did she actually say, in her final moments, "Too much happiness"?

ALICE MUNRO: I rather think she did. I don't think I thought that up myself.

AFTERWORD:

Our meeting with Alice Munro took place over Christmas holidays; my husband Tom Good and I were visiting his parents in London, which is not too far from Goderich. He offered to chauffeur Kim and I to our very exciting rendezvous so that we could review our questions enroute. An engineer, he also set us straight on some mathematical principles that were key to our queries. Inveterate pickers-apart of fiction, we promised ourselves we would not spend the interview telling Alice Munro what we believed was happening in her story. You saw the mixed results of that pledge above. I, for one, was nervous: I'd spent much of my adult life reading and mulling Munro's stories, which, when it comes to human nature, are unforgiving. I feared an author with a distant, hard-nosed air. In fact, Munro joined us at her usual table in the back corner of the genteel Bailey's with an open smile and a quick humour, and delved wholeheartedly into conversation as her glass of white wine was being poured. She seemed to presume, rightly, that we were as puzzled as she was by the questions she raises in her fiction. What followed was a lively back-and-forth that ultimately involved Tom, who began lunch as an unobtrusive observer, and Munro's warm and dignified husband Gerald Fremlin (who has since passed away), who arrived an hour into our meeting. We suspected the plan was for him to whisk her away if she felt the need to escape us and our queries, but she waved him into a chair and promptly told him Tom was a combat engineer who'd recently returned from a tour in Afghanistan. This keenly interested them both: we talked of war in different places and times. Munro had recently read that Samuel Beckett was involved in the French resistance: "Beckett, who doesn't seem to have a good word for humanity, was a hero. I was very surprised." We learned how Munro and Fremlin had met. We wrestled with how things had changed for women through the three generations we three women represented—if, fundamentally, at all. She reminisced about the early days of Munro's Bookstore in Victoria: "It was just the beginning of the hippie era. I could go in on a Saturday afternoon and the smell of pot would just lift you." She recalled her long-ago gig as writer-in-residence at the University of Western Ontario and the photo that was taken of her when she received her honorary degree there. Fremlin: "It's a marvellous picture." Munro: "Is it the one where I'm looking dubious?" Fremlin: "Yes." We heard about her family trips to Goderich as a young girl, the car usually breaking down on the way. "It's a great harbour," said Munro. "People are sailing, there's a lot of swimming, but there are the great boats coming in from the lakehead, they're getting offloaded with grain onto the train to take them further into the interior. It's a real working port." I remembered this teeming, Munro-esque description the following summer, when a tornado swept through Goderich and flattened the very restaurant in which we'd sat, long known to be a favourite of Munro's for her meetings with journalists and others from the outside world—the world outside those thrumming ones she builds inside her books.

The Lure of the Gallery Wall

with John Barton and Stephanie Bolster

John Barton's collection *West of Darkness* (1987), recipient of an Archibald Lampman Award for Poetry, was a poetic autobiography written in the fictional voice of Emily Carr. It was reissued as a bilingual edition in 2006. Stephanie Bolster's Governor-General's Award-winning first collection, *White Stone: The Alice Poems* (1998), was largely based on Charles Dodgson's photographs of Alice Liddell (the inspiration for Alice in Wonderland, which Dodgson wrote under the name Lewis Carroll). Her second book, *Two Bowls of Milk*, contains poems based on works in the National Gallery of Canada's permanent collection as well as paintings by twentieth-century Québécois artist Jean-Paul Lemieux. Several poems in my own first book, *Out to Dry in Cape Breton* (2006), address works by Alex Colville, Molly Lamb Bobak, Mabel May and others.

I met John and Stephanie in the late nineties, while we were all, either full-time, part-time or freelance, in the employ of the National Gallery. We also each knew the Ottawa poet Diana Brebner, who died in 2001. Diana's ekphrastic poems engaged with artists ranging from Vermeer to Mary Cassatt, and most notably include the series "Eleven Paintings by Mary Pratt," which won the 1992 CBC Literary Award for Poetry and which appears in her 1993 collection *The Golden Lotus*. My conversation with John and Stephanie took place via email, between Montreal, Pointe-Claire (Quebec) and Victoria in late 2009 and early 2010.

ANITA LAHEY: I've thought a good deal about what is compelling about writing from the starting point of a work of art. Is it the chance to imagine how someone else's imagination is working? That's one idea that I kick around. Another is something I used to say to students when I was leading "art and creative writing" tours at the National Gallery of Canada: that a piece of art is a contained world you can enter, poke around in and explore. It has an idea and a perspective already proposed, as opposed to the WHOLE world, so this immediately offers a path to begin wandering. I'm wondering what ideas you two have about why we commit ekphrasis. Is it a deliberate process or is it something that catches you unaware?

STEPHANIE BOLSTER: Like you, I've asked myself this question often and never been satisfied with my answers. One pat and not untruthful one is that I wish I had talent in the visual arts and that I get vicarious pleasure through engaging with the work of visual artists in this way. But that begs the question of why I wish I could paint, draw, make sculptures. Ekphrasis is really a metaphor for how I see the world: through framing, through focus. I'm very conscious that many of my poems use windows or doorways or simply the notion of a snapshot in time. One advantage of drawing inspiration from, say, a painting by Vermeer rather than from a glimpse of a man huddling in a doorway on Crescent Street is temporal: I can stand in front of the painting or look at a book depicting it for hours and can come back the next day to see the same thing. The object won't have changed, but I will have changed.

A friend pointed out to me years ago that after I moved away from B.C., I began to write about paintings rather than about the natural world. This is not entirely true, as I wrote most of my Alice poems—many inspired by photographs and all of which borrow their subject from the artwork (albeit literary) of another—while living in Burnaby and Vancouver. But his insight still strikes me as important. In part, I turned to the already-depicted image as a way of coping with the alienation that I felt in a landscape, urban geography and climate that I didn't understand, surrounded by vegetation I couldn't name. I think, too, that I find in paintings the calm that I often find in nature. When I encounter an artwork that will give rise to a poem, my initial response is that my constant internal monologue stops. And in that silence, another voice can begin.

A couple of my favourite definitions of poetry come to mind here: Charles Simic's "Poems are other people's snapshots in which we recognize ourselves," and Seamus Heaney's "Poetry is a revelation of the self to the self." The artworks that initially prompt responses from me are ones in which I see something of myself reflected but transformed or renewed by having been created by someone else. I'm thinking of those images we drew in elementary school of overlapping circles; there is an area where my "set" and the artist's "set" overlap. There's an immediate, intuitive, often visceral sense of kinship. And yet some of my ekphrastic poems actually arose from being encouraged by our dear, mutual friend, Diana Brebner to write about works that didn't initially engage me—even ones that I found alienating. From that I've learned to listen to all my responses to a work, not just the "I feel a poem coming on" moments. That said, my "usual" ekphrastic poem begins with an encounter with a work of art that just stops me. In that moment, I understand myself and the world differently.

JOHN BARTON: The word "ekphrasis" is not one I encountered until I started to work at the National Gallery in 2000. I was a very young and perhaps naïve poet when I wrote my initial Emily Carr poem in the fall of 1978 when I was twenty-one. My mind was not loaded by theory or by the second-guessing that an awareness of theory can engender. Instead, one day I had a eureka-like awareness that Carr's life and work, both as a painter and as a writer, would consume me. I never asked myself why. However, over the course of six years, poem by poem, I became aware that Carr was a convenient mask that allowed me to appropriate her issues in order to work out my own. I believe that *West of Darkness* is a portrait of the artist becoming aware of his or her vocation. Writing it allowed me to discover and articulate the values that I felt should be important to anyone about to commit him- or herself to a creative life. And what better illustration of such a life than Carr's, which is full of aspiration, disappointment, failure, self-actualization, and even triumph.

Stephanie, I am struck that you found solace from the alienation you felt in an unfamiliar landscape in the "already-depicted image." I was attracted to Carr because she was the one thing I knew about Victoria when I moved there in 1978. And I initially knew her principally through her writings, for my mother made much of them when I was growing up. Also, in August 1972, on the way home to Calgary from Eastern Canada on a family vacation, my parents and I listened to a CBC documentary about Emily in the driving rain somewhere along the Trans-Canada in Manitoba. Those broadcasts stayed with me and only six years later, like a seed planted in one of Carr's forests, my book took root.

A key word in what I said earlier is the word "mask": we wear masks to conceal our own identities. By wearing one we divert the attention of our readers away from what's underneath, which is vulnerable, perhaps ugly. Line by line, poem by poem, they become so preoccupied with the mask's revelations that they fail to realize that its story has really been our story all along. Or at least we, as writers, hope they will be so easily and so magically misled.

Twenty-five years after I completed the Carr collection, I find myself writing a book where poems about paintings also form a large part of it. Today, I am much more deliberate and self-conscious and see the paintings of Paul Cadmus as opportunities to explore the homoerotic predicaments I believe he enunciated through them. Unlike the poems about Carr's paintings, the twenty-six I have written about Cadmus' paintings are, for the most part, arduously articulated facsimiles. Even still, despite my apparently brushstroke-perfect fidelity to the paintings, I can't help seeing fragments of "my stuff" bleeding pentimento-like through the layers of varnish.

ANITA LAHEY: That this is a way of plumbing one's own artistic motivations makes perfect sense, but I still find it interesting that so many of us would turn specifically to visual art. Perhaps it allows us some distance. There may be a freedom in engaging with an art form that we know less about. When I regard a sculpture or a painting, I'm not dissecting it as another practitioner would. I'm free to respond emotionally and imaginatively, as opposed to academically or critically or even enviously.

Stephanie, you saying that your poems happen through windows and doorways reminds me that I've been told that my poems are sometimes like little stories. When I go into the art gallery, it is the portraits to which I'm immediately drawn. When you see a compelling portrait, it feels as though a person has somehow been stolen from the world. It's an astonishing thing to behold. Who is this person? Who took them and put them here? Why? How? Under what circumstances? I really, really want to know the answer to these questions.

Diana once said something that has stuck with me, about the conversation that goes on when a person beholds a portrait: between the viewer and the subject, between the viewer and the artist, and between the subject and the artist. The possibilities here, of history, of fiction, of gaps that need filling in, are exciting and almost overwhelming.

STEPHANIE BOLSTER: That three-way conversation is certainly part of what makes the process so dynamic. To simply translate the work onto the page is not only impossible but not interesting to me, as the artwork already exists. Part of what made the Alice poems such a lasting project for me was that I identified—as a woman and as someone who at that point in my life felt constrained, albeit more by my own character than by any historical or familial expectations—with Alice Liddell the subject, with Alice the character (who wanders through a world over which she has little, if any, control), and with Dodgson/ Carroll the creator (who couldn't resist attempting to stop time by pinning the child Alice in place). Perhaps it's as you suggested, John, that by taking on a mask we can speak more truthfully and discover new facets of ourselves. That slant-telling that Dickinson named and engaged in has great resonance, and ekphrasis is one way to get at that slantness. We can attach our thought bubbles to someone other than ourselves.

JOHN BARTON: I wonder if some of our concern about why we write about visual art, "we" being ekphrastically inclined poets in general, is a legacy of the cultural appropriation debate that ensued in the late 1980s and early-to-mid 1990s? A debate that made many writers second-guess themselves and made readers question our motivations. For me, personally, it was a loss of innocence, even if that innocence was a naïve understanding of what speaking in someone else's voice meant. And as a gay writer, it has made me very conscious of who I am speaking for.

When we write about Jean-Paul Lemieux, Paul Cadmus or Pegi Nicol McLeod, should we be hesitant to simply render the work in good faith? Are we embarrassed to be mistaken for copyists? I suspect that many readers might expect a reasonably exact transcription of a work, especially if they know it well, and might therefore feel that the poet is "using" the artist should the poem stray too far. I found myself considering this while also paying heed to a self-imposed obligation to the "work" that developed when I "worked" with the curators at the National Gallery, who seemed to foreground the motivations of the artist before anything else, especially when exhibiting and interpreting the work of a living artist—boy, could I tell you stories! I began to feel a responsibility to provide readers with a lasting glimpse of the original. However, who's to say that I start the eye where the artist or any other viewer would. Nor would I necessarily move that eye over the canvas as the artist would. There is one Cadmus poem, based on his painting *The Architect*, which, in my appropriation of his voice, has him declaim a vision of New York as a future gay metropolis—a gay capital, if you like. I am very aware that this is not his view but mine: from the perspective of almost sixty years after Cadmus stood at his easel to paint this work in 1950, I know that the immediate postwar period was crucial to the emergence of a confident gay consciousness. Gay and lesbian veterans were attracted to and stayed in the cities after they demobilized and in turn attracted more people like themselves to move to "the big city." The rapid urbanization of North America served the gay community well. It's a perspective that Cadmus could never have adopted. He may only have noticed his own friends returning to New York after the war. Still, it was impossible for me not to see the architect he painted as an architect building homes for a growing and ever more visible gay community. It is this impossibility that vitalized the poem.

Returning to the question about why we write poems about art, I feel it is a way to escape the confines of our own genre while staying faithful to it, as if we were lifers craning our necks to look at greener pastures through the bars in the prison's air vent—now there's a window for you, Stephanie! I read somewhere that the choreographer and dancer Twyla Tharp once said, "Art is a way to run away from home without leaving home." It's a way to expand our world, especially as so much of twentieth-century poetry seems overwhelmingly concerned with the self. To write about someone else's poetry is such a small step outside our own heads. Writing about art is a few steps farther. Also, when we write on another poet's work, we have to compete with how well that poet writes. Why take on John Donne, for example (though Mary Novik does it so well in her novel *Conceit*)? However, to write about someone else's art is liberating—we find ourselves walking in those green fields, however briefly, and we don't have to measure up. Who's going to compare my iambic foot to Cadmus' brushstroke?

STEPHANIE BOLSTER: You may be right about the voice-appropriation concern, John. That came up at a pivotal time in my development as a writer, in the context of an undergrad workshop I was taking with Daphne Marlatt at UBC in 1989-90. The discussion arose in response to someone else's poem, written in the voice of a First Nations woman. The poet was not aboriginal; another woman in the class was. As you can imagine, it was an intense discussion and quite devastating for many of us. Suddenly, doors I hadn't even imagined opening had been closed. And yet, I'm just realizing the irony of this now, the major project I ended up writing during that course was a series of narrative prose poems in the voices of female characters drawn from fairy tales. I suppose because there was no "real" Cinderella, I felt no sense of limitation and I was encouraged rather than chastised for what I'd done. The first Alice poems began as part of that series. She was one of the few speakers without fairy tale origins. Only later did I begin to write about the historical Alice Liddell and I was certainly aware of the dangers of appropriation. I'm not oblivious to the fact that I "used" Alice in ways that resemble Dodgson's use of her.

It's interesting, given this aforementioned sense of responsibility, that I don't feel I need to render the visual work faithfully in words as you increasingly do, it seems, John. I think, if I were a painter, I'd rather read what my art had inspired in a writer than read a literary imitation of my work. Coleridge wrote of the difference between imitation and copying, of the fact that a waxwork figure prompts disgust whereas a work of "genuine imitation," a compelling oxymoron, imitates "that which is within the thing, that which is active through form and figure." This is, obviously, tied to theories of translation; most translators say that they strive to translate the poem's essence, not its words.

JOHN BARTON: My favourite poem about art is Auden's "Musée des Beaux Arts," which seems to strike a balance between fidelity and personal perspective. Auden expresses a timeless awareness of ordinary suffering that seems greater than Brueghel's *Icarus*, but nevertheless is articulated within a frame that includes the painting itself. For me, the poem has great pathos, and while having seen Brueghel's painting, if only in reproduction, does enlarge the poem for me, having done so can't diminish it either. It's as if poem and painting are facing each other like mirrors and, as a result, reflect one another infinitely and create possibilities for infinite reflection. I see how carefully and economically Auden has rendered the painting's essentials for his purpose and therefore can more fully appreciate how he has allowed the painting to stand both on its own and inside the poem. I particularly love the poem's title, for it evokes a leisurely visit to a museum. I see him moving from room to room—"In the room[s] the women come and go/ talking of Michelangelo"—and I am following in his footsteps.

STEPHANIE BOLSTER: The ekphrastic poems that engage me most are ones that not only stand on their own, but that function in a broadly ekphrastic way without necessarily pinning themselves to "art" or to specific works. I'm thinking of Aurian Haller's "Song of the Taxidermist," for example, which cites museum specimens (e.g. "*Tago*, Iditarod Trail Sled Dog Race Gift Shop / Museum, 1959. / Siberian Husky in taxidermy.") at the opening of each section rather than paintings, photographs or sculptures. Another project that functions even more loosely as ekphrasis is Cole Swensen's *The Glass Age*, which John Ashbery describes as a "long meditation on glass, windows, vision, and various writers and artists who have used these in their work, especially Bonnard, Apollinaire, Wittgenstein, Hammershøi, Saki, and the Lumière brothers." Her series in *Goest*, "A History of the Incandescent," includes poems like "The Invention of the Weathervane" and "The Origin of *Ombres Chinoises*" that are about made things, but not necessarily art things. The poems' connection to their subjects may be oblique and is always dynamic. For me, ekphrasis is very much an eye-of-the-beholder situation, which brings to mind Karl Shapiro's comment that "Poetry is a way of seeing things rather than a way of saying things." Ekphrasis is a perspective, a process, and for me, more intuitively, a *feeling* of being so moved by a work that one must write. Not necessarily *about* it, but from it, to it, after it.

I also love Charles Simic's poems on Joseph Cornell, *Dime Store Alchemy*. There is a compelling match of poet and artist there; Simic can inhabit Cornell's sensibility because it is, or seems to be, his own. But when it comes to individual poems, my favourite is the same as John's. Also Rilke's "Archaic Torso of Apollo." I read this as an ekphrastic poem although it lacks the acknowledgement of artist, year and materials that I find so tantalizing. I'm not even sure whether the poem was a response to a particular sculpture (it would be easy to check, but I'd rather not know). As one of Rilke's "thing-poems," this poem reinforces my sense that one can write about any made thing ekphrastically: a train station, a lamp. Though I worry that in defining the process so broadly I'm diluting its meaning too much. Certainly I would say that a poem about a stone would not be ekphrastic, unless that stone had been shaped by human hands.

I realize that there's a bit of re-inventing the wheel going on in our discussion. Scholars have written about all this; were they listening in, they'd no doubt wonder why we didn't just turn to their theories. Yet I'm resistant to reading theories of ekphrasis by non-practitioners. Self-consciousness about craft, the kind that our conversation is engendering, is useful to me, but self-consciousness about interpretation less so.

JOHN BARTON: It's intriguing how this conversation is becoming preoccupied with our responsibility to the work of visual art, whether or not we, as poets, are obliged to be faithful to it. It turns out that the answer is yes as well as no. Why do I seem more inclined toward the affirmative? When I worked in the Publications Division of the National Gallery, I was trained to provide high-fidelity quality assurance and often did press checks. I would go to the printer's plant and work with the pressman to guarantee that colour reproductions in books, magazines and brochures were as "faithful" as possible to the original. After all the work that had gone into making the publication in question as flawless as could be, mine was the final approval required before anything would be printed. As you can imagine, signing off was fraught with anxiety, for the reputation of the Gallery itself, as well as my own skin, was implicated in my decisions. The irony is that the many rounds of colour corrections made prior to going to press seldom involved comparing a proof against the work of art it was intended to represent. Instead, we depended upon transparencies or scans that were presumably created under appropriate lighting. In other words, to echo Plato, we manufactured shadows of a shadow of a shadow. When you flip through a *catalogue raisonné*, there's no way of knowing how accurate its plates are without having a prior intimate knowledge of the works themselves. However, I have become so experienced at colour fidelity that I now look at illustrations in a catalogue and analyze their flaws—too much black, say, or not enough cyan or magenta. After visiting an exhibition, I like nothing better than to pour over the accompanying catalogue and, like a forensic criminologist, reconstruct what went into it.

Doubtless, this is where my preoccupation with fidelity comes from, an allegiance forged in the pursuit of accuracy against the possibility of failure. I hope, as a poet, that I have not painted myself into a corner and turned into a mere copyist, stuck before a work I admire, slavishly reproducing a lifeless likeness. I hope instead that I am engaged in "genuine imitation"—yes, Stephanie, it is a marvellous oxymoron—an engagement where every poem, like the colour plates I signed off on for the Gallery, is ultimately inaccurate. However, perhaps inaccuracy, masquerading as fidelity, is where the "artistry" comes in, with perspective shining through the most minute gaps in the truth.

On a conscious level, at least, I am less and less interested in myself and my own story, both of which seem to be perennially deficient sources of inspiration. However, this is not always true. When I was sitting beside my father's bed watching him die the last day of his life, his greying pallor reminded me of the true-to-life sculptures of Ron Mueck, whose works I first encountered at the Gallery. This awareness transformed witnessing my father's death into an aesthetic experience. Perhaps it allowed me to think about something else. However I might wish to frame it, I found the experience profoundly moving. It was an honour to see my father out of this world, in appreciation of his seeing me into it. I did end up writing a poem about this, inspired by Mueck's sculpture, *Dead Dad.*

ANITA LAHEY: The problem of "using" other people, as a writer, is something I think about a great deal, as I draw from my own life and the people I know and care about extensively. I also "use" strangers in my poetry—that I don't know them doesn't make them any less real or less "stolen." This question of using is one of the compelling aspects of Colm Toibin's novel on Henry James, *The Master*, which I read—and loved!—earlier this year. I don't know enough about James to know to what extent Toibin is creating fictional connections between James' fiction and the people in his life, but the way he illustrates how life feeds and leads to art and how uncomfortable this can be, is fascinating. It's also worth noting that Toibin, too, could be said to be using James and indirectly all the people James already used. It's like an endless game of mirrors.

The other thing I'm reminded of is more directly relevant: Between 2002 and 2004, I was leading writing tours at the Gallery with high school English classes. A few of the regular stops on my tour were connected to poems written by the two of you, in Stephanie's case most often the sculpture Dog-woman by Peggy Ekagina, and in John's case an Emily Carr painting, usually *Autumn in France*. John's poem "Autumn in France," like many of the poems in *West of Darkness*, is written in the fictional voice of Emily Carr. The poem begins with the line, "My eyes shrink from this canvas,/ my attempt at light." And "Carr" goes on to describe the experience of creating the painting, what she saw, how it felt, what she tried to do. One day when I finished reading this poem to a group of students standing before the actual painting in the Gallery, one of them became agitated. She asked me what right this poet had to act as though he knew what was in Carr's head. I responded that it was an act of imagination, an attempt to understand human nature and the artistic process through another person. She wasn't convinced. Nor did it escape her attention that this was a man taking liberties with a woman's mind. I wish now that I'd also said this to the student: when you create a piece of art and put it out in the world, you tacitly allow others to enter your psyche or to imagine they're doing so. To go back to Stephanie's metaphor, you're providing a door or window. The piece of art is the portal. What's beyond it is going to look and feel different to every person who goes through, but you are absolutely inviting them in.

It's interesting that Stephanie's poem "Dog-woman," from *Two Bowls of Milk*, is also built around the artist's process. In this case the voice in the poem is the viewer of the artwork, imagining herself being shaped, cut from rock, by the artist—but also imagining herself as the artist creating the sculpture. This dual fantasy is managed in the first tiny stanza, by the help of a brilliant line break: "Who's to say I'm not/ that dog, that small/ woman low to ground." The "dog" is a small woman low to ground but so would Ekagina have been while carving. That opener has never failed to entice, surprise and illustrate how complex this question of who we really are can be.

I have imagined myself as the subject of a work of a art, such as in my poem on Edwin Holgate's "Ludivine," and as the artist, such as in a poem I wrote on a war painting by Molly Lamb Bobak. I think somehow all this leads to that question of creating and being created—do we have any control over who we are and what we do? Entering the realm of the artist, as maker of things or as made things, seems a pretty fruitful way to get at this question. Here's one last question: Do you ever resist the urge to write on a specific work of art? Or have you been compelled to write from something and found it took you nowhere? I have resisted, and I have failed. Resisted works include Janet Cardiff's "40-part Motet," which is an installation so sublime I fear ruining its magic. Failed works include several prints and paintings by Alex Colville, including *Child and Dog*, the source of a terrible attempt at a villanelle, and *Köln Express.* Colville's works are so much like freeze-frames from stories that I'm dying to get at the whole narrative and often I just can't.

STEPHANIE BOLSTER: Yes to both resistance and failure. I have many a notebook filled with jottings that thought they could become poems; in some cases, the magic vanished as soon as the work was out of sight. On the flipside, I've resisted the pre-Raphaelites because my long-standing attraction to their work doesn't feel deep enough. I've adored Waterhouse, an embarrassing admission in many circles, I realize, since I first saw a poster of *Hylas and the Nymphs* as an undergrad, but when I recently went to the show of his work at the Montreal Museum of Fine Arts I knew I was beyond writing about any of those paintings. Not that one can't have a complex response to them, but they are so much about surfaces, yet the technique isn't as dazzlingly invisible as Vermeer's. Though the latter's paintings also have gorgeous surfaces, they move me much more, in part due to their extraordinarily technical prowess and to their restraint. Like Colville's paintings, they suggest and resist narrative. They are all subtext. And yet the gazes within them acknowledge the viewer more than is the case in Colville's work. Does the subject meet the viewer's gaze in any of his paintings? In the most straight-on one I can think of, the woman is holding binoculars, which not only intercede but efface the viewer. But back to Waterhouse. In his paintings, everything—myth, flesh—is there to be seen. And many of them are working with myths and literary works that already have a life, so the painting is itself a kind of ekphrasis; the adaptation/ translation has already happened.

I remember Diana—a ghost voice in this conversation—once telling me about some books on Mary Cassatt that she had been accumulating toward a project that she wasn't yet ready to write. It struck me as surprising and wise that one could want to undertake a project but realize that one wasn't yet mature or skilled enough to do so. I feel that now with certain projects. On some level, the Cézanne poem I submitted for this ekphrasis issue is about not "getting" him until recently and an awareness that the lack of connection was a failing on my part. Over the years, I've attempted many poems on Robert Polidori's photographs, none of which have transcended description. I have, perhaps always, been drawn to still images; my frames frame a moment, not a motion. Diana once observed that the speakers in my poems rarely moved. The challenge I'm posing to myself in ekphrasis now is: how to transcend the still moment?

JOHN BARTON: I had toyed with writing on Josef Albers's work in the National Gallery but I could never find my way into this nonfigurative painting. For a long time I resisted writing about Paul Cadmus' remarkably grotesque series, "The Seven Deadly Sins," until I found the right form and context; it's now cast in Lincoln Kirstein's voice, who bought all seven paintings. The canvases for each sin are explored in short Italian forms and sequenced in the order Kirstein hung them in his hall.

I've reread Rilke's "Archaic Torso of Apollo" and certainly still admire the poem; however, I found myself stopped by its close, "You must change your life," which serves to suggest what art exhorts us existentially to do.

Far be it for me to doubt the depth of a master's response but I don't believe any work of art can ever do this; nor do I write my poems for that reason. To change someone's mind, perhaps, or at most to engender empathy, if not for myself then for my subjects. I immediately recalled Auden's line, "For poetry makes nothing happen." On the surface, it seems almost to have been composed to refute or act as counterpoint to Rilke. However, I don't agree with Auden either, or more properly with the popular interpretation brought to his most famous epithet. If you go back to "In Memory of W. B. Yeats," the poem from which it is drawn, Auden suggests in the third part (the line in question is from the gloomy second) that the real impact of Yeats' legacy is how it affects us, how his poetry, and all poetry, can "Still persuade us to rejoice." In other words, art does change us, if only in some small way. Perhaps writing about art, by being the self-aware ekphrastic poets we are, allows us to articulate the subtlety and wonder and terror of that change.

AFTERWORD:

Myself, John and Stephanie all live in different cities now, but there are times when we converge and visit galleries together, or other urban settings that invite looking. Stephanie and I once spent a morning roaming solemnly through an exhibition of photographs by Robert Polidori at Musée d'art contemporain in Montreal (he has a cameo in my last book, while Stephanie continues to feel her way more deeply through his charged landscapes, which contain the visual residue of traumas such as Chernobyl and Hurricane Katrina). We wandered, with her young daughter, through Montreal's Royal Botanical Gardens, as well as through a lush exhibition of urban gardens flanking the Lachine Canal, in the shadow of a massive silo in Old Montreal. Awkwardly but gamely sharing a set of earphones, we followed a podcast walking tour around the west end of downtown Montreal, narrated in a literary style that offered a compelling mixture of personal observation and local history. There is a dreamlike quality to my memories of those hours: our keen gazing interspersed with conversation about what we were seeing, and also about many things that we weren't. With John, I once took in a retrospective of paintings by British artist J. W. Waterhouse at the Musée des Beaux Arts in Montreal: all those nymphs and fountains and foliage, all that fuzzy cinematic light, gradually playing on my senses in unsettling ways, and eliciting wry commentary from John. He also introduced me to Fredericton's Gallery 78, housed in a Queen Anne Revival mansion just down the block from the grander, provincial institution, the Beaverbrook Art Gallery. At Gallery 78, you might discover a small gem by Molly Lamb Bobak—which John did, and ferried off to Victoria with him—a scene rendered with uncommon clarity by Tom Forrestall or a shape-shifting clay vessel by a contemporary potter. Upstairs, we poked our heads into artist David McKay's studio: he was literally watching paint dry, fanning a small canvas so he could resume work on it. He chatted with us about the misty, tree-branch-traced riverbank scenes in various stages of progress around the room, the St. John River itself flowing lazily by across the road and dominating the view through the thick, wavering glass of the room's windows. Both Stephanie and John have served as poetic mentors to me and—what is the best way to put it?—literary confidants. But during all of these "artistic" outings we have never touched deeply on our collective addiction to reeling poems out of paintings and other works of art. The conversation above was a welcome chance to hash it out.

A Little Nibble Before Writing:
Reviews, 2001-2006

Anne Simpson

The Marram Grass: Poetry & Otherness (Gaspereau 2008)

In her book of essays, *The Marram Grass: Poetry & Otherness*, poet and novelist Anne Simpson describes her attempt to write about the suicide of a teenage boy in the Nova Scotia town where she lives. This segment of "Season of Ice," the second of six pieces that make up the book, is profoundly disquieting. She finds herself "imagining him in the garage with a coil of rope, or an orange extension cord, trying not to waken his parents as he shook off his boots and got up on a chair, an old table saw, or broken dryer."

Like pretty much any collection of essays by a poet, this is a book for writers: it relates a winding, associative journey through its author's writing mind and reading habits; it delves into the mechanics and philosophical underpinnings of literary devices such as metaphor; it relates the elements of fiction and poetry to political, spiritual and day-to-day matters, the stuff of life away from the page.

Given that, Simpson's discussion of her attempt to write her way through the boy's suicide, whose mother was an acquaintance of hers, feels like part of the lifelong conversation or interior monologue that runs through the life of a writer. Reading it raises familiar, troubling questions: what right did she have to creatively re-enact this private death? Was she reducing someone else's tragedy to a "writing project?" These are questions most writers ask themselves at some point, and Simpson likewise appears to be tackling them as she "confesses" the impetus behind her poem, "A Woman, An Owl, A Boy," which appears in *Marram Grass* following the essay. Is this impulse to turn the shrapnel of others' lives into "art" empathetic or voyeuristic? Is it honesty or is it theft? I am reminded of the poem "Coal Deliveryman" by Ramón Cote Baraibar, translated from Spanish by Craig

Arnold, which appeared in *Poetry* in April, 2009. The poem is ostensibly about the speaker's incredulity at finding the same man doing the same dreary job for decades, "determined to show the heavens that a man might do that job his/ entire life, that he scraped in the mines, that he stole thread from his wife to sew/ his sacking, that he dreamed of infinite excavations ..." Stole from his wife? It becomes clear that the poem is really about the job of the poet himself, about whether that job is as dirty, futile and relentless as that of the coal deliveryman, and about whether the heavens might forgive him for not having done more than that.

This notion of duality, the flipsides and doubles that populate both literature and life, forms Simpson's main concern and line of inquiry. In her lead essay, "A Hundred and Fifty Psalms at Twilight," she contrasts the language of the wilderness with the language we have trained ourselves to use. She asks what a world without grammar would be like, and conversely: what if we could comprehend the call of the mockingbird? Poetry, she decides, is not a purer form of language but exists "somewhere between order and chaos, thriving on both." As a writer who explores and exercises her craft through engagement with the natural world, Simpson falls into a school of Canadian writing that includes, some might say is led by, the poet Don McKay, whose essay collections delve into poetics and meaning in a similar fashion: down a woodsy path, where ideas nestle under curling fern branches, waiting to be uncovered or flushed out, as by a dog tracking grouse. A deliberate awareness of the interconnectedness of all things informs such writing, in a way that feels at times exciting, at times obvious and at times a touch smug. It can seem as though the traipsing writer feels he or she is the only one who hasn't forgotten, for example, that those clumps of long grasses on the beach are called "marram," and that if only everyone were as attentive as they, the world would be a far more harmonious place.

Simpson, to her credit, mostly avoids this righteous tone, in part by extending as deeply into the work of others as she does into her own creative process, with its starts and stops, its surprises and uncertainties. In "World at Play," Simpson spends a week at Elizabeth Bishop's childhood home in Great Village, Nova Scotia: writing, walking, and boring into Bishop's poetic mind. For any writer interested in some hard thinking on the transformation that takes place between reality and the page, this essay alone is worth the price of the collection. Bishop, Simpson tells us, "goes through things to try to locate the ineffable." She quotes Bishop's description of poetry as that which "proceeds from the material, the material eaten out with acid, pulled down from underneath …" Like Bishop, Simpson makes leaps and associations that suggest faith in underlying meaning that might emerge into clarity. In "Looking at Paintings," her interest in a sixteenth-century altarpiece by the German artist Matthias Grünewald connects with a suburban Ontario landscape that includes two steel plants and a golf course. "I was pulled inward by my thoughts about Grünewald's altarpiece … and I was pushed outward into the manicured landscape of the golf course … I was creating my own vision of an altarpiece, without realizing what I was doing."

In "The Dark Side of Fiction's Moon," Simpson casts the disturbing concept of the literary double against her own experience attending public hearings on a proposed petrochemical complex and walking the still-rural land slated to become its home. She writes: "None of the experts seated behind the tables wanted to do harm; they weren't against the land … As I looked at them, it was as if I saw my own face in the faces of those around me." I wish she had gone further. I wish she had asked herself in what ways, in her own life, she might use items made from the spoils of such a chemical plant. (We are talking about things made of plastic.) But her acknowledgment of the connection across the table embodies the kind of awareness that forms the underpinning of all art and literature—that both makes it, and makes it necessary.

This brings us back to that young boy and the poem his suicide spawned. Simpson tells us she walked repeatedly over the ice of the frozen harbour that winter. She examines the dangers that thinkers such as Hobbes and Locke felt metaphor posed—Hobbes, for one, labels metaphors misleading "absurdities"—and delves into philosopher Paul Ricoeur's idea that metaphor "shatters the previous structures of what we call reality." Ice, suicide, metaphor: all things that destruct or self-destruct and thus leave a space (or a hole) that needs filling. Simpson ultimately judges her poem "as nothing" in the face of a boy's death: "It simply revealed a desire to understand." That desire, though, is everything. As Simpson explores in her final essay, form is emptiness and vice versa—one depends upon the other, just as absence and presence are bound and as loss and possession somehow equate. "This is the twofold thinking of poetry," she writes. But what happens when the poem is over? One last flip: words become silence. It's the silence at the end of a poem into which Virgil and Dante emerge, at last, from the underworld. Simpson writes: "They see the night sky with a clarity they did not possess before. They stand poised between worlds, hardly daring to breathe, as if they were waking—still trembling—from a nightmare."

There are moments in Simpson's essays when one walks smack into this kind of clarity.

AFTERWORD

The reference to the poem "Coal Deliveryman" by Ramón Cote Baraibar was a bit sneaky. The poem was legitimately on my mind and affected my reading of Simpson's essay about how poets mine the lives that touch our own. But there may be a false impression offered, of a widely read critic who effortlessly, when called upon, pulls together disparate threads. In fact, in the days when

I wrote this review, though I was editing one literary magazine, I was reading few if any others: the laws of irony, and of time. It was the Montreal poet Susan Gillis who put Baraibar's poem before me, at a hotel bar on Sherbrooke Street where, from 2008 to 2011, we occasionally met with a group of fellows, among whom Leon Lukashevsky and Judith Hertz were most dedicated, to talk about poems. Not our own poems, but poems written by other people that had bowled us over, infuriated us, or confused us—poems we wished to revisit with the aid and company of other minds. As I recall, Susan was distrustful of Baraibar's piece. Her initial reaction upon reading it was pleasure and affinity, but then she began to wonder what trick he had played. Was it too easy? Too satisfying, this poem? Did it play to expectations? Did it push just hard enough for us to feel a tug, but not so hard we were forced to make a choice: to either stand our ground or allow ourselves to be yanked off our feet? This problem was picked at over pints around a high, polished wooden table and I remember thinking that I didn't care if Baraibar had lured me in with some obvious flourish. The poem had worked on me. It stuck in my mind that week and the week after. To this day, like some of the essays in Marram Grass, *it stays with me. Am I just an easy mark?*

Final Words: Skelton's Last Poems

Robin Skelton, *Facing the Light* (Ekstasis 2006)

I am compelled to stop on the poem "Craftsman," halfway through Robin Skelton's final collection of poetry, *Facing the Light*, which was published nine years after his death at seventy-one. A single stanza of nine short lines, it begins: "Because of this/ I make, the day/ won't go amiss/ or lose its way." An unadorned declaration of faith expressed using impeccable line breaks and a blatant rhyme most poets today would avoid. A more subtle rhyme, swinging barely detectable along the trajectory of colloquial speech, would currently be favoured among those who dare to rhyme at all. But Skelton, who published more than sixty collections of poetry in his lifetime, would not have cared. For this I admire him. *Facing the Light* stoops to no fancy language, no fancied-up form, no ostentatious dance. The right combination of the right words can open a crack in the consciousness; this is what good poetry does and is meant to do. Sometimes, as Skelton illustrates at his best, all it takes to effect that crack is one swift strike with the right tool in the right place, nothing remarkable required.

Not being a West-Coaster, I came to Skelton as an outsider. I confess that the blurb on the book gave me pause, with its hyperbolic declaration that, "In these last poems, completed shortly before his death in 1997, Robin Skelton completed the journey he had begun over seven decades previously: he created his birth." Had his champions lost perspective? By the time I got to "Craftsman," sixty-something pages in, I was worried; by then I'd read many poems that bore a suspect tone of profundity. One example is "Death," which works through a series of the usual morbid personas—the figure with the scythe, another "pallid in the shadows/ at the ball"—to conclude that "death is an ampersand/ linking this word, that word,/ beyond the silence." It sounds deep, very "Death Be Not Proud," yet it does not truly seem so to me.

But—and this "but" is significant—there was a fine line between Skelton's successes and failures, and the writing falling on the right side of that line couldn't be more right. *Facing the Light* is a book written by a man who knows his days are numbered; death lurks both literally and metaphorically throughout. Sometimes he descends into sentimentality and false revelations, but fine poems also emerge like lights in the distance, assuring you that you are, and he is, on the right track after all.

Consider the rest of "Craftsman": "because of this/ it will not stray/ and I dismiss/ the need to pray/ because of this." It's a simple, quiet sliver of verse. But this doesn't negate what is really a moment of poetic perfection. In a style that harkens to such circular, sing-song childish prayers as "Now I Lay Me Down to Sleep," Skelton expresses a pure faith—but one that flatly dismisses the sort espoused by the juvenile prayers it mimics. Those cute rhymes that few would stoop to use and the repetition of the clumsy "because of this" make the poem both an excellent marriage of form and content and a near-radical act, for it relies on tools most would normally consider naïve.

Moments such as this kept me believing in Skelton even amid my frustration over his more self-indulgent tropes. I was seduced by "In the Allotment, 1930," from its tactile, well-wrought opening onwards: "The gates swung shut./ I was alone/ with cabbages, pea-sticks, shallots." In the couplet poem, "A Matter of Time," Skelton critiques and forgives in equal measure the kind of everyday failure of human relations we all commonly enact. The simmering anger softened by compassion in "Reading the Palm" is chilling and convincing, barely held within the lines, as in these first three stanzas:

> No one can tell you
> what is not to be told.

The leaf buds on the tree;
the leaf drops from the bough.

Your son smiles at the sun;
the sun destroys him.

Facing the Light was compiled and edited by poet Harold Rhenisch. In his introduction, Rhenisch reveals that an earlier version was sent back to Skelton by one of his publishers because "some of the poems were not up to snuff." He also writes that those who know Skelton's work will find some of his best poems collected here, and that the book's final poem is the one "he waited his whole life to write." When Rhenisch and Skelton's daughters found it in a heap of papers and passed it around, they "each hushed in turn." Titled "24.III.88" the poem begins:

This is a time
when the cat walks through the mirror
and all the mistletoe berries
fall like snow.

This is a time when the
red wine turns to silver
and the pillars of the house are black.

This is the time
when, opening the cupboards,
we discover only crawling children.

No wonder they hushed. The absolute surety with which Skelton puts forth these unsettling lines do indeed mark this poem as a true accomplishment, one that demands attention in a quiet room. Its second half, in fact, begins in a quiet room, with the light turned out. A buzzing fly disrupts the peace; the penultimate couplet reads:

There is no fly. No sound. No room;
no bed; no house; no life, no death.

See how the elements, beginning with a fly and ending in death, descend through periods to semi-colons to commas—away from the safety of the full-stop to the useless comma, which stops nothing, only allows an extra breath, a half-second in which to see, helplessly, what's coming (and I don't mean the concluding period!). What a difference from the earlier ampersand personified as Death. This poem is both a life's work and a life's end, placed gracefully on the page, an astounding final word from a long-celebrated poet.

AFTERWORD:

I must have read and reviewed this book around the same time I read Margaret Edson's Wit, *then watched Emma Thompson gloriously hit the mark in the movie version of the masterful play. The action revolves around Donne scholar Vivian Bearing's struggle with a fatal cancer, but the central metaphor hinges on an erroneously punctuated edition of Donne's* Holy Sonnets. *In the last line of* "Holy Sonnet Six", *the comma and period are replaced by a semi-colon and an exclamation mark, which Bearing's academic mentor deems "hysterical," utterly missing the point of the poem: that "Nothing but a breath—a comma—separates life from life everlasting." I fear I "borrowed" Edson's insight when deconstructing Skelton's last poem. But then, once you see it you can't argue with it or pretend it away: such is the power of punctuation.*

Oana Avasilichioaei, *Abandon* (Wolsak and Wynn 2005)and her translation of Nichita Stănescu's *Occupational Sickness* (Buschek Books 2006)

"It wanted a mortum profundum." From this, the mildly menacing first line of "Dragon," the long poem that begins *Abandon*, it's clear that Oana Avasilichioaei's first collection will be no ordinary book of Canadian poetry. Avasilichioaei's dragon resists bribery by cornmeal and red onions, eats diseases for breakfast and wants "drunkards to sing its glory." It rises bold and cruel from her Romanian background like a doomed political movement. The dragon promises a trip well beyond the familiar Canadian lyric into a hard reality, a subversive, myth-like poetry swirling masterfully about its secrets and clues.

Or does it? This was the question I asked myself after my first heady foray into this seductive but ultimately only partly successful book. To read *Abandon* alongside Avasilichioaei's impressive translation project, *Occupational Sickness*, a collection of poems by late Romanian poet Nichita Stănescu, is to encounter an apprentice who has yet to successfully integrate the lessons gleaned from her mentor-poet into her own work. Stănescu died in 1983 and remains one of Romania's most popular poets. Avasilichioaei writes in the introduction to her translation that for Stănescu, "words were alive; they had all the qualities of life—birth, struggle, breath, joy, tumult, respite, death; they were corporeal, carnal. If cut, he often thought, they would bleed." Through the intimate work of translation, Avasilichioaei well knows Stănescu's every wounded syllable; but she has yet to consistently break open her own words, to give them scars and breath.

Avasilichioaei's potential for a commanding poetic voice rears again and again in "Dragon," particularly when her creature comes into contact with humans, such as the "blue-eyed wife" who "let it take a swig of slivovitz spiced/ with peppercorns and two swigs of her breast./ I want my man back, she begged./ It tossed a bone and asked,/ Why want him when you can have me?" Throughout *Abandon*, Avasilichioaei repeatedly displays this talent for the stirring dialogue of the absurd, a technique still more fully realized in the work of Stănescu, such as in this exchange in "Psyche":

> An angel came to me and said:
> "You are the pig of a dog,
> a mutt and a snout.
> Grass stinks below your oppressing shadow,
> your breathing is a bog!"
> "Why?" I yelled. "Why?"
> "For no reason!"

Equally maddening and powerful is Stănescu's "Giving up the hearth," built with escalating variations on the following exchange: "A horse, he dreams a horse,/ a kind of horse of a horse./ 'What kind of horse?' the child asked/ the soldier, who was fast asleep./ 'I dream no kind of horse,' the soldier said/ 'I simply dream a horse, a horse, a horse/ a horse.' Avasilichioaei's dragon doesn't quite achieve the aura of the soldier, nor that of his dream horse. And when he is spoken for, rather than speaking, it is difficult to maintain a faith in his reality. "Dragon" at times reads like unfiltered exposition. For example: "At lunch, outlaw street children,/ the handicapped and gypsies./ And do away with the light. Excluding times/ when foreign dignitaries visit, export/ electricity from eight to six each day." A passage such as this doesn't convey corruption or its attendant strife so much as provide a list of examples; it spells out rather than breathes, in dragon-fire, its damaged world.

In other instances Avasilichioaei is more successful. The first two stanzas of "At the train station," the second poem in the section "Abandoned Markets," are rich, compact and evocative:

I stare at a woman who feeds
yoghurt to a meager kitten,
the two-dollar, first-class ticket stiff in my hand
The dismal skylight, ruptured tiles weigh
        a spider makes his home in the sharp
        edges of broken glass.

People slouch, hands rough and empty
eyes dark to spots and slipshod scraps.

The poet returning to her homeland is taking in the sight of its open wounds. And just as we begin to lump this scene neatly in with notions of post-communist economic hardship, Avasilichioaei introduces the worst image of all: a dog, its tongue blackened from dragging on the ground because "The entire lower jaw is missing." Here, the poem ends.

You could read this final image as a metaphor for an entire country's debilitation by a brutal political history. At the beginning of the poem, the narrator is staring. By the end of the poem, the reader is staring as well, and at something far more searing than a woman feeding a kitten. The shift from the kitten to the dog is important: some things can be helped and we are compelled to help. Other things, usually those most troubling and horrific, are lost causes. So the poem travels some distance in that tricky, alchemic way poems can, while staying put in the train station. Even its plodding gait and spiritless tone could be defended as concrete manifestation of dull acceptance—of a dismal reality that long ago ceased to be abnormal.

Equally arresting and politically charged is the last stanza of "A collector's burden": "See that woman in the corner/ lurching with each movement of the train?/ In that bag she hides people's used stories./ She will hide yours in exchange for your shirt." The way the bag and the woman become something out of a dark fairy tale, matter-of-factly there and utterly realistic, calls to mind how the work of Stănescu grips at the reader's wrist and hisses: Wait! You must hear this!

One of my favourites among Avasilichioaei's translations is "Longing for man," which begins "And I hammered down on him/ I made him a sword/ and I took the sword in my hand until the hand/ that lifted the sword/ became his sword./ And I looked at him with contempt/ until he grew beautiful[.]" The necessity for subversive storytelling lends Stănescu's poetry its strength, as well as his near-deification of words themselves, which crop up as subject matter throughout his riddle-addled verse. Stănescu writes in one poem, "Mother, I fear words!" Yet he uses words fearlessly, with flawless calculation. In "Requiem for a mountain's burial," he writes: "I say rip out their tongues/ those who cry with tongues./ And those, who no longer see words/ rip out their eyes,/ eyebrows/ will do for seeing."

"Dragoness," the third section of Avasilichioaei's book, is a long sequence written in the voice of the illegitimate daughter of Stephen the Great, a fifteenth-century prince of Maldovia, in Romania's north. The second stanza, a fine couplet, stands out: "I am half peasant half queen/ ablaze on a hunt for my own mythology." This is Stephen's daughter speaking but it is also Avasilichioaei, making her declaration through the voice of her adopted historical figure, becoming her own dragon-myth. Her hunt thus far feels incomplete and too much like hunting for sport than for survival. But there are glimmers of Stănescu's brilliance here, enough to suggest that she could someday achieve as much as the poet she describes as one who "handled words with tenderness sharpened on the edge of a knife." Avasilichioaei has yet to break the skin of her lines—but she has the knife in hand, the blade firmly pointed.

Was is fair to review Avasilichioaei's first book alongside her translation of Stănescu? How would I like it if my first book had been compared, say, to my own translation of Wisława Szymborska? (If my Polish were good enough, she's the one I would attempt.) But then, Avasilichioaei must hold Stănescu's work up as a standard, at least in some respects; the through line between her work and his was unmistakable. So to put the two side-by-side may have offered a useful perspective, if not for the author than for her readers. It also served a purpose for me, as reviewer: it clarified those usually nebulous gaps between what was happening on the page and what might have happened.

Lynn Davies, *Where Sound Pools* (Goose Lane 2005)

"Testing," the first poem in Lynn Davies' second collection, *Where Sound Pools*, masquerades as a little poetic game, announcing: "Here is a poet who is not afraid to play!" A hand-clapping moment it is, reading this playful little poem, for those weary of earnest, self-important verse. But the game is a front, and why Davies ought to be crowned the Queen of Subtlety. For "Testing" is truly a manifesto, the switching on of a sound machine, a radio, a poet with a bottomless ear.

A two-stanza portrait of a sunflower, the poem "tests" all the directions this active poet's mind threatens to lead. The flower could be "an ember minus heat" or a "disembodied eye," two dramatic recastings that Davies tosses off and dismisses, like a poet revising an early draft deleting distractions. But this is no early draft and these "distractions" build up the possibilities of the sunflower, make it capable of almost anything—of fire first, then of sight, widening the possibilities inherent within anything to which Davies may turn her attention. This open experimentation with metaphor is typical Davies. It's disarming, almost self-deprecating, the way she writes that a thing is this, no wait, maybe this, or perhaps that. You read on, thinking, "Ah, here's a person who knows no better than me—but she's not afraid to guess. Let's stick with her, see where this goes."

Within the first few lines, Davies transforms then re-transforms the sunflower in clear, un-muddied language she's fit to a tap-tapping lilt that tugs and won't let go. And things only get better. She settles on sunflower-as-microphone, giving the poem's title a two-pronged meaning and conferring great import to the power, not just to the sense, of hearing, as well as of passing on what one hears, broadcasting it far and wide. The sunflower "transmits to an alien ear/ cat bell, the kid on the roller blades/ snapping gum, tires on gravel,/ the trembling aspen." When Davies instructs, "Imagine hearing/ all this for the first time," she becomes the sunflower, the reader, the alien. She's pressing play on her yellow-petalled stereo, turning up the volume, inviting us to press our ears close.

What follows is a rich, deliciously imaginative soundtrack of ordinary life—heightened, slowed down, rewound in places for repeat listening. Ordinary life Davies'-style means not just verses on the Canadian seasons tied to scenes of family and home, but encounters with the tuneful inner world of a parking-lot attendant, a dwarf guide, cascading angels, carved pumpkins. Violin bows become branch tips; squash flowers are "alert" to a "meticulous clock." Here we have a blues song for bananas, an ode to a mushroom-gatherer followed by one to hiking boots. The poems reinforce the praise accorded Davies' first collection, *The Bridge that Carries the Road* (1999), which was nominated for a Governor General's Award for Poetry and prompted critics to use such adjectives as "sublime." Though Davies' subject matter sometimes borders on "been there, read that"—heaps of snow poems, pardon the pun—she pulls this off by the idiosyncratic way that she angles in. She has successfully followed Rilke's advice in *Letters to a Young Poet*, where he counsels us, "as if no one had ever tried before, try to say what you see and feel and love and lose."

She accomplishes this most completely in "Composing Winter," a brilliant long-song of a poem in the second half of the book. Against a background of seasonal daily life amid snow and storms, she overlays a study of 14th-century Italian painter Giotto. The "grieving angels" in the Master's works echo the snow angels laying beneath bird feeders. The snow angels themselves take flight as snowy owls, a flight that is echoed by the flight of birds in his *St. Francis Preaching to the Birds*:

> The other monk Giotto includes cannot
> believe what he sees. Birds stilled by syllable
> when Francis calls to them. A chattering flock,

now a feathered ear. Except for the ghostly doves,
it's hard to identify the fading birds. Eliminate
the obvious: no crows or herons. Maybe painted

birds fly away too, their withdrawal a slow
takeoff into the fresco's blue hills. Or out
the church door, looking for the likeness of trees.

Davies animates the artwork without effort, then gently stills it by reminding us that the departing birds will only find the painted likeness of the trees on their journey. Next, a deer is observed nibbling the frozen pear trees in the yard—our own wintry tree likeness? That Davies can blend the biblical, arid world of Giotto's saints with the immediate whitened chill, that she dares to try, reveals an openness, a fearlessness, a deep-seated patience, and an understanding that the connections murmuring beneath disparate surfaces can be tapped, deciphered, translated.

Davies has a convincing way of turning one thing into another simply by letting us in on the revelation-in-progress. In "Vows of Silence," a fallen leaf becomes the beginning of certainty's end because it landed during a game of codes and messages: did it really fall or was it placed? Because the whimsy of childhood appears frequently in her poems, there is danger of reading in something like nostalgia. But much more is going on. Davies brings up the bass and drumbeat beneath her soft melodies. She can be wrenching. Despite its gentle cadence, "Falling Angels" is physical, brutal, and more about human failure than otherworldly beings: "you suspect that what you see/ of angels depends on what they/ fall through or against. The ones/ in front of a building about to buckle/ / under the wrecking ball or winged figures/ around a person blown to bits, these/ are the angels hardest to see. Some fall/ in pairs, wearing flames. You've dreamed/ of them talking to gravity, giving it features."

The entire collection is arranged with a deft touch, the poems moving rhythmically and meaningfully together. In "Quartet," after she evokes a forest of instruments at a concert in an old church, Davies writes "I won't place deer or a bobcat/ at the edge of the trees drawn by sound./ I'll put myself, cold, probably lost,/ bringing fire so they'll keep on playing." That willingness to be cold and lost for the sake of hearing the music makes Davies the poet she is, one who listens with intent to both the external and the internal and sends out, like a transmitting sunflower, a strange and honest blending of the two.

AFTERWORD

I *can't find my copy of* Where Sound Pools. *Did I loan it out? Slide it permanently from the shelf it in a ruthless pre-move cull? Sadly, this is possible. To move from province to province with a hefty book collection is no simple affair. When I dug up this review I couldn't recall any impression the book had left all those years and authors ago, an occupational hazard that could lead to a discussion about the sheer volume of poetry collections published annually, but not now, not here. I began to read, idly curious. As soon as I encountered the sunflower, the book as a whole resurfaced, complete with Davies' disarming voice and the intense delight her poems had offered with their inventiveness and whimsy, qualities grounded in a hard reality that made her work that much more affecting. Davies' words were still in me, unobtrusively "pooling," if you will. So. Wherever you are, my* Where Sound Pools *review copy cluttered with pencil-notes, may I transmit this message through a willing sunflower? I miss you. There's a gap on my bookshelf just your size.*

Catherine Owen, *The Wrecks of Eden* (Wolsak and Wynn 2001)

Not long before reading *The Wrecks of Eden*, I participated in an online debate about the political role of poetry. The topic emerged in light of the recent raft of "poets against the war" websites and compilations. Though hardly a warmonger, I was annoyed at the pervading assumption that all poets would hold the same view of the situation between America and Iraq, simply by virtue of their being composers of verse. Aside from its arrogant righteousness—when have any of us, huddled in our little writing nooks, had to make choices that might affect the stability of the world?—such herd-like thinking is precisely what good poetry strives against. As one colleague wrote during our debate, "In political poetry the positioning often becomes more important than the poetry itself. The politics of the message override the art." The expectation that we, good little poets that we are, all sit down and write lines of protest makes me squirm, makes me want to shake someone nearby and shout: Doesn't anyone know poetry is more than this? Or what can happen to good poets when they let politics muscle its way to the front of their work?

The whole thing made me, well, ready for a fight.

When I picked up *The Wrecks of Eden*, Owen's sixth book and a title shortlisted for the 2002 Dorothy Livesay Award, I was hardly in the mood for banner-waving. See me as the weary politician walking unwittingly into the path of a lone, passionate dissenter. Owen stomps about the page furiously, aghast at the extinction of species and the environmental degradation wrought so thoughtlessly by humans—a poet of protest if there ever was one. But she won me over from page one and held me through a long series that serves as a litany for lost creatures. Though it fumes, her poetry does more; it has become that finely wrought thing on the other side of anger: what we call art.

This is a significant accomplishment. Many assert that poetry, regardless of its subject matter, is political action. Don Domanski wrote in our debate: "breathing life back into a world drained by human greed is as subversive as it gets." But to combine rage against society with poetic *umph* is a rare feat that elevates both the message and the means through which it is delivered. When you can filter what might otherwise be helpless, righteous or partisan sentiment into a series of truly fine, wrenching couplets, as Owen does time and again, you have achieved artistic grace. (It doesn't hurt your cause, either.)

Owen performs brilliantly in the first poem, "Antenatal (a memo)," in which she urges the reader to "Give birth to an extinct species," for example:

> Let the
> diploid cell of a dodo enact division
>
> in your uterus, an auroch expand the fetal
> sac with softly-cloven hooves. Feel the kicks
>
> of bison bonasus, the undulations as a hare-
> lipped sucker fish turns in the amniotic inlet

Owen is neither afraid of biology nor sounds; she blends them into a forceful music, a chant, a sung command:

> … Have a caesarean section for a mammoth,
> an episiotomy if it will ease the heath hen
>
> back into the world. Abandon human conception.

Owen is also brave. She tries to push herself to the limits of her anger by taking up midway through the book with the anti-humanist Robinson Jeffers. Unfortunately this series of poems does not rise to the level of the rest of the book. Though it contains sharp, intense moments, it feels forced—or perhaps not forced enough. "Man dissevered from the earth … often appears atrociously ugly … the greatest beauty is organic wholeness" contains a truth that ought to take the reader by the throat. It begins:

> The morning bird
>   and the morning car
> begin their separate melodies
>   at the same time

And closes thus:

> We think the city depends on its machinery   to endure
>   but it does not—
>   it relies on its birds

In between, Owen establishes how the sounds of humans are "conjured" in the bird's song, and vice versa. The message is simple yet startling and the piece itself is meticulously laid out on the page, perhaps to suggest the machinery or a musical score. But the choppy display, all that deliberate placing of gaps and brackets, detracts. This poem is too careful; it has become essay first and lost something on the way. Perhaps the experiment proved Owen couldn't quite give in to Jeffers' coldness.

The optimism of the book's last section, "The Found," with its engaging, slightly anthropomorphic odes to bees, butterflies and snails, testifies to this. As does Owen's unexpected empathy for Audubon, who killed the birds he drew, in "The Naturalist." She cannot entirely disown a man who appreciated creatures as he did, "a self-styled frontier man" who "passed years around lakes/ and marshes." "Ballets he made from these birds, and/ battles," she writes adoringly, unable to help herself. In "Slippage," she writes of the meeting of natural and man-made worlds with stunning compassion:

> There is a bird who opens ruins with its beak
> like nuts in a season sharply being invented, and
>
> slipping through the loopholes of speech and metal
> holds court in both worlds to keep the wild
>
> from the amnesia of builders and its eggs
> as warm as ghosts.

Owen succeeds as a political poet because she cannot help loving humanity while trying, without compromise, to knock us off our throne.

AFTERWORD

I love what Jay Parini writes in Why Poetry Matters *about poetry and politics: "Poetry is by its very nature political, although it does not necessarily advocate one policy over another, side with a particular party, raise a fist in defiance, or hold a banner in a parade of protest. Poets may do all of the above, but in their poems they supply something that comes before the polemics: a sense of direction, a spiritual grounding, a place to stand where the pressure of reality will not overcome imagination, thus limiting possibilities." I read this recently and immediately thought: aha! He has articulated what I was clumsily trying to say all those years ago in that review and in that terrible debate. So there you have it: what that guy said. Especially the part about reality not overcoming imagination. Had Owen let that happen, there would not be an entreaty in her book to give birth to an extinct species—and some wild sense permeating the whole collection that this might be possible, that it might even be our rightful penance, our duty, our chance to make amends.*

Susan Glickman

Running in Prospect Cemetery: New and Selected Poems (Signal Editions 2004)

I turn to the title poem in Susan Glickman's *Running in Prospect Cemetery: New and Selected Poems* with anticipation. Being both a runner and a graveyard explorer myself, I am seduced by its title. I am impressed by its length: long poems take guts, and those that are successful demand a heightened skill for breadth, for paring, for the cultivation of momentum and suspense. Being, in some senses, a "student" of the school of Bronwen Wallace, I am attracted to this elegy to the late Kingston poet, who was once credited by Dennis Lee for having created "a new poetic instrument" with her distinct narrative style. Knowing Glickman has borrowed this poem's title for her selected works, I think: ah, this will be her pièce-de-résistance. Here, I will fall into the soul of this book, the knot within which is twisted the impetus behind a quarter-century of verse.

By the time I read "Running" on page ninety-seven, I have read the poems pulled from Glickman's first three books—*Complicity*, *The Power to Move* and *Henry Moore's Sheep and Other Poems*—and been struck most by their range of subject matter. A one-topic poet Glickman is not. Having come to her *Selected and New* with a rudimentary familiarity with her work along with an awareness of her status and accomplishment, I have been by turns impressed, puzzled and hopeful. If Glickman could close a poem as deftly as she did "Living Alone" in her early twenties—"You wake up dreaming you're asleep beside the fridge/ there's so much white space beside you,"—surely she must have reached new heights by her mid-thirties, when she published "Running" in *Hide and Seek* (1989).

By now I know Glickman to be capable of unpredictable metaphor and those insights toward which every poet strives: the ones that startle with both truth and originality. She allows herself the freedom to stumble on unexpected associations and to run with them. She can string together a solid line and can carry a poem to its logical—or, even better, illogical—end. Her toolkit contains wisdom, perspective, humour and the ability to use an exclamation mark, a rare skill! She balks not at expansion, whether intellectual or emotional: she travels Mexico texturally and socioeconomically; she delves into Henry Moore's notebooks and bravely extrapolates her own meaning by comparing his sheep drawings with his sculptures of women; she mines the history of the camera obscura. She judiciously exploits the personal; she is not a navel-gazer. Her subject matter is neither self-indulgent nor small-time.

But I also know that while she frequently achieves grace, she also tends to explain her big ideas or work her way through them the way you might in an essay or a letter to a friend: in prosy lines often containing awkward or flat language. She is fond of flabby phrases such as "in particular." Section V of "Henry Moore's Sheep" begins with the uncompelling, "And this is the strange part—." Section VII begins with the un-poetic "How to account for this contrast?" and wends toward this lazy stanza: "So his tenderness goes to the sheep/ and his ambivalence to/ the human figures."

I am hoping, as I begin to read "Running in Prospect Cemetery," that Glickman will have grown into her strengths and out of her weaknesses. This thirteen-page poem begins with inklings of a Bronwen Wallace-style narrative, those intimate revelations that seem to meander but lead you to moments of clarity, the way conversations over coffee between friends often do. It contains, as expected, some marvellous lines, such as "the machinery of praise rusting/ in my tears." But reading on, I find that between bright spots much of the poem, while sound in meaning, is constructed from phrasings and verbiage that bring to mind an early draft. Its sentiments are of the sunny-side up brand: to be taken for what they seem, unturned, unsliced. Where is the under-layer? The deft Glickman metaphor? The particular image? One disappointing excerpt:

and I "missing" her as though I had arrived a little too late,
thinking as usual there was plenty of time
and she'd just left, a hand waving goodbye from a window,
the bus gone down the lane
in a cloud of dust

A bus in a cloud of dust? Glickman at this point has been building her reputation as one of the more "intelligent" young poets in Canada for more than a decade. Yet this is the language, the imagery, for which she settles. I see neither Glickman nor any echo of Wallace in this passage, but a generic narrator speaking of a generic friend. There is no thrill of recognition reading this passage, simply a been-there-done-that thud. She ambitiously links three major elements: the loss of Bronwen to cancer, her own struggle with infertility, the setting of the cemetery. But her circular movement through all three, both physically and spiritually, is, except in isolated places, plodding rather than exciting. She may mean it to be plodding. Certainly that is how she must have felt in her state of dual mourning. If so, all I can say is, it is less than interesting to read.

I look up Glickman's old reviews. I want to know how she was read when she came on the scene, when she wrote about Henry Moore. I find her described as intelligent, sympathetic, graceful, imagist, light, more concerned with things than ideas, low-key, technically skilled, balanced, self-aware, tender—praised more than criticized. But I also encounter references to weak line breaks, to a cadence "a bit too colloquial, a bit too Purdyish," complaints that remain relevant. Writing about *The Power to Move* in *The Fiddlehead* in 1987, M. Travis Lane suggests Glickman gets into trouble when she tackles weighty subjects: "the lightness of her tone is a problem." Lane continues, not necessarily negatively but hitting my own misgivings bang on: "Typically [Glickman] writes as if addressing an acquaintance in a pleasant and unpressing manner. The poetic impulse seems amiable, almost idle . . ."

Reading *Running* through to the end, I conclude that Glickman is too comfortable. She is enjoying herself, her rhythms and insights, but a little too much, a little more than she has earned. The section of new poems betrays the same uneven quality: some are as slight, as wordy, as unrealized as some of her earlier work. Disappointingly, they are included alongside such strong, lovely constructions as "Reading in Bed," which is expertly shaped, indulges in not a single extraneous word and closes flawlessly on a metaphor that rewrites the closing of the day in a way only Glickman can:

> Reading in bed, Oh reading in bed!
> the day gives up; turns around once, twice, three times
> tucks its nose under a paw
> and goes to sleep

If Glickman had worked all her efforts to this level, I may not be looking at poems such as "Reading in Bed" as a glimpse of her capabilities, as an indication of the deeper, more mature talent her reputation has led me to expect. While casting about, ever valiantly, for new subjects, Glickman has not employed the same energy and sense of exploration in terms of craft. She has not been tough enough on herself to realize her own poetic potential.

AFTERWORD

This review is uncomfortable for me to revisit. It is cranky and impatient. I was thirty-two, old enough to be judicious, thoughtful and fair. Did I misread Glickman? Am I simply not her ideal reader—do we have a sensibility disconnect? These are questions I wish I had asked in the review itself. I was so wishing Glickman had pushed through her own initial feelings and impulses to a more difficult, "truer" truth, but I fear I did not do this myself when considering her work. John Barton, editor at The Malahat, *assigned this review and worked through revisions with me, helping me to clarify my points without turning them into swords. After a recent discussion of my lasting misgivings, he reread the review and wrote me this: "I think its strength rests in the personal burden you carry as a close reader of this book, one so wanting to love Glickman's poems, but one who is unwillingly unable to, based on the evidence. The review is a kind of quest, and you rally the reader to join you on your journey from first poem to last. As you proceed with the reader in tow, you become ever more uncomfortable, writing down the last line of the review with a sense of anguish as well as disappointment. The fact that you are still uneasy almost nine years later is testament to your ability to get under the skin—not only the skin of the book, but also your own. Criticism as a sliver that's difficult to get out." I offer this review here because it makes me question my rights as a reader and reviewer—what are we within our rights to demand of the poet we meet on the page?—and because I know it to be honest. It reflects my real, visceral response to this poet's work and to my high expectations of her. I'm aware that part of the reason I doubt this review is simply because it isn't a ringing endorsement. Perhaps I should be equally mistrustful my more enthusiastic assessments, which don't cause the same squirmy unease when I look back on them.*

Short Reviews and Notes
from Arc Poetry Magazine

Triny Finlay, *Splitting Off* (Nightwood 2004)

The skinny on Triny Finlay's literary raison d'être lays itself out halfway through her exquisite first collection, *Splitting Off*, at the bottom of a poem called "Self-Portrait as Ekphrastic Tension"—a tight, image-rich, eight-couplet instructive on hope (which she likens to a vase carried in a backpack through Asia, cracking enroute.) She closes with: "The morning light in your living,/ room will catch every gap/ in the vase if you glue it back together." This is what Finlay is about: "splitting" things apart, gathering up the fragments and piecing them meticulously into place, knowing that what she's engaged in is not repair but something both more difficult and more complete. That unforgiving beam of light on the gaps gives up the whole sorry tale of the vase: what it was, what it endured, how it has become, like a person tested, damaged and used, both less and more than its former self. *Splitting Off* is a tour through a talented early poet's rigorous testing of her own voice, through a range of poetic styles and devices, from momentum-heavy prose pieces to taut couplets and sonnet-variations to one of the best glosas I've ever read: "Winter Ritual," which avoids the standard pitfall of paling in comparison to the four-line quotation around which it is built. Instead, Finlay finds the gaps between the lines she's taken from Leonard Cohen's "You Have the Lovers" and fills them, without mercy. Lovers are her territory, after all. Divided into five strong sections, the book deals in sensual, tactile imagery; in food, sex, memory, perception, colour. What was that moment, that encounter, that strange time? How did it taste? How does it taste now? Finlay is sharp, rhythmically masterful and playful. Her opening section on pink is a joy to read, with its wealth of tangents and absolute disregard for limitation. She handily uses props to anchor existential business: weakness to milk, separation to bread crust, willpower and survival to the colour red. She knows shape and how to use it: how to shape her words on the page to her theme, or against it as required. "Making Ends Meet," a perfect square on the page, is a perfect circle in content. The circle butts up against the edges of the lines. Finlay sometimes sets up a mystery, a possible discovery, then veers off inexplicably. She can be annoyingly coy. A few poems feel like false or abandoned starts. Finlay does most justice to her talents in the title section, a series of wonderfully inventive self-portraits—as Toronto's Gooderham Flatiron building, as the hungry dog on Bloor St., as Sonnet 54, as conjoined twins. This is where she lets herself go. Here, the poet is enjoying herself immensely while at the same time getting somewhere—to where the answers probably lie. At the closing of "Self-Portrait as One More Potato," Finlay writes, "Yeah, I was Irish once. Then I split/ off into something over here,/ something gold,/ something with too many eyes." Too many eyes: the poet's curse and what she couldn't function without. Finlay is well on her way to using them all.

Alison Pick, *Question & Answer* (Polestar 2003)

The first work I read by Alison Pick was "Shoulder Check," a finely honed, deceptively conversational twenty-two-line poem that appeared in *Arc* 47, in winter 2001, and is included in her first book, *Question & Answer*. The poem is something of a travel tale, a journey back into a four-year-old self from where Pick relates, without qualm or flourish, an early memory of unwelcome change: the sale of the family car. Hardly a monumental event, the episode becomes, through Pick's gentle yet honest telling, a small but significant rite that colours all those yet to be endured: "Maybe the first loss/ simply repeats like a tape/ stuck in an old car's tape deck/ / something outgrown/ that I love nonetheless/ being driven away into the night." *Question & Answer* is divided cleanly into three sections, the second of which offers the most satisfying marriage of Pick's passions and talents. Titled "Still Life," the sequence begins with "Apple," a declaration and tender lament balled up tight as a seed: "You are born./ Of a hard dark pip,/ of semen,/ it hardly matters." The poems alternate between the "fruits" that ripen the stages of the narrator's life (orange for recklessness, pineapple for love) and visitations of the lives and deaths of relatives victimized by the Holocaust. The best of these is "Beef Fondue," which in three brief stanzas encapsulates a grandmother's unsettling response to her unspeakable past, a granddaughter's frustration-laced empathy and the well-appointed dinner table over which they quietly collide. In this accomplished set, baby steps toward the understanding of family history are juxtaposed with giant leaps in the life of the narrator. Reading them, we begin to understand one of the everlasting plights: how we wrestle with our own propulsion forward as we look back, trying to conjure the lives from which we have sprung, and reconcile the two. Pick's work, an ever-shifting blend of lyricism and narrative, is direct and refined. It plays without trivializing and ponders what it chooses without undue fuss. Pick does not vary vocabulary for the sake of it; instead she repeats and reuses images and words with the deliberation and skill of a hypnotist. Her play on a pantoum, "'Anyone for tea before the night falls?'—Gwendolyn MacEwen," is mesmerizing. In "Nocturne," the opening poem of the final sequence in the book, Pick writes, "there is inhale, yes, exhale, true, but the space/ between holds no name." Pick places herself and her many unyielding questions in that space: "Would you still love me if I had six arms? If I burned down the library? If I was an axe murderer?" and "Tell me who you are. What you want." The questions, which she phrases and rephrases into oranges, apples, kiwi, water, cars and canoes, are Pick's echo, her call. Her ability to exquisitely delineate the eternal quandaries of humanity—who we are, what we are and why—without unnecessary dramatization, indulgent complication, or coy answers is something to behold, something to read and reread.

Carla Funk, *Head Full of Sun* (Nightwood 2002)

Anyone who has swallowed the general view that religion is tame and boring, the bible dry and sexless, need only pick up Carla Funk's *Head Full of Sun* to be proven woefully deceived. Her first sequence of poems, borrowing the voices of Christianity's more notorious women, introduces a Bathsheba who admits "the way newly washed skin calls out/ for another body against it/ makes it impossible to keep clean," and an Eve who tastes the apple in her lover's skin thinking "desire/ isn't what it used to be." Such post-coital ennui at the beginning of time! We are dealing here with a poet who believes in God without irony or apology and who takes him on with the boldness of a questioning child, with all the feisty defiance, tempered with humility, of the old prophets. Funk's "Alphabet of Psalms," the long sequence that anchors the book, serves as a non-sequential chronicling of a life, from adolescent experimentation, travel, childhood traumas large and small, to marriage, adulthood, parenthood and infertility. I love the way the set jumps from "Psalm of Easter Break Vacation, 1981" to the "Psalm of Falling," from the particular to the monumental and back, from Peru to questions, regret to shoes. There is an honesty in Funk's writing that is almost painful to face, something like listening to a child who doesn't yet know to be embarrassed by certain notions or feelings. This honesty puts the lie to so much poetry and memoir and the careful filtering and processing it has been subject to; it makes irony seem not sophisticated but rather cowardly, a tool we use to mask our true missteps and naiveties. Funk, in short, is not trying to be cool. Her writing bursts with reverence, guilt, shame, confession (even of what would look from a distance like inconsequential sins). It allows itself to be naïve and brims with desire, craving fleshly pleasures and the soul's redemption with equal measure. The tension between the two makes for fervent reading. Not all the poems are fully realized or properly vetted. Funk offers original and piercing observations; for example, in "Tongues of Men and Angels" she writes, "because silence is a dialect of nuances I'm longing to perfect." She is adept at the rhythmic and textured image. But she needs to curb herself. In too many selections, she lets herself create long lists of examples, lists that—perhaps because of the absence of punctuation in the hands of a still-developing poet—rely on the line-end as a comma and become more prosaic than necessary. She can get too caught up in language play, in each little lexical gem, to see the poem whole, to see that her many flourishes water each other down, like a faith spread over too many gods. Nevertheless, Funk's invitation to join her as an "anxious tourist in strange weather" is well worth accepting, whether or not, as she writes so musically, so ominously, "you see or do not see/ the lamb with its torn throat/ standing at the centre of every story."

Susan Gillis, *Swimming Among the Ruins* (Nuage 2000)

Epicurus, a Stoic, wrote, "Death is nothing to us, for that which is dissolved is without sensation; and that which lacks sensation is nothing to us." This was a rather stark proclamation meant to put to rest that persistent and irrational fear of death and the dead that tends to nag at the living. Pity that Epicurus never encountered the poetry of Susan Gillis. What would he have made of this poet, standing in the echoing tomb of Clymnestra, feeling the ancient dead breathe into her, entering "places the wind could not"? I don't believe in ghosts any more than Epicurus did, but I'm hard-put not to believe in Gillis' poem, her remarkable solidification of that airy haunting we've all felt: "They breathed/ into the space between my skin and skeleton./ My spine lengthened/ and lengthened again./ My hips widened./ My ligaments eased and bones realigned." Gillis is deft at conjuring and giving weight to this sort of indefinable sensation: be it the murmuring of lost civilizations or the clinging ruins of love. We think she is writing about watching an eel spiral "like a lost necklace" or a brook being scratched and broken by its rocks. But in the face of the eel she confides, suddenly, "I miss you." The brook becomes "a noisy lover." Watching men with leaf blowers roam the streets becomes, improbably, an exercise in learning to love. Gillis spares her readers, thank goodness, the particulars of these failed relationships in favour of details that elevate moment and emotion. We don't need to know what has immediately led her to consort so intimately with a seal that "if it opened its snout/ I'd have fallen in." We have all seen, as Gillis does in the streets and markets of London, the world around us glimmer with brutal vitality while parts of our own lives slip through our fingers. It is difficult to read "Vapour Trails"—in which Gillis writes, "My cupped hands: I turn them, open, to you./ They come back bruised"—without unfolding your palms to seek the red and purple markings of your own life. Gillis seems at times too comfortable in her own rhythm, too dependent on easy joiners between clauses. But her cadence is both hypnotic and foreboding, filling the emptied holes in the world with just enough sound, scent and colour to prove that even in nothingness there is something: "a bead of water falls/ whether from a lintel or a bird's wing/ or an eye/ and the dead can hear it,/ it falls onto their throats."

Sue Sinclair, *Secrets of Weather & Hope* (Brick 2001)

Reading Sue Sinclair, one is struck with the impression that nothing she can see, touch or taste is in any way separate from her consciousness and being. She does not merely eat a green pepper; she identifies with it, compares its reflection of light to that of a dented fender, declares it was "born/ with its eyes shut tight." She does not simply cross bridges, but feels their pain, seeing them as "architectures/ of longing, chance." Collar bones evoke wings, desire and symmetry—a completeness—that their wearers lack. Sinclair's poetry, vivid, lively, crisp, and packed with delicious surprise metaphors, goes beyond its empathy with objects to urge convincingly that they are part us, and we part them, that somehow they embody the facts of existence with an enviable, clear-eyed integrity. She finds in "things" a natural courage, respecting them for their ability to express with eloquence and dignity all that we strive to keep carefully hidden. On bridges: "They rise publicly, aching/ with effort, to risk everything." On peonies: "they force you to look/ into the place where colour/ submerges, gives itself up, and you might/ find out what you're willing to risk." Sinclair explores her obsessions with purity and delicacy and, in the series on clouds that forms the core of the book, with reverence. Neither solid nor entirely inanimate, clouds get the full Sinclair treatment, a vigorous exploration of their true characters and plight. They bear the responsibility of "earthly memory"; they are stillborn; they "breathe more deeply" than us. "Bodies hanging in the sky," they murmur and collide, "opaque and fractured by light." Sinclair's sensitivity is striking. In her hands, light both illuminates and obscures: it misses its targets and threatens embarrassment. Light can appear as a fist "moulded onto darkness." In "Stained Glass" the world is "fuelled by light." In "André Kertész," "every lit form proposes/ not just the doing but the falling/ into doing." Sinclair's poetry is often exquisite but sometimes too loosely formed. Some lines and phrases work so admirably for their right to be that it's annoying to encounter those that don't. Weak qualifiers such as "sometimes" and "seems" appear frequently. And too often she engages us with a beautiful, original idea that she doesn't push to its potential, as though she is satisfied with one unexpected insight rather than accepting its invitation to travel yet farther. But Sinclair brings imagination and intensity to her writing, and a keen awareness of her own participation in the act of looking. In "Calcereous" she writes of a shell—and a person—who "doesn't comment on the light/ but absorbs it." Through her poems, she urges herself, and anyone who reads them, to do the same.

S.D. Johnson, *Hymns to Phenomena* (Thistledown Press 2000)

My first encounter with S.D. Johnson was a poem called "But Quietly," in which rain "has many quiet chambers" and a drooping willow tree harbours a mind "like that of a woman/ searching a crowd for her lover." The poem is a medley of arresting images, delicate confessions and utterly, deliciously dense spaces wedged between the lines. The poem is about absence, an absence that Johnson fills and fills and fills—with things, with sounds—until, paradoxically, the emptiness encompasses all. What a feat to live up to in an entire book of verse. Johnson does it, with grace and absolute surety. In *Hymns to Phenomena*, "But Quietly" is just one achingly beautiful song to humanity among a concert of sophisticated, passionate and tender compositions. Inside the cover, the dedication reads: "for you." What can one say but thank you? Such an excavation a reading of this book becomes, an uncovering of a deep, holy, thrillingly inventive respect for the glories of life. Johnson's poetry looks loose at first brush, the punctuation scattered and unpredictable. In fact, Johnson's words are so carefully chosen, their place on the page so determined, the text begins to seem carved or set down like a complex score. Her unorthodox punctuation, commas before dashes, for example, becomes familiar and necessary, part of a meaty language of observation. Within this sturdy scaffolding, Johnson brilliantly and judiciously stretches the bounds of vocabulary. She chooses rare words with aplomb. Though I ran frequently to the dictionary, I did so happily, with anticipation, for I inevitably found a meaning that added layers to a line or a poem, that proved this was the only term to employ. Consider the angel of white in "Lessons for the Body," who leaves in his wake a feeling of "intercostal loneliness." Look it up. You'll know what I mean. Ordinary words, meanwhile, are nudged into places they have never been: pomegranates wait to "live" inside your mouth, ideas "clot" into sounds, there is a "mood" to love inside a tin cup. To convey the richness and range of Johnson's poetry is like trying to describe views through a kaleidoscope. She displays an infectious faith in the miraculous and one of the most free-wheeling, authoritative imaginations going. Ever considered entering the mind of a spider "bored with a simple geometry" who contemplates "a room/ which moves infinitely, like a blind dancer"? Johnson will take you there in a way that leaves you wondering: Why have I not thought to take this trip before? What did I see before reading this? How did the world look?

Sharon McCartney, *Under the Abdominal Wall* (Anvil 1999)

"It's like dreaming about someone/ who's dead; I want it to last." With this confession tucked almost slyly about halfway through her book, Sharon McCartney puts plain a truth hovering beneath her deceptively simple language. McCartney writes about pain, psychological and physical: from the child witnessing her sister's slow death with a sharp, unforgiving eye to the new mother relentlessly reliving the gruesome shock of giving birth. But her poems do not whimper, they're not even mildly regretful. McCartney is concerned with the beauty of pain's paraphernalia, with recreating the plots of grief in all their stunning, awful glory. She is at her best in unapologetic reportage. In "As if We Knew Each Other," a woman describes giving birth, the child "pried" from her as "through a split envelope" while she "stared, conscious/ up the nose/ of the anaesthetist." A more subtle example is "Between 8:30 and 9:00, Saturday Night," a poem that begins, "He chops knotty oak into kindling;/ she reads under a knitted blanket./ He wants her to be as she once was;/ she wants him to be as she is now." Using the right details, properly situated, McCartney is able to conjure all that has and hasn't happened without tiresome chronology or lessons. Unfortunately, she doesn't always use this skill. The voice in this book is singular, relentless and almost claustrophobic. I found myself enduring the poet's attempt to document personal experience and "work through" issues, wishing she would venture outside her world more frequently, just enough to negotiate other realities, as she does impressively in "Exotic Hardwoods," an encounter with a murderer selling handicrafts. McCartney's sharpest weapons are the spaces between lines. In "October 1967" a man approaches a girl in the park: "he stops me and fingers/ the hem of the dress my mother/ trimmed with a blue fringe./ There was a doll I once loved to abuse." The skill evident in this passage, the astonishing leap, makes it difficult to tolerate less polished attempts, in which potentially powerful moments are crowded with explanation. In "My Father Tells Me the Story of How I Was Conceived," we are told "My father is clearly embarrassed," an emotion far better related by subsequent lines describing his laughter and moving hands. McCartney succeeds more frequently than not, placing words on the page in a way that they can be grabbed hold of, by the fists, the senses. In "New Mother" we learn the smells of boredom and love. In one of many unflinching accounts of childbirth, snapped arteries wag "like broken/ kite strings." By the time you read that McCartney's narrator doesn't want to stop dreaming of her dead, you know it's not just because they will vanish when she wakes. The voice in these poems wouldn't dare move through life, waking or sleeping, without acknowledging the sorrows that trail behind, that etch vivid scenes in the back of her skull.

Shawna Lemay, *All the God-sized Fruit* (McGill-Queen's 1999)

Shawna Lemay must keep a little garden of Lewis Carroll fungi next to her desk. A little nibble before writing scales her down to fit the proportions of a painted canvas. For here is a woman who slips into works of art and watches them swell into multiple dimensions, who revels in snooping, poking into crevices and unexpected cracks. Poets often trace the thread of what they see in a work of art back into their own souls. We are blessed with some exquisite practitioners of this often subtle craft: Stephanie Bolster's National Gallery poems in *Two Bowls of Milk* and Diana Brebner's Mary Pratt poems in *The Golden Lotus* come immediately to mind. Lemay is up to something more mysterious and playful, more deeply meshed in visual art while at the same time disregarding the frames that hold it in. In Lemay's world, art forgers keep diaries containing oddly thrilling confessions such as: "I have ink recipes/ calling for crushed beetles, squid ink,/ dried partridge blood, a rusty nail." A still-life painter works in the kitchen with "the smell of dying flowers always in her hair," while a still-life painter's wife bears practical offerings: "here is a lemon carefully peeled/ the rind a curling ribbon." A drowned prostitute rumoured to be the model for Carravagio's *Death of a Virgin* speaks eloquently: "I learned to feel the difference/ between velvet, brocade, organdie/ when a dropped cape brushed my ankle." Rubens' fleshy models, meanwhile, ruminate on those who ponder their hung likenesses: "The stickpin women come to look at us now." We are led through the sensations of the woman who restored Da Vinci's *Last Supper*, the paint persistently flaking "the way paper floats up from a bonfire." In Lemay's artistic universe, women demand recognition, be they historically neglected painters, subjects or wives. Her depiction of German artist Paula Modershon-Becker's struggle between wifely duties and artistic calling is breathtaking: "I was on fire with how many tiny fires./ Some for him, some for my paintings./ I thought it would become one large fire/ and then I would become someone." Lemay's accomplishment is not just one of imagination but of reigning fancy in with precision. Her language is rock-solid, images whole and textured, line breaks often startling and fragments used judiciously, to great effect.

AFTERWORD

I was very new to the Canadian poetry world when I first began to write these reviews. I came to most of the poets above completely blank: I knew nothing of them or their work before something in the title of their book or first poem or overarching theme drew me. Now some of these poets are acquaintances and friends. I suspect my reading of these books would be different now, perhaps richer, because I'd bring to them—I'd have no choice—a cache of personal context and emotion. But I'm glad the poems got the chance to stand on their own terms without the tint of my later relationships with their authors. The reading was more like venturing into an unknown world: I had no idea who I would meet or what to expect with every page I turned. I was in a position to be surprised, and I often was.

Notes from *Arc Poetry Magazine*, 2004-2011

Unlike a poem that bows its way regally off the page, a poem that is indubitably complete, a poetry magazine is never done. Each issue is an entrance and a publication senses in its very spine, stapled or bound, when it's time to refresh the wardrobe.

⁂

Turn the magazine over and shake gently. Mutter your spell, whatever it is. A poem may just fall to your floor.

⁂

If there is no refuge to be had in words, there is, it seems, no safety anywhere. Anything could be or mean something other than what it is or what it was.

⁂

We revel in double meanings, in the hidden undersides of words: we seek these and use them to our own ends, planting little bombs as we lay our lines down along the page.

⁂

It may very well be the birth of a poet: the narrator understanding that she can use words with as much force and devastation as her antagonist.

⁂

By thirty, one is aware of the contradictions that dog us, of the good that comes with the bad and vice versa; that no plan is foolproof; that life, above all else, will surprise. The best poetry is aware of these realities. Indeed, it plumbs them. God willing, the best literary magazines, shoestring budgets and all, find that poetry.

⁂

In Arc 1, a thirty-page volume of 8.5 x 11 inch stapled sheets with a thick stock cover, appeared a set of short lyrics by Sid Marty, whose work had been included seven years earlier in Al Purdy's 1971 anthology Storm Warning. Revisiting the issue recently, I noted the following stanza from Marty's "News," which seemed to embody a manifesto for the new magazine in which it appeared:

> Tattered, the sentences and phrases
> drift to earth like prayer flags
> held in the long fingered grasses
> washed and eaten by time

⁂

I recently learned from co-founding editor Christopher Levenson that the name *Arc* was chosen because it was short and punchy and at the beginning of the alphabet—but also because it lent itself to metaphor: "We don't pretend to cover the whole circle."

⁂

One of the things I love about reading is the relationship one builds, amid lamps and shadows and bookshelves, with one's favorite authors. If the alchemy that takes place during an act of reading is pinned in that space between the mind and the page, where reader, writer and imagination meet, is there such thing as pure objective judgment of a literary work anyway?

⁂

Swift and Pope understood the marketing value of mystery and cultivated their own anonymity to stir curiosity and speculation. The reason this worked is simple: people want, by nature, to place a thing made. That joy in "Anon" is in part a basic joy in the life of the imagination: the invisible author is free to be created in one's mind. Gwendolyn MacEwen writes in her poem "The Garden of Thieves," that the "Great poem," "the one we all know/ Never gets written" was in fact "written by Anonymous who was my favourite poet/ And who I thought was a Byzantine king."

⁂

Maybe reading work by known versus unknown writers is simply the difference between that intense conversation over coffee with an old friend, complete with the undercurrent of shared histories, ancient shorthand and inside jokes, and that unexpectedly riveting discussion at the party with a stranger. Both etch into the self. Both claim their space.

⁂

I was fortunate to hear Brooklyn author René Houtrides speak recently in Chicago. She began by describing the 1940 collapse of the Tacoma Narrows

Bridge in Washington State, how it rollicked and swayed and came down a mere four months after it had opened. She spoke of a soprano shattering glass; of a military officer—via one powerful, self-made sound—causing soldiers to break rank. These are all examples of resonance, Houtrides said. Everything is in motion. That motion works back and forth between and against different forms, such as the way high winds took hold of something unsettled in that faulty bridge. When a piece of writing pokes or bashes or even gently moves against something "already oscillating" inside the person reading it, stuff happens: the glass explodes; the bridge comes down."

⁂

This is why we write and why we put what we write out in the world in books or in little magazines. You take something in; it becomes something else in you; you pass it on; it becomes something else in someone else. Dominoes, but dominoes that alter in form when toppled, that ding the table and leave chinks.

⁂

The way to measure the significance of these endeavours is to pick up their resonating pitch and somehow follow it through time and space. Who wrote these contributions? Who will read them? And then what? And then what?

⁂

Contrary to some of the more familiar black humour in contemporary poetry circles, we all chose to believe that, despite the generally accepted view of things, doctors, scientists, plumbers, pharmacists, mechanics, consultants and so on actually do read poetry and might have some worthwhile things to say about it. How would we know if we never went looking? If we never asked?

⁂

You might ask why we, the poets and critics, should care about what the entomologist or the hobby farmer thinks of, say, Charles Bruce's "Back Road Farm." Would or should the entomologist have any interest in what I have to say about a moth? When I show my work to other poets, they want to talk about line breaks, word choice, that thing we call "voice." Doug told me that the pupal case for the moth looks much rougher in nature than I had depicted in the poem. He described to me in detail how the adult female attracts a mate. And he asked me a pointed question: "So we have these adults emerging in the spring 'for no great acts.' I don't know anything about your personal life, but some people believe that lovemaking is a great act. Do poets?"

⁂

We live as poets in this age amid a peculiar tension. We work at a craft that we wish counted more, but keenly know the value of the sidelong glance we are afforded by our apparent marginality.

⁂

A person close to me once suggested that what we do in an age such as this is "keep the line intact." There is no glory in this work. But glimmers of that through line flash when, for example, the poet in the family is called upon for solace at the funeral, hope at the wedding. When someone like my older brother, not the poetry-reading kind, requests a copy of my poem that appeared on the bus so he can hang it in his office.

⁂

One night I sat up in bed, racing through poem after poem in my copy of *Final Harvest: Emily Dickenson's Poems,* edited by Thomas H. Johnson. Obviously this is not how respectable people read poetry, but the brevity of Dickinson's poems, their rhythmic quickness and the em-dashes that propel them forward, can render the impulse to gulp them down in speedy succession difficult to resist. I read as if in a trance, all those Deaths and Years and Realms and Winds. Then I hit "We like March," (#448 in this edition), which seemed to be printed twice in a row. A look at the margin told me this was no mistake. The first version had been written in 1872 and the second in 1878. Here is the original:

We like March.
His Shoes are Purple—
He is new and high—
Makes he mud for Dog and Peddler,
Makes he Forests dry.
Knows the Adder Tongue his coming
And presents her Spot—
Stands the Sun so close and mighty
That our Minds are hot.

News is he of all the others—
Bold it were to die
With the Blue Birds exercising
On his British Sky.

The poem is 65 words long. This doesn't change. But by 1878, Dickinson has joined the first two lines as well as the stanzas, making a 12-line poem beginning, "We like March—his shoes are Purple." (Note the period/ dash exchanges.) Both "Peddler" and "dry" are now followed by dashes. "Dry" is capitalized. Line seven has become "And begets her spot—"; "exercising" has been replaced by "buccaneering"; and the final word's gone lowercase.

⁂

How did "presents" become "begets," along the lines of a wholesale switch, from "offering" or "showing" to "creating" or "causing"? I looked up "Adder Tongue." According to Culpeper's *Complete Herbal and English Physician*, published in 1814, Adder's (or Serpent's) Tongue grows in moist meadows, "quickly perisheth with a little heat" and "hath but one leaf, which grows with the stalk a fingers length above the ground ..." The stalk resembles a snake's tongue. "Begets" definitely does more to evoke this slightly sinister plant, as well as activate the poem, just as March itself tends to "activate."

⁂

"Buccaneering," unlike the flat "exercising," bursts with rhythm and connotation. We've gone from ho-hum duty to exuberance, with a hint of the outlaw. "Buccaneering," while calling back to "begets," brings the alliteration in Dickinson's final few lines nearly to excess. Excessive is sometimes how March feels. "B" is also the sound of "birth" and "beginning." With these few changes, Dickinson has turned her poem from one that describes to one that acts out. It is more like a living than a dead thing on the page.

⁂

To properly "finish" this poem, took what? Just a few judicious, inspired alterations. Okay: six years and a few alterations.

⁂

I can't count the times I have said of a poem, "This ending isn't earned," or "The poet copped out," or "It should have ended sooner," or "It didn't go far enough."

⁂

Dickinson did not spend six years staring at the line "With the Blue Birds exercising." She left it; she came back to it. We know that some balance between attention and space will get us to the end of the poem, some mixture of driving the poem and letting it drive us.

⁂

The urgency that propels us to work at all is dangerous. We want to be able to say "I did this" and move on. May I use this space, in this hopeful and imperfect journal, to plea for patience? That the poets all hedge a little, stem the rush to publication, balk at birthing a book every year, or even every two? That we take a few poems we've written, put them away, and not look at them again for six months or six years?

⁂

There is an interesting tension at play between poetry and fiction. Fiction we drive forward with plot—even in the most plot-light tale things vanish, undo, rearrange or slightly shift. The poet tries to forestall the coming incident, to stop us in our tracks before we absentmindedly walk away. This is not for the sake of nostalgia but to hold the thing down so it can be examined, plumbed, transformed and thus revealed anew.

⁂

Metaphor. When it works on us we can feel it unbending our joints, rearranging our insides, turning back our ears.

⁂

In a folder in my office, I keep a poem by Czeslaw Milosz that I tore out of a copy of *The New Yorker*, from when, I can't say, though the paper is definitely yellowed. Called "Realism," and translated from Polish by Robert Hass and Milosz himself, it begins with these lines:

> We are not so badly off if we can
> Admire Dutch Painting. For that means
> We shrug off what we have been told
> For a hundred, two hundred years. Though we lost
> Much of our previous confidence. Now we agree
> That those trees outside the window, which probably exist,
> Only pretend to greenness and treeness
> And that the language loses when it tries to cope
> With clusters of molecules. And yet this here:
> A jar, a tin plate, a half-peeled lemon,
> Walnuts, a loaf of bread—last, and so strongly
> It is hard not to believe in their lastingness.

This passage, for me, embodies and dramatizes the question: What about visual art casts us under its spell so insistently (by "us" I mean poets) that it causes us to write, to throw words back at it?

⁂

Way back in 2001, before *Arc* was part of my life, I was assigned, for the National Gallery's magazine, *Vernissage*, interviews with three poets who had "dallied" with artists. One of these, the now-late Diana Brebner, discussing her series "Eleven Paintings by Mary Pratt," explained the process like this: "You have this whole world, and it sort of looks out at you, and you look at it. There's a correspondence. You see different objects as landmarks. There might be an apple, a knife. You look at it in terms of colour, the way maps have colours that denote territory or geography. And there's a psychological overlay, it's the one you can't see, it has to do with how the different colours or objects are organized, the intensity. There's the narrative overlay. Often you read the painting from left to right. There's a way of seeing, it's not exactly a story, but a relationship. And then also the associations you make, with oranges, jam-making—personal history. My personal history and Mary Pratt's are intersecting in this artificial space. But it isn't artificial. How can you not, after having seen a work that way, write a complex poem?"

⁂

Umberto Eco, in an interview with the German magazine *Der Spiegel* in November 2009, described a painting as a "cutout of infinity." We love paintings, he said, because of the paradox of the frame, which makes us believe we can see more than what's inside it: "A person contemplating a painting feels a need to open the frame and see what things look like to the left and to the right of the painting."

⁂

Science, I felt, was too rigid, all its answers spelled out. Since my aspirations were literary, I planned to drop science as soon as the rules allowed. Which I did, not long after peering keenly into the organs of a dissected frog.

⁂

I research scientific subjects all the time—from the mating habits of seahorses to the health impacts of industrial waste sites to the safety of genetically modified foods. I am constantly humbled by how little I grasp about the way things work. I ask myself: how can I be a legitimate writer with such a deficiency of fundamental knowledge?

⁂

What if a poet or novelist plunked her adult self in the sandbox with a magnifying glass? What if she squinted mighty hard at the principles underlying quantum physics? Our calls prompted an avalanche of enthusiastic response. It was buoying to discover our hunch was correct: the literary scene is teeming with writers who have salvaged that unencumbered inner explorer (and many who are scientists themselves).

⁂

In the grown-up world, relations between the arts and the sciences can be fraught. But anyone who has genuinely delved into both worlds sees the limit in any hard line drawn between them. The creative force, the tangents and false starts, the spectre of futility—all belong to both. Scientists feel it, writers feel it: that sense that what we're reaching for will ever be just beyond us. Adam Sol hails that outstretched arm when he writes, of one of Pluto's three moons: "Even Oblivion has an orbit. / Even Oblivion bends the light."

I did not think deeply about the competitive aspects of poetic life. I preferred to view the writing of poetry as a singular engagement with one's world: a private effort undertaken in the hopes of honing a creation worthy of sharing with a reader, should such opportunity arise.

Some would say that embedded within the act of writing, some spark of competition must always be found. We compete against our peers, against yesteryear's masters, against our own selves.

Much is at stake in the realm of prizes, contests, awards and in the underlying atmosphere of competition under which many of us toil: not just egos, dollars or even legacies, but the very nature of the poetic pursuit.

As an "emerging" poet sending out my work, I suspected that one ought to be circumspect about any rejections or honours received: for who, really, could legitimately decide what work was "best?" My experience on the other side of the desk has hardened this suspicion into conviction.

We mustn't give each poem we accept, each award we bestow or each issue we compile too much weight. We're working along a continuum that will shift and evolve, that revises itself just as we revise our own work. Some of our decisions will stand the test of time; others won't.

The Real Ones are More Expensive:
Personal Essays

Poland's Hereafter

In August of 2005, I was walking down Ulica Nowy Świat, which roughly translates as New World Street, a boutique-lined avenue in Warsaw's chaotic core. One moment, I was staring at a nun who had stopped to chat with a man on a bicycle; the next, I was face-to-face with Pope John Paul II. He was waving from the top of a folding card table. He was wearing white and smiling like a movie star. He was very very small.

Behind the table stood a white-haired vendor with the look of a man who was guarding rather than selling. Among his trinkets were decorated boxes, embroidered tea towels and the requisite display of wooden dolls with bowling-pin hips that house smaller and smaller versions of themselves. Because this was Poland, though, one of these dolls was the grinning former pope.

Nuns and popes. Already I felt surrounded. It didn't help that I'd spent the night in the guest room of a residence for an order of priests. I should have guessed this was how it would be. Poland, after all, is the most Catholic country in the world, where a good ninety percent of the population remains devout. What I couldn't have anticipated, however, was that, twenty-four hours into my first trip here, I would already be reacquainted with my doubting-Thomas anxieties. My lack, that is, of whatever it takes to cross to the other side. The holy side.

I picked up the pope and twisted him open. Inside was a smaller John Paul, in a different pose. Inside that, another. And so on, until his tiny face was a mere blur of colours. I turned the doll in the air, not knowing whether it was meant to be funny or reverent—or simply mercenary. The doll was light and cheaply made but cost ZL60 (roughly CDN$20), enough for a reasonable meal for two, even in price-inflated Warsaw. I slipped the doll back on the table, thanked the sour-faced man and walked away.

Two days later I was in Krakow, where Karol Wojtyła, before he became the first Polish pope, had spent his youth. The place where, in defiance of German occupation, he studied underground for the priesthood in the early 1940s; where he taught theology; where, as a priest, he pushed for the construction of the first Catholic church in the Soviet steel-town development Nowa Huta; where he served as archbishop; and where, as pope, he once wept before getting on the plane to return to the Vatican after a rare visit home.

I can't help but compare that record to mine. As a teen, I considered my babysitting gigs in the meeting room of my church a legitimate substitute for actually sitting through mass myself. When I did attend, which was rarely, I often showed up late. Let's not get started on my eight years of living with a man out of wedlock (not always the same one). I have also been known to heartily criticize the late pope's stance on birth control, gay marriage, the ordination of women—you name it.

Ho-hum. Your typical fallen North American Catholic. But here in Poland, I was way out of my depth. In this country, Sunday mass in many churches is offered every ninety minutes and people stop off for confession on their way home from work. I do have a reverent streak, but all this Catholicism was beyond me. A few weeks in Krakow and I was beginning to feel nostalgic over that little pope doll back in Warsaw, standing there stoically among all the other souvenirs.

John Paul II died on April 2, 2005. It was now August. In a country such as Canada, four months would have been ample time for the mourning of a celebrated public figure to peak and wane. In Krakow, the months had only heightened and intensified the loss—and thus, ironically, his presence. He was in or on (or both) every local church, sculpted into statues and onto plaques. Heaped at the base of even the smallest such tributes were hundreds of candles in coloured-glass jars. The windows of every local bookstore burst with dust-jacket reproductions of his face; piled inside were his poems, his essays, his likeness and his prayers. He was in the historic Jagellonian University, where he once studied and lectured and where it was possible to peer at his transcripts in a long glass display case in a hushed room.

He looked out cheerfully, or solemnly, from postcards crammed on racks in Krakow's main square, the Rynek Główny. He was deep underground inside the historic salt mine at Wieliczka, carved entirely out of salt. He waved jauntily from the balcony of the Sukiennice, the historic cloth hall, in the form of a blown-up reproduction advertising a photographic exhibition of himself. He was on two trees in the garden outside the Franciscan church: someone had screwed plastic-sleeved magazine covers into the trunks, featuring images of you-know-who.

He could not be found, however, in a particular window at the stately Palac Biskupski—3 Franciszkanska Street—where, on each visit to Krakow, he would appear with a greeting. Before this window, Poles had gathered in the thousands while he was dying in far-off Rome. The whole "far-off in Rome" thing didn't stop them from standing quietly on the street with candles, looking up as though he might at any moment pop his head out to offer a blessing. You still couldn't walk by without seeing a cluster of people on the sidewalk, faces upturned, mouthing prayers.

On every city block was graffiti about Krakow's rival football teams, Cracovia and Wisła. Every time I noticed such artwork on an apartment wall, I recalled the historic truce my friend Eva, a German student who'd been in Krakow at the time, had described to me: the two teams and 15,000 of their frequently violent supporters stood together in honour of the ailing pontiff. The Planty, a winding ribbon of parkland that was once a moat surrounding the city, reminded me of another tale she'd told me: on the night of April 8, a live performance of Mozart's *Requiem* by the Krakow Symphony and Philharmonic Choir was broadcast through the old town starting at 9:37 pm, the hour of the pope's passing six nights prior. The lament floated through the stone-paved medieval streets where Krakowians, in the thousands, paraded solemnly with lights.

He came to life in a lecture I attended, "The Roman Catholic Church and Poland," given by social anthropologist Annamaria Orla-Bukowski, who had moved from Chicago to Poland in the 1980s. Orla-Bukowski explained how it was the church that improbably kept Polish culture alive while the country was partitioned for 123 years—that's four generations—up until the end of the First World War, thus neatly tying up national identity with religion. Further oppression of both people and church under German and then Soviet occupation from 1939 on solidified the Catholic Church's position as "a symbol of the Polish people, sharing the same fate." Orla-Bukowski explained how the Pope's visit here in 1979 was on the lips of "every other person" in Gdansk one year later during the Solidarity strikes that would ultimately turn the tide against Communism. "They said they were doing it for him," says Orla-Bukowski.

He had even been transubstantiated into a little clump of melted, hardened wax on the ground outside the famous Mariacki church. As Orla-Bukowski explained one afternoon over drinks in a nearby café, the city had laid sheet metal beneath the part of the church wall on which a plaque depicting the pope hangs, one of the many spots locals had transformed into a shrine by placing lit candles on the ground. The metal was meant to protect the stones of the ancient market floor from molten wax. But it failed to contain the endless flow. Wax had run down the metal into tram tracks, which Orla-Bukowski remembered watching workers scrape clean in the early mornings on the days leading up to the pope's death. City officials diligently rounded up tens upon tens of thousands of burnt-out candles each night and pleaded for people to stop. They pleaded, but the candles kept coming.

By the time I was taken by goodhearted relatives to Wadowice, John Paul II's hometown, in the same spirit that Canadians ferry visitors to

Niagara Falls, I was poped out. Visiting the crowded church in which he was baptized, walking through the rooms of the second-floor flat where he lived as a boy, partaking of the recently established tradition of eating a Wadowice kremówki, the local cream pastry John Paul once mentioned enjoying as a child, I couldn't muster a single ounce of appreciation. I mean, what do I know about sustained faith in heroes? About believing in leaders and saints? What do I know about actually needing them?

After five weeks of overkill—shrines, shrines, everywhere I turned—I realized I would likely never understand what it was the Poles needed and were getting from the extreme remembrance of John Paul. I hadn't lived what they'd lived; I'd only been told. And so I asked a cousin who was with me in Wadowice, as we hovered near a crowded souvenir stand in the local church, what she thought John Paul would make of all the fuss. She smiled and said, a little ruefully, "He always told us not to put up statues for him. Just to live good lives."

Good advice. But if his habit of beatifying and canonizing saints is any evidence, the Polish pope also understood the need for heroes, particularly local ones—particularly in hard-done-by places. If Karol Wojtyła is now where everyone in Poland thinks he is, if that "presence" I felt was inspired by more than just statues, postcards and dolls, he must understand that need more than ever.

AFTERWORD

My grandparents boarded the Stefan Batory II in Gdansk, Poland in the fall 1938 and set sail for Canada—you might say just in the nick of time. They disembarked at Pier 21in Halifax where they were processed by Polish-speaking nuns and took a train west to Ontario, where they spent some years on a farm on the Hamilton mountain with my grandfather's brothers before acquiring their own piece of land, first in Vineland and then in Burlington. Ours is an example of an immigrant family whose connection to its history and culture shrank to a mere thread very quickly. We grandchildren numbered sixteen and not one of us could say much more in our grandparents' tongue than "dzien dobry" (hello) and "dowidzenia" (goodbye)—nor could we make our way around a farm. In part due to the cold war, the extended family back in Poland was almost otherworldly, existing on the other side of so many divides, geographical and political. My visit to Poland as an adult was revelatory: the essay above, focusing on the country's reverence for John Paul II, who still hangs smiling in a frame at my parents' house in Burlington, barely touches the experience, particularly the thrill of being welcomed into the homes of relatives who'd been so remote in my childhood as to seem fictional. Visiting meant hearing firsthand tales of my grandparents' younger selves, and of those who were close to them. My second cousin Agnieszka told me what happened one year when her grandmother, my grandmother's sister, needed new boots. After train trips into the city at the break of dawn three days in a row, she still came home empty-handed: each day, she could not reach the counter before all the boots had been claimed. The fourth day, Agnieszka rode in with her and, being young and strong, pushed to the front of the line and raced up the stairs as soon as the doors opened. Success! "You went to the counter and took what you could get," she told me. "They might not fit, they might not be a style you liked, but you needed boots." Agnieszka and I are of the same generation. I still find the contrast between this event from her teen years and the far more trivial struggles I endured during my own adolescence—I was not allowed to go to this or that party, I had to wear discount BiWay jeans instead of Levi's—striking and humbling. I was fourteen in 1984, when Pope John Paul II visited Canada. We attended a giant mass for Polish-Canadians at the Canadian National Exhibition in Toronto. In this country, we had no need of stirring words to spur a revolution; instead, I came home with a JPII felt banner, the triangular kind that fans wave at football games, Karol Wojtyła's smiling face framed in a little circle near the tassels.

How to Be Friends with a Redhead

With each whir and snap of the scissors, I hold my breath. On the chair next to Joana I've laid out a series of navy blue ribbons. My job is to collect her rich red hair as it drops from her scalp, divide it by length and tie it into bundles. The growing piles of cuttings shimmer against the chair's vinyl covering, long and short, gingered and mulled.

What am I doing? Why am I letting this happen? I'm supposed to be the helper, the friend. Please tell me—good God, no—this haircut wasn't my idea.

We're twenty-two. I'm fresh out of journalism school at Ryerson University, working as a reporter on a monthly Toronto newsmagazine in Cabbagetown and Regent Park. It's a rough place to work and I like that: I'm cultivating my own anti-establishment streak, growing less and less polished by the day, or so I fancy. Joana, meanwhile, has taken a leave after her second year in the Ryerson School of Radio and Television Arts program, and is working part-time at Eaton's in Vancouver, developing what seems to me, "Miss Anti-makeup" if there ever was one, an alarming expertise in cosmetics. She's cultivating beauty; has a knack for it.

Well, she was cultivating beauty. She hasn't taken a shift at Eaton's in weeks. Now she's on leave from that as well.

Four years ago, during our final year of high school, a lump was surgically removed from the tiny hollow under Joana's lightly freckled arm. It contained two iffy cells. No biggie, her doctor said: it was out. A year later she found another, further down her arm. We celebrated her twentieth birthday, August 27, 1991, in the Toronto General Hospital. A bunch of old friends drove in from nearby Burlington. We took over one of the colourless lounges and Joana's dad, who'd carted in a cooler of pop, ordered pizza. We should have been in a bar; we should have been dancing. Malignant melanoma, they'd said this time. They'd used the "c" word. Not the one she and I had decided as fourteen-year-olds was the vilest piece of language on the planet, but this new one, equally ugly, worse.

Joana, who looked and felt no more diseased than the rest of us, made us all laugh about the foul-smelling patient with whom she was stuck sharing a room—some unpleasant gastrointestinal problem—though neither her plight nor her roommate's was really very funny. By then she was lump-free once more, thanks again to surgery. She got defiant. *Dear my Cancer,* she wrote in her journal, *You are not going to get me!! I'm sorry; I know you are trying to put a damper on my wonderful life, but it's not going to work. You might as well quit now.*

It didn't. What began as a supposedly harmless, easily extracted tumour when we were eighteen had spread to her thighs, spine, head, ribs and midriff. After I don't know how many surgeries followed by round after round of varying chemotherapies, plus a side tour of naturopathic remedies such as injections of mistletoe extract (a fine source of lame-o jokes for a while), her breasts have shrunk down to the nipple and morphine is part of her everyday, meaning pain is too. She is now on a last-ditch, super-strength chemo treatment. And this new drug, unlike its predecessors, is claiming her hair.

We're saving it on the off chance that it grows back a different colour. We've heard stories about this happening. It's one thing to be born with, say, brown hair. You learn to take comfort in its soft, mulchy blahness. But to have brownness thrust upon you after a lifetime of red—the red of fall-fired leaves, sharp candied cinnamon—is unthinkable.

She didn't need to explain this when she handed me the ribbons in her seventeenth-floor Vancouver bedroom yesterday, before we left for the ferry. We fell into efficiency mode—get the job done—like we did when we fought the school board in grade thirteen or threw parties while my parents were away, or planned her seduction of Rob, now her boyfriend, in our first year at Ryerson.

I threw out a question: "All of it?"

"As much as you can."

"No problem."

The hairdresser pauses between each snip, dangling the scissors like a pair of crossed swords. She's older than us, thirtyish, her own hairdo long and black, down to the chest. She parts Joana's hair in places and peers down, doctor-like, to survey the resident obstructions: four or five wide lumps, some of them split and rimmed with puss, that protrude as high as an inch or more from her scalp.

When we warned her about these, she waved a hand in the air and said, "Don't worry. I'll be careful." She seemed so sure, it would have been insulting to insist. Now, with the lumps in her sights, she betrays nothing. Neither shock nor disgust. Not even dismay. She passes me a fresh cutting; she's thoughtful enough to try to catch the longer strands before they fall to the floor.

I want to grip her by the shoulder. This doesn't faze you at all? You think this is normal?

I'm still recovering from the moment I spotted Joana in Vancouver's crowded airport two days ago when I arrived with Ross, my boyfriend. She was standing behind a railing in frayed jeans. She wore her hair in a bob, as she had when I'd last seen her back in January when she came to Toronto for a visit. But it was now more airy than sleek and a milder red, as if someone had turned up the orange. And though her eyes were still that fresh, bottomless blue, her face was misshapen and swollen. It was like looking through a mask to see her own much smaller face, far beneath. I wove through a throng of people, leaving Ross behind, and tapped her on the shoulder.

"Hey," I said. She smiled and the real Joana flashed through. I stepped forward to hug her. She stiffened.

"Careful."

I lightly circled my arms around her shoulders, trying not to notice whether my hands brushed over any tumours. I moved back and she looked at me.

"Anita, your hair!"

"I know," I said. "I got it cut off."

"Wow. You look so sophisticated."

"It was liberating," I said, showing off my neck.

I wonder how she felt seeing me march effortlessly through the airport, my health and strength intact. Sophisticated, she said. That's how I looked. But I was tired and rumpled from the flight, and, upon seeing her, even more rattled than when she'd told me a few weeks earlier that she had literally stopped breathing: two tumours in her neck were growing toward each other, cutting off her airway. She'd had emergency radiation, which seemed to have helped, but her breaths were still shallow and rasping. I would never have grouped myself among those who rush off to the salon after every fight with a boyfriend, every disappointment at work. Yet, there I was, in the face of Joana's latest disaster, freshly transformed.

Years from now, I will come across a book with the intriguing title *Big Hair: A Journey into the Transformation of Self*, by social anthropologist Grant McCracken. In it, I'll read that one of the weapons a woman puts to use in the face of upheaval is a new hairstyle. According to McCracken, this is "one of the ways they negotiate the endless succession of changes that make up even the most tranquil of contemporary lives: career shifts, marriages, births, divorces, retirements." No mention of watching close friends have it out with a persistent, escalating cancer.

Before I left Toronto, Joana told me that scar tissue from the radiation on her throat might eventually cause as much of a problem as the lumps themselves. Someday soon she might simply stop breathing. The air will have no way in. The kicker is, now that it has almost happened she isn't afraid to die. "It wasn't scary," she said on the phone. "It was really peaceful."

I'm glad she isn't scared, truly. But as she sits here so serenely in the salon chair, exuding her new willingness to "go" gracefully, I panic. Hurrah for grace. Fuck grace. I have to stop myself from abandoning my tidy arrangement of clippings and leaping up to shield her sore-addled head from the woman with the scissors: No, no! She isn't willing. She is afraid. You've got it all wrong.

Joana pulls the hair from the brush and lays them both side by side on the sun-yellow comforter. They wait there between us, the brush next to my leg, the hair next to hers. The apartment is quiet. Ross has gone with Rob to Safeway to buy Joana some Popsicles to soothe her throat: the tricolour kind that look like rocket ships.

I start pushing the hair around on the yellow fabric, smoothing it out, holding it to the light. The sun seems to give it life, the redness brightening strand by strand. I once heard that people used to create jewellery from the hair of the dead and wear it as a symbol of mourning. Our hair will outlive us, simply because it is already dead. How depressing is that?

"Imagine finding this in your brush every day for a month," I say.

"It won't last a month. It'll be long gone."

My eyes on hers answer, "This sucks." Hers reply, "You have no idea."

She looks into her lap. So do I, though I've been trying not to. Her legs are bare: she's been working up the energy to finish getting changed. We're going to Stepho's for dinner, their favourite Greek restaurant, and Joana wants to wear jeans. Her thighs are milky, dappled with orange. But these are no longer her legs. They're broom handles with skin.

I turn my eyes back to the hair in my hand. It just falls away. Lets go. When she lifts her head from the pillow in the morning, a tangled layer stays behind. It collects on her shoulders throughout the day. You don't feel it losing hold, she tells me, and then you look down at the brush and the bristles are full, or you absent-mindedly run a hand through your hair and discover a patch of baby-smooth scalp.

The year before we met, Joana won the regional speech competition with a presentation entitled "Being a Redhead," an honour that meant giving the speech in front of the board of trustees. In a photo from the event, wearing a lemon-yellow patterned dress that lent her a look of innocence as well as an air of maturity, she is gesturing, mid-sentence, to a particular member of the audience—a dour man in a suit who would have frightened me into shyness purely by his age and attire. But Joana's expression is almost sly, her posture playful and her presence palpable, even in that battered old print. She seems as classy and captivating as Julie Andrews in *The Sound of Music.* Stick her on a mountaintop. Give her a song.

I don't know what she wrote in that speech. Sitting here in her Vancouver bedroom, nine years into our friendship, four years into her life with cancer, I have yet to ask her what it's really like: having red hair. All I know is she once used Flirt, that '80s-era tinted mousse, and relished her few days of purple with an enthusiasm that shocked me. I had thought red was colour enough. There was also the time I sat down beside her in the cafeteria and asked what was wrong. She was quiet, deflated. She slid her yearbook toward me, flipped it open and showed me where some jerk had written, "Hey, Jo, is your hair red all over?"

"She was a redhead." One day I'll notice that's the first thing I ever tell anyone about my friend Joana. In my mind, that lost speech will contain everything she never told me, all the subjects we never got around to. In my early twenties I'll catch myself following a redheaded woman on Elgin Street in Ottawa: past the Courthouse, past the grey-black Bell Canada office building, past the formidable Lord Elgin Hotel, coming nearer and nearer to the National War Memorial that crowns the boulevard. Block after block, I'll be terrified the woman will sense she's being stalked; yet I'll want her to turn around, needing to see Joana, real or not—hallucination, visitation, whatever—propelled by a gale of questions blowing in too late.

Without my primary source, I'll be stuck combing books such as McCracken's *Big Hair* for answers. In it, he writes that we see redheads differently because they make up just two percent of the population: "There are just enough of them that they cannot be classified as freaks; but so few of them that we never really get used to them. They are always exceptional." He describes red hair as a "flag of warning" and a "potent symbol." The colour of the hair, people tend to believe, is the "temperature of the soul."

In the periodical databases, I'll turn up a 1988 *Seventeen* magazine article called "The Redhead Revealed," a lighthearted tour through the gruesome history of redheads, who were once routinely burned at the stake or buried alive and whose bodies were pillaged for their supposedly poisonous fat. "Red," I'll learn, was seen to equate with "loose." Egyptians buried ruddy-haired men alive.

All of which would have been news to Joana, too.

In my thirties, I'll go online, thinking idly how this was something Joana never really knew either—the Web—and scrounge around on the website Realm of Redheads, reading comments such as Kaicen's from 2004: "I can't say that I was or am really so different ... I have ten toes, eight fingers, two thumbs. [Red hair] gives me icebreakers for meeting new people and I feel sexy knowing I'm a rare species." And Jill's from 1999: "Please, do not say that I am attractive for a redhead, or that my white skin looks good on me ... Try, 'Your hair's what caught my attention, but I'm sure there [are] more wonderful things beneath the hair!'"

After hours of this, I'll decide that "sweetgirl's" cheeky 2004 posting comes nearest to what Joana felt: "I'm hot-tempered, stubborn, passionate, prone to fits of rage, self-centered, and [I] expect the world to revolve around me. Society has made me this way. If [people] had not made such a big deal about my hair colour and singled me out as 'special' because of it, I would be as well-adjusted and normal as any other human being in this world :)"

But I won't really know how Joana felt. I'll just be pretending. I'll have long before noticed in myself an ingrained preference for a certain fiery shade of red. And I'll find vindication in such unlikely places as a *Coronation Street* episode in which a character obsessed with Rita Hayworth displays some locks of hair belonging to his ex-wives, also redheads, and declares, "Neither quite pulled it off. Auburn and strawberry blonde. Not proper flame red, like Rita."

Here, in Joana's apartment, I don't know any of this yet. I've merely sat through enough John Hughes films—seen enough Molly Ringwald sticking it to the rich kids, defiantly creating her prom dress from scraps and mesmerizing bad boys, good guys, geeks, the lot, all while adorned with supercool, iron-red hair—to get another idea, an idea of redheads being less destructible than the rest of us. Less vulnerable to the hazards of life on earth.

"What are you going to do? About your hair, I mean."

"I don't know."

"It'll get worse. You'll lose more all the time. Bigger clumps."

"Great."

"But if you get it cut off, it's like 'Fuck it. I don't need it. Who cares?'"

There is a lineup outside Stepho's when we arrive. I'm ready to say we should go somewhere else but Joana just leans against the wall. I worry that her legs will give out. I can see them beneath her jeans, the denim billowing about their thinness like giant capes.

After an agitating fifteen-minute wait, we're led to our table. Joana pulls me aside and whispers a request. I walk to the washroom, enter a stall and hover above the toilet seat. Is it low, medium or high? I sit and stand, sit and stand, trying to imagine doing so with pipe cleaners for legs. Would

I make it back up? I plan for the day when we'll laugh about the night Joana turned me into her bathroom scout. I plan for it hard.

When I return to the table, they're all talking about how, tomorrow, we'll take the ferry to Victoria and spend the night. "And while we're there," I say, "we'll find someone to chop off your hair." I grin to indicate I'm joking. Half-joking.

"You're right," she says, without enthusiasm. But then Rob and Ross get involved and the four of us start to trash-talk her cancer the way we like to. Before the tzatziki and pita arrive, the haircut has become a ceremony, a battlefront; we'll all be there, weapons and jokes at the ready. By the time we get on to how tough she'll look, how skater-boy, and the effect she'll achieve with her blue paisley bandana and super-short, red-hot crop, everyone is convinced. It makes sense. It's the only way.

"Is it made of actual hair?" I ask Joana.

We're sitting in a narrow cubbyhole of a shop on East Pender Street in Chinatown. The walls are lined with faceless Styrofoam heads, some bald, others adorned with blue, brown, black, red and yellow wigs. Some curled, some straight. Spiked, piled, beehived. Long and shiny and far too real. A woman has marched into the back to fetch the one Joana ordered a couple of weeks back.

With all the talk of haircuts, I forgot she was buying a wig. We face a mirror. I look at my hair, which falls heavy and straight around my ears. It never occurred to me before: what do they use to make wigs? Where does the hair come from?

"I think it's a mix," says Joana. "Part synthetic."

"Really? Like what, polyester or something?"

"I don't know. The real ones are a lot more expensive. They last longer but—" She shrugs. I'm glad she doesn't finish the sentence.

"I'm having a weird thought."

"What else is new?"

"Seriously, they could have used your own hair."

Joana looks at me as if to say, "You're kidding." But I can't stop.

"Then it would be the exact right colour. What kind of red are they giving you?"

"Well they saw me. I told them I wanted it the same."

"Hmm."

"They said they'd do their best. I gave them a picture, too."

Now we're both worried. Way to go, Anita. Excellent work. The wig's arrival does nothing to lift our moods. It's meant to be put on from back to front, pulling the mesh cap snugly over the skull. Joana struggles with it. She's sore and tired and aware that the wig will fit more easily once her own hair is gone.

"It takes practice," the saleswoman says. "Don't worry."

The wig is a solid, dark red, slightly more metallic in colour than Joana's. It's a perfect bob with perfectly even bangs. I like it and hate it at the same time. I focus on the like side of the equation, going so far as to call it "perfect," asking myself why I suddenly think Joana is too fragile for the truth.

Seven years later, I'll find myself researching an article about Canada's foremost wigmaker, Donna Gliddon. She'll tell me the same thing about hair that the fictional version of Vermeer in Tracy Chevalier's novel *Girl With a Pearl Earring* tells his maid about the typical cloud: it appears white but contains greens and pinks and blues, purples, greys and yellows. Behold the secret to a fine wig. My hair qualifies as plain brown—"blech," says Gliddon—but even this is merely an illusion. It is in fact teeming with hues, some nutty, some woodsy. There is even, according to Gliddon, a "rich undertone of red." This startling information will come my way too late to bring it to Joana. It's one of those things that, once drawn to your attention, you can't imagine not having known before. Hair is many colours. It's so disgustingly obvious.

What would we have seen had we spread out a handful of Joana's hair? We'd have teased out all the softer reds, the pinks and unripe berries. There'd have been the browns—not so different from mine, just fewer and lighter. We might even have discovered, you never know, that her particular shade of red was laid over a dirty blonde base that lurked inside like a delicate secret.

The atmosphere in the shop is almost festive. Snip, snip. I watch each finger-full fall away.

Joana sits quietly and straight-backed in a blue plastic smock while Rob chats with the hairdresser about their favourite local restaurants. Meanwhile, Ross is squeezing in between chairs and fixtures to get a better angle with his camera, taking photographs as though we're on a weekend holiday: two young couples on the lookout for adventure.

Joana widens her eyes, flattens her palms against her oversized cheeks and shapes her lips into a shocked O. She is hamming it up. Ross focuses and clicks. Focuses and clicks.

Is this really so easy?

The stylist lifts her fingers through the partly chopped hair, causing it to muss. Sassy. Playful. A little gel and it'd graduate to chic. "It'll look good on you," she says. "Trust me."

Confessions of a Eulogist

Let death and exile and every other thing which appears dreadful be daily before your eyes; but most of all death: and you will never think of anything mean nor will you desire anything extravagantly.

—Epictetus, *The Encheiridion*

She grew up on a farm in southern Ontario, learned to drive on a tractor and always described the killing of chickens with horror and relish. She didn't like my father when they first met; loved to tell us he was boring, dry, an utter nerd. At the drive-in on their first date, she ate, to his astonishment, a hot dog, a bag of popcorn, pop, peanuts, and a bag of chips. On their second date, he asked what religion she was. "Thank God I answered Catholic," she always said of her response. "Otherwise he probably would have stopped the car and let me out." She gave birth to four children and never let any one of them forget the pain she endured—while giving birth, but also during all the anguish-filled parenting years that followed. She kicked smoking for twelve or thirteen years, then picked it up again in some sort of undefined rebellion. She was weepy, might have carried some gene responsible for the unlimited production of tears. She was Polish but hated making cabbage rolls, preferring a casserole that contained all the same ingredients, layered rather than tediously rolled. "It tastes the same. What's the difference?" she'd say, leaning into the counter, one hip raised, her milk-chocolate eyes flattering you, daring you to call her lazy.

I am walking on a paved path along the Ottawa River as these thoughts whirl. It's early June, a muggy evening. People bike, jog and rollerblade past me. This is the sort of normal, summery thing I imagine the people around me are doing: admiring nature, absorbing heat and sunlight. Nothing more complicated than moving or being still. I, meanwhile, have been composing a eulogy for my mother.

She is not dead. In fact, she's only fifty-one years old and relatively healthy. I'm beginning to think I am ill, however, caught in a morbid fantasy: If Mom dies, when Mom dies, what might I say about her at the funeral?

And it's not just Mom. One of my not-so-rare daydreams involves the death of someone close to me and the oratorical role I might play in marking his or her departure. My one living grandparent, my father, my siblings and a number of close friends have all been victimized on my morning jogs, in the dentist's chair, as I finger peaches at the local farmer's market, and of course those foggy, early-morning moments when I lie on my back in bed, not yet ready to rise.

Some days I think this may be grounds for some serious psychological excavation. We live in a society where death is hardly top of mind. Am I suffering from some affliction? A pathological desire to perform at funerals? I try to see it in more benign terms. There are people who can be counted on for certain things in times of mourning. The aunts and neighbours who bring casseroles. Those women in church basements everywhere, cutting up the tuna sandwiches to offer after the service. People who sing at the graveside, who bear the coffin, who listen intently and sympathetically to outpourings of grief. People who pray. Food, muscles, hugs, fresh Kleenex—these are all gifts people proffer to help their dear ones and themselves wrestle death. I am a eulogist. I bring words.

EULOGY ONE: THE FRIEND

It's my twenty-second birthday. My friend Joana Fraser and I have been napping in my snowed-in basement apartment in Toronto. We now sit, still somewhat groggy, in the dark living room, discussing where we should go for supper. I have the Yellow Pages open to the restaurant section.

Joana has been my closest friend since we met waiting for the school bus in the nearby suburb of Burlington during our first week of grade nine. She was the cheerful redhead who seemed to know everyone and who had already, somehow, personalized her Catholic high school uniform. I was the quiet one with slouching shoulders and dull, brown, wretchedly winged hair. We both wore glasses for distance and this somehow solidified things. That, or she was in need of a faithful listener. Within a week, I was in the living room of her mother's townhouse, being led through the pages of her parents' wedding album. (They were now divorced.) She introduced me to Billy Joel, Mr. Noodles with melted cheddar cheese, horoscopes, the delicate art of popping zits and good old-fashioned spontaneity, from dancing wildly in the living room to trying on all the clothes in your closet in different combinations.

We have been inseparable ever since, through high school, university, and her six-year ordeal with cancer. Well, until four months ago anyway, when in September 1993 she moved to Vancouver to be with her boyfriend. This is our first visit since then and I am trying not to notice how thin she is. She has always been beautiful but now seems translucent, lit from within. Her cheekbones, once masked beneath the roundness of her face, are delicate sculptures. Her navy eyes float above them like planets on a mobile. I could spin them around.

I can't think about supper. We talk about the treatment she's taking to augment chemotherapy, an extract from mistletoe that she injects to stimulate fighting cells against the hard tumours sprouting just beneath the skin all over her body. I can't believe she's giving herself needles. Remember, I prod, how afraid you used to be of swallowing pills? That ridiculous ordeal with the spoons and the juice?

"Yeah, that," she says. There's a pause. "It's come back, you know. I can't do it anymore. Well, I mean. I think I have a lump in my throat."

She looks at me and I look at her. I make a lame joke about hanging her from the ceiling so people can stand beneath her stomach to kiss. She laughs weakly.

I remember the fat phone book in my lap but can't bring myself to move it. Joana straightens her back and says something about elephants in the living room, how she needs to be able to talk about this stuff and I say OK, not knowing or wanting to know what I'm agreeing to. Then it happens. Her funeral, she instructs, should not be a depressing affair, because she hasn't had a depressing life. It's been good and full and she does not feel cheated. So there. No black. Spring flowers, she is saying. Tulips. Daisies. And that nice hymn, she thinks, about the sea and the sky. I know the one she means. And, Anita, I'd like you to write something for me. She slips it in. Somewhere around the tulips and the hymn. You don't have to read it yourself, if you don't think you can, but would you write it?

"Of course. Of course I'll read it myself."

"Well, you don't know, you might not—"

"I will."

I do not think to ask her any questions. I am too intent on making sure she understands I'm unfazed. Maybe I am shaken, but I don't stop to try to figure this out. I focus on not thinking at all. Therefore, I don't learn a thing. For example: What would she like me to say? Or not say? Why me?

This is how I come to be standing at the pulpit in St. Raphael's Catholic Church in Burlington, Ontario, before 450 people on the evening of May 4, 1994, six days after Joana's death, on the verge of delivering my first eulogy.

I have had little exposure to eulogies, or funerals for that matter. My uncle died when I was seven; I remember touching his cold, dead cheek, but of his funeral I recall nothing. My grandfather died last fall. His funeral was a high Catholic mass, said in Polish. I didn't understand a word of it. The only eulogy I've ever heard was for a boy I used to play with across the street who was hit by a car. The idea that someone other than the priest or minister would address those gathered in a church flabbergasted and impressed me. But I remember nothing of what was said.

One of the first things I think when her father calls to tell me the news is: OK, Anita, it's time to do that thing she asked. I buy myself a new notebook, a nicer, more expensive one than I've ever owned, a black spiral with thick pages and a wine-red textured cover. I make notes. I am single-minded, dogged, sure. If anyone can write about her, it's me.

I spend the days approaching the memorial in an underwater state, with moments of clarity and stillness occurring while I write, as though gripping a pen in my hand means I've come up for air. The motif for my speech: all the things I "learned" being friends with Joana. I don't know how I chose this theme but it seems to work: appropriate anecdotes emerge in my thoughts frequently and send me reaching—or running—for my notebook.

I know too little about this business to be daunted, am too green to be aware of what might go wrong, to consider jealousies, politics and family conflicts, and all the people I might neglect or offend. When the moment at the memorial comes, I approach the podium and heed some long-ago remembered instruction about public speaking: Look slightly over the heads of your listeners, never at their faces, and never, ever into an eye, no matter how tempting.

I open my mouth and the words resound, splashing through the church, one on top of the other. It's easy. Easier than it should be.

Almost instantly I have people laughing about Joana's obsessive admiration of Anne of Green Gables, her lack of organizational skills, her vanity, her ability to embrace her "geeky" side, even her specific instructions on how we should mark her death. I speak of her gumption and spirit, describe her exploding into dance on a crowded sidewalk, her refusal to let a nurse pronounce her name wrong. In what I will later see as a manifestation of denial, I insist on speaking of her in the present tense, an affectation I explain with one of those jokes meant to soften the edges: I know she's here. This is Joana we're talking about. As if she'd miss a party that's all about her.

I quote from her last journal entries. She had urged me to read them. In one of the entries, she describes "the most important thing in life," which, not earth-shatteringly, is rooted in love. She expresses her epiphany toward this understanding by referencing, without irony, a line from the movie City Slickers: "It's that one thing that Billy Crystal refers to—'that thing on the end of your finger that's the most important thing in life.' I remember watching that video and being perplexed. What could it be?"

I look up at the congregation and close with the following words. "I just want to say that of all the people in the world, only my friend Joana could take the most important thing she's learned in life and put it in the context of a blockbuster Hollywood film about some middle-aged men and some cows."

With that I step away. I have just spent several minutes talking about my best friend behind her back, or in front of her ghost, depending what you believe, to nearly every person she's ever known. I have praised her and poked fun at her. There is nothing left to do. Halfway to the pew, I break into gut-wrenching sobs. They smack against the walls of the silent church.

EULOGY HAZARD NUMBER ONE: FRESH-SQUEEZED GRIEF

Seven years pass after Joana's death. I am living in Ottawa, a twenty-nine-year-old journalist trying to transform herself into a poet and playwright. I have weathered other losses, recently delivered another eulogy, for my grandmother, and suspect the next funeral is not far off, for a middle-aged friend beginning to weaken in that now-familiar duel with cancer.

I realize that while those around me approach funerals with dread and the gritting of teeth, I can't hate them. I find them fascinating and have to consciously subdue my interest in the proceedings. It's the gash they tear into our everyday existence that I appreciate, how they force us out of complacency and routine. But it's more than this. I have borne losses through which funerals have helped me, and I think I know why. What are the patterns, the pieces of a funeral? There is music, of course, sometimes heady but often disappointing. There are prayers, in which I can't believe, try as I might. Then there are the usual Bible readings to do with, ho-hum, God's mercy, his promises to the righteous and faithful. But if the funeral includes a eulogy, there is a story. Story, for me, is a thing to revel in, even when it ends in sadness. Even when it's made of your own pain.

When attending a funeral, it's the eulogy for which I wait, and the lack of one that leaves me grasping. I begin to think that long-ago tribute to Joana whet my appetite, that she accidentally pinpointed my skill in mourning. Once I allow myself to indulge this theory, I find myself in the throes of discovering a new literary form—new to me, that is. And wildly, thrillingly different from any other I've tried.

The writing, giving and consuming of eulogies, which I begin to do voraciously of any printed examples I can find, seems a questionable pastime, particularly for a writer. The eulogy's definition alone—"speech or writing in praise of a person"—renders it suspect. Compare it to some more highly regarded forms of literature. A poem is a polished jewel and feels that way, rubbed and loved. A story is meticulously chipped into fine definition, like an aging profile from a blank-faced stone. A eulogy is a blurt. Sappy, incomplete and awkward, dripping love and exaggeration.

Though we all listen intently when a eulogy is being read, outside the funeral's insular circle of shock and grief the eulogy is held in popular disdain, slotted into that dangerous realm of touchy-feeliness. You won't find a Norton anthology of eulogies, nor a category for the eulogy in a broader volume. Death scholars either ignore it or abhor it. Typical is *The Funeral: Vestige or Value*, in which author Paul Irion mercilessly dissects American funeral customs, without neglecting the smallest detail. Except, that is, for eulogies. He mentions them only when he must and then only with desperate caution. He speaks of the "perfectly legitimate desire to avoid the pitfalls of lavish eulogies." After asserting that a funeral offers the chance to honour the deceased and his or her contributions, Irion quickly covers himself: "This does not necessarily require a glowing eulogy."

But Irion must suspect he's indirectly making a case for eulogies. Why else would he keep trying to convince us—and himself—that he's not? Irion tells us that according to anthropologists, there are three basic rites that must be carried out after a death: the rite of separation, the rite of transition and the rite of incorporation. There is no handy History of the Eulogy to tell us how, or how long ago, this particular mourning ritual began. Anthropologists and scholars have been far more concerned with what we do to a corpse—cremate, mummify, bury, dance around—than what we say to or about it. But I submit that, aside from being clearly rooted in the ancient practice of storytelling, one of the earliest ways we humans tried to make sense of our existence, the eulogy shows remarkable potential to serve each of Irion's rites and indeed stems from these necessary acts.

Separation is the cruel, initial jolt. This person was here and is suddenly, irrevocably gone. But on some level, particularly at first, this absence is not so different from that created when a person departs the room where some gathering has taken place—say, Thanksgiving dinner. The turkey is eaten; the table cleared. Aunt Martha says her goodbyes. Those who remain are now free to analyze Martha's contribution to the evening. We will say we were impressed by some witticism she uttered, alarmed at her treatment of Cousin Jeff, or once again shocked by her greedy consumption of stuffing. She made us laugh; she made us boil. Confused us, bored us, taught us something lovely.

This is what we do. We assess. We grope for our reactions to people when their presence is no longer here to weigh us down with vulnerability. The process is no different when a person dies, merely more urgent and utterly final. When the eulogist stands up to speak, it's as if she's saying, formally, officially: "It's OK, she's gone. We can talk now. Just us."

Once we begin speaking to one another in this way, we embark on the next rite: transition. Relationships change as we feel our way around this gap in our midst, explaining to one another what the life that once filled it meant to us. Our sentences stretch across the emptiness, fill it with new moments and shared thoughts. Like it or not, we adjust.

After Joana's memorial service, her father came to me, wrapped his big bear arms around me and said, "You're my new daughter now." These were words of uncorrupted grief, not entirely meaning what they said. Joana's father and I had a new reality to navigate and we found, at first, that speaking about Joana was the easiest way to do this. As the years passed, when we saw one another, we spoke more about ourselves, less about Joana. Our relationship evolved to the point where she became not an absence between us but a silent presence, solid and sure, made whole but unobtrusive by the earlier work we'd done.

Which leads us to the third rite: incorporation. That is, as Irion describes it, "incorporating the deceased into a new form of existence." This is not the business of the afterlife as some religions see it; this is memory work. I once heard the earnest and intelligent minister Brian Kopke, of the First Unitarian Church of Ottawa, eloquently describe, while presiding over a funeral, "our duty to memory." Our purpose here, said Kopke, rubbing his cropped beard, is to "build and solidify our memories so we can take them with us into our new lives" and in that way grant a friend a form of immortality. This may sound a degree too pat. And Kopke's voice does bear some of that suspicious breathlessness of the late-night, mush-hour, radio DJ. But his words made plain, psychological sense. Learning to replace a life force with memories, to live with this diminishment, is no easy task. Yet we must use memory, for we have nothing else, to transplant this person from physical space into our minds.

Such work is fraught with danger, for we become impatient. We think our memories, when they don't flow fast enough, have abandoned us. We also manipulate them into truths we prefer. After Joana died, I raged at myself for not being able to recall a single conversation with her. I saw scenes in my head, dozens of fragmented scenes: It's her sixteenth birthday, and we sit in a cool, damp crevice in the Niagara Escarpment. We are eighteen, standing in a dingy student co-op in downtown Toronto, surveying the dreary room we will share during our first year at university. We are standing together at a railing, wind whipping our hair, as we ride the ferry to Toronto's Centre Island for a rare afternoon in the park. These are painfully, infuriatingly, silent scenes in which I know we spoke—deeply, earnestly. In the days and months after her death, the temptation to fill in the blanks was nearly overwhelming.

No wonder then that an intellectual like Irion, trained in measured, passionless prose, would be wary of the eulogy. It gallops into our loneliness bearing on its back all the statements of comfort we could ask, all the fumbling admiration we might hold up to our lost companion. I shudder to think what Irion might have thought of Justin Trudeau's eulogy for his father after the former prime minister's death in the fall of 2000. Justin revealed to us, with a theatrical flourish, that his dad was a looming figure, a force to negotiate. He described himself and his siblings as "the luckiest kids in the world" with a father who "loved us with the passion and the devotion that encompassed his life."

Ugh! Cringe. Puke.

I loved it. The eulogy was not remarkably cohesive or beautifully written. Nor was it tempered with references to Pierre Trudeau's failings, of which there were many. (He was arrogant, a know-it-all, likely a workaholic, and so on.) It was emotionally naked, nothing more or less than an expression of love, minus inhibition, hesitation, checks, balances, or buts. You knew it was true, in that deeper sense—the soul's truth—by the way Justin dissolved into sobs when it was over, as if something had been removed from his centre, and he knew, finally, there was no getting it back.

For me, in the throes of such loss, the eulogy's more reserved cousins won't cut it. Consider the obituary: the chronicling of a life, anchored by educated but tempered guesses at its impact on some field of study or profession. And that's an obituary marking a so-called notable life: it is not even this much for the supposedly average among us. For most, obits simply list the date and manner of death, surviving family, and the place and time of the funeral. Perfectly practical, bland. The epitaph—pithy, sorrowful, sometimes witty, always carved in stone—wins hands down in the dignity department. But its brevity and habit of quoting literature and scripture can seem defensive, a holding back. The elegy, a verse of lament, is arguably as personal and unreserved as the eulogy and it might even achieve decent wallowing. But an elegy is a poem, as is its musical twin, the blues song, a status that lends these tributes credence and respect.

The eulogy is not after respect and neither are freshly skinned mourners. We are raw, and raw is what you get. This can result in beauty: thick, haunting, heavy. The sort that will bruise you.

Phyllis Theroux, a writer of magazine columns and children's books, is a rare public appreciator of the eulogy. In 1997, she edited *The Book of Eulogies*, an unabashed homage to the form. One of her more remarkable finds is by John Conrad Sr. about his son, who died at fourteen, having lived with a difficult disease called tuberous sclerosis. In his opening, Conrad asks, "How do you find any redeeming value to the life of a retarded boy who suffered from severe bizarre emotional problems?" When Conrad does uncover something redeeming in his son's life, you buy it and rejoice, because he took the hard way to find it. "In the end," he says, "we got nothing that we wanted in our child John and everything that we could ever have needed." You wonder to what extent Conrad wrote his way to this redemption.

Other gems include William Makepeace Thackeray rhapsodizing over Charlotte Brontë: "I remember the trembling little frame, the little hand, the great honest eyes." Philosopher Hannah Arendt laments poet W. H. Auden's demons, admitting she "found it difficult to understand fully what made him so miserable, so unable to do anything about the absurd circumstances that made everyday life so unbearable for him." Mark Twain wrestles with the loss of his daughter, and former slave Frederick Douglas lauds Abraham Lincoln (after taking him down a peg or two). Among these, many lesser-knowns are sketched by spouses, parents, children and friends. Revealed are broken hearts, failures, betrayals, swift but indelible moments, acts of red-eyed courage. Reading them gives a sense of the grand continuum, that fleeting taste of the greatness of life, and at its fringes the niggling, relentless reality of death. Author Richard Selzer writes of his mother, Gertrude: "When it came, that last breath, it was as though a lamp in whose circle I had lived all my life had been extinguished. Now I was free to live anywhere. In the dark."

Writing a eulogy is the real thing, honest-to-God "blast-it-out-sucky," a mantra a group of writers I meet with developed to describe our goal of not hedging on the first draft of a work. The idea is not to edit as you compose but to squeeze words from the elbow, the shin, the skull—dump it all on the page. You never know what might emerge. The eulogy forces this sort of honesty. No danger of your internal editor getting in the way—she's on shock holiday as you process this loss. And what time is there for revision? They've booked the venue, published the time and place in the newspaper.

There's bravado to this, a conscious choice to give yourself over unexamined, unsieved. That's one of Theroux's guilty delights in this form. "Eulogies are always double portraits … We are aware as much of the eulogist as the eulogized … we are given glimpses into the recesses of their minds and hearts that under ordinary circumstances are concealed."

After Joana's memorial service, I reprinted my eulogy on purple paper and pasted it into the fancy red journal. I didn't dare scan it. I feared almost immediately that rereading would reveal some syrupy crap that I had been blind to in the after-death shock.

I still avoid it, still fear what it may reveal. For rawness can also sting, like a scraped knee.

Three years before Justin Trudeau's tour de force, I rose very early one morning to watch the televised funeral of Princess Diana. I still can't shake the image of her brother, Earl Spencer, speaking so bitterly of the royal family, the media and the photographers who plagued his sister. He described the princess as "the most hunted person of the modern age," vowing to protect the souls of her sons from being "simply immersed by duty and tradition" and not permitted to "sing openly as you had planned." At the time I thought, better if he'd not spoken at all. Anger in grief I can accept, but what good does it do to spew it to the world? Yet a part of me understood his need to blast—in all directions—his rage at having lost his sister. And I've spoken to people who admired his outpouring. Good show, they said, finally let those royals and the predatory media have it. Much of the world, for better or worse, mourned Diana's death. If Earl Spencer ever evolves beyond his anger, he may recoil at the acidity of his words. And yet there may be something of value in the way he seethed. It certainly said more about human nature than most sociology textbooks. One hopes it was the beginning of letting go.

In the introduction to her anthology, Theroux raises what I've called a "blurt" to near glory. "The eulogist," she intones, "is the first person to step forward, in a formal way, to hold a lantern above the loss." And that little speech he or she offers, dangling above our stunned selves, "has a natural majesty."

"As a powerful container for human feeling, it may not be surpassed."

No one promises that the eulogy will be pleasant to listen to. Nor that it might be illuminating, articulate, transcendent or even interesting. This is death we're talking about, and, while death is the only truly reliable thing about our existence, it is seldom tidy and never predictable in the way it stomps through, nudging and knocking us about.

When the eulogist steps up to the lectern in the church, or wherever a funeral or memorial service is being held, the congregation sits stunned, eyes puffy, fists gripping balled tissues. I imagine they are thinking to themselves, "What can she possibly say that could mean a bloody thing in the face of this?" They are thinking: "Look how small and red-cheeked she is. Surely she's going to break down. That's the last thing I need to see right now."

Mostly they're thinking: "What on earth will come out of this one's mouth?" And why not, I ask myself, add suspense to the proceedings? Give us some uncertainty to steal our attention for a few thankful moments from the biggest certainty of all.

EULOGY TWO: THE GRANDMOTHER

Six years after Joana's death, my grandmother, Beatrice Lahey, known to all as Beat, succumbed to breast cancer. She was seventy-five years old, a wiry creature no taller than a nine-year-old girl. She lived in Cape Breton and I had grown particularly fond of her throughout my twenties, visiting several times from my home in Ottawa and relishing early mornings in the kitchen with her, drinking tea and flipping through the flimsy *Cape Breton Post*.

After she died, I travelled once more to the fishing village where she lived. For three days, I hovered as my father and his seven siblings wrestled with all the marginal decisions necessitated by death, details that seem to grip the forearm and twist the punishment of loss all the more tightly: who would sing which hymns, what rings would or wouldn't be buried with her, which grandsons had agreed to act as pallbearers, who else should be approached, and so on.

The absence of something (other than the familiar bemused exclamations of Beat) nagged. Halfway through the second day I understood. There had been, to my knowledge, no mention of a tribute of any kind, by anyone. I took my father aside. Eulogies, he told me, just weren't part of the norm around here. A funeral consisted of a Catholic mass followed by internment. Any thoughts to be expressed would emanate from the mouth of the priest.

This was long before I'd begun to examine the nature of the eulogy and my attraction to it. I was operating on instinct, troubled by the likelihood of my grandmother being sent off without a word to distinguish her life from the multitudes that passed each year, without some account of her own trials and triumphs and, most of all, her idiosyncrasies. But I was also keenly aware of my status here, as a usually absent Ontario relative. This woman had eight children who were, with dignity and restraint, orchestrating her send-off. Who was I to step in and suggest the traditional Catholic service wasn't enough? And yet, as the hours passed I was seized more strongly by the feeling that a failure to properly eulogize my grandmother would constitute a larger failure, not just against her but against life itself, those lives already extinguished as well as the mad pulsing that persists all around. It would be an act of neglect, that quaint Catholic concept known as a "sin of omission." And it would be mine. For I understood that not only did I desire an oral tribute to my grandmother, but if there was to be one, I would write and deliver it.

I knew that whether or not they felt it right and proper to include such a speech in the service, no one else would want the job. But there was more to my assumption of the eulogist's role than that. I believed this was my job, and that I would perform it admirably—indeed I might have hesitated to trust another in my place.

After Joana's memorial, people ranging from complete strangers to my mother had told me I was "so strong" for having delivered a eulogy. I was wary of this assumption. I did not feel strong. I was normal but for my grieving: I was still young enough to think loss the exception in life. And I did not think of myself as anything other than a person who had simply, in faithfulness, fulfilled the wish of a friend. But now here I was thinking perhaps I ought to do another, this time for a person who hadn't asked me to step forward and star in her show and for a group of mourners who didn't think it necessary; in fact, who hadn't thought of it at all.

Would my aunts, uncles and cousins, not to mention my own father, think I was claiming some right to Nan, trying to turn her event into my own? If one of them had made such an accusation, I couldn't have said with assurance that they were wrong. How far would I have to plunge to uncover my own motives? There was no time for such serious excavation; Nan would be buried in two days.

I decided the impulse ran deeper than the doubts. An exchange with my aunt, the wife of my father's brother, made some difference as I balanced and weighed. A friendly, polite woman, she is not one to speak her piece in a crowd. When we were out of earshot of the ever-present crowd in the kitchen, she smiled, gently whispering her reservations. "You do know it's going to make it sadder for everyone, don't you?"

At first I thought, yes, she's right: this is an imposition. And then I thought: Yes. It will make it sadder. And I nodded to myself. We should not, I decided, be left to wade through this moment untouched. If it be sadness that must gather for this woman, this death, then bring it on.

We say our goodbyes to Beat in a small wooden church facing the ocean. After the service the pallbearers will carry her body across the street to the narrow plot next to my grandfather's, at the back of the cemetery, on a moist, grassy patch overlooking the salty bay.

I sit gripping my folded speech, printed out from my cousin's computer just this morning. This one was difficult to write, perhaps because I agonized over my right to do it. Perhaps because I feared I didn't know her deeply. She wasn't my wisdom-sharing elder and we'd never had any truly heart- or mind-revealing talks. I asked myself whether I was embellishing when I wrote certain things, such as "Beat was one of the few adults I had known when I was growing up who didn't talk to me like a child—and whose presence didn't require censorship of the sometimes daring banter of youth." Did I really remember her this way or did I just want to?

But as I culled my memory and strung together anecdotes, a theme began to emerge that felt true, of a woman of habit and determination, who took comfort in small rituals and who had her own peculiar ways of doing things, from how she killed flies, addressing the pest before swatting it with satisfaction, to how she drank her tea, with Carnation condensed milk, the spoon always in the cup. Moments came to mind as I wrote, most not destined for the eulogy, from the times she'd shared her bed with me (she did not move at all in her sleep) to the times I'd seen her angry, worried, or frightened. In many respects, she had been frank about her feelings and her fears. I knew her more than I had thought.

Having learned this much, I almost feel, sitting in church as the funeral begins, as though my work, at least the part of it that concerns me, is over. The reading aloud will be something of an epilogue. At least, I think so until I stand up.

I falter somewhere on the first page, in the section about how as a child I'd come into the kitchen and she'd say good morning "just as if I were completely grown up." The tears well and I must stop. I lower my head, press my eyelids with a thumb and forefinger, shake it off. I get through the part about her love of solitaire and the many varieties she taught me, and how meticulously she would scratch her cherished Bingo lottery cards. But then I start talking about how small she was and yet still able to give a proper dressing-down to each of her seemingly gigantic adult sons. This story is meant to be funny and people do laugh, but she's down there in the coffin in front of me, never to be teased for being short again, never again to be crouched down to for a hug. I have to stop, breathe, squish my voice back into some stable shape.

And so it goes. With every characteristic and quirk I describe, every anecdote I share, it strikes full force that these are things of the past. There is nothing shocking about losing your elderly grandmother. Yet I'm breathless with the notion that this woman's life is over. She no longer resides in that little house on the hill to which we will soon return. This can't be! It simply can't. She was so real, so Beat, even a few days ago when I spoke to her on the phone.

I finish the speech but deliver the final lines in a thin voice. This is what I get for wishing to force this death down people's throats. It is thoroughly lodged in mine.

EULOGY HAZARD NUMBER TWO: THE AUDIENCE

I don't mean the audience itself is dangerous. It's the eulogist's response to having one that's a more likely cause for concern. A eulogy is an oral form, after all. And not everyone is good with oral.

As Theroux fondly remarks, eulogies are often delivered by "rank amateurs." These people are not accustomed to standing at a podium or opening their mouths to a room full of attentive faces. The prospect may terrify them. That's no fun to watch. Nor is uncontrolled sobbing. Many priests and ministers regard this possibility as they might a plague of locusts after God has promised one: They expect it—smugly, but with dread.

For her 1990 study, "The Acceptable Face of Human Grieving? The Clergy's Role in Managing Emotional Expression during Funerals," British sociologist Jenny Hockey found that British clergy, though they expressed a desire to lead funerals that offered some therapeutic value to mourners, greatly feared uncontrolled outpourings of emotion. One minister fretted over eulogists who cry, introducing "an upsetting thing to the service." Another described eulogists who "break down" as "embarrassing" for all.

Thank God I didn't know this before delivering those two eulogies. Was the priest, each time, back there wringing his hands while I spoke? As I wavered? Hard enough to deal with my own worries, let alone those of the man who's supposed to be lending some spiritual serenity to the proceedings.

Worse than nervous Nellies, in my opinion, are people with issues. People with issues are emboldened by microphones and audiences. They spend their lives waiting for such opportunities. I'm not knocking Mark Antony here. So what if his eulogy to Julius Caesar was a call to arms, an exploitation of the podium, of the vulnerability that death leaves in its wake. It was true. And it was breathtaking in that familiar but never ordinary Shakespearean way—

> My heart is in the coffin there with Caesar,
> And I must pause till it come back to me.

Everything—pain, love, our bizarre, futile existence—is crammed into that "pause." It heaves and breathes like a giant bear.

I once, as a reporter, attended the funeral of a man in Ottawa who had been chased by police and had, in his attempt to escape, drowned in the Rideau River. Wayne Johnson was black, the details surrounding the incident were foggy, and his death had followed other, similarly tragic incidents involving black men and local police. Much of the community was outraged, and the main speech at Johnson's funeral focused on that rage. I don't blame the man who spoke; perhaps his words were unavoidable, necessary, even welcome. But it seemed to me Johnson had died twice: first in rushing waters amid horrible circumstances, and then once more, by his absence at his own funeral.

The hijacking of eulogies with political rhetoric is nothing new. African American activist Amiri Baraka published an entire volume of eulogies a few years ago. In his foreword, Baraka describes the collection, which spans thirty years, as "a summing up of a period of history." But it is more than this. It is one attempt after another to summon the anger and energy of a people against injustice. Perhaps Baraka is wise; perhaps he knows the aftermath of a death is the best time to seed change. But his words seethe and boil, and his subjects drown beneath them: "Once again, we come together to mourn one of our fallen children. Today, another man-child slaughtered by imperialism. Again, a wanton bleeding of all of us, through our babies. These same babies we swore to transform the world to save!"

At least Baraka's preoccupation is about something larger than himself. Let's whip back to 10 BC, to meet Roman senator Quintus Lucretius. Lucretius is believed to be the man behind the famous—in classical scholarship, anyway—"Funeral Eulogy of Turia," in which he hardly gives his poor dead wife the chance to jump into his watery prose, never mind drown.

Lucretius speaks of his wife's character, but only from the perspective of how she fulfilled her duties to him. "Why should I mention your domestic virtues: your loyalty, obedience, affability, reasonableness, industry in working wool ..." Soon his speech is all Quintus: "You provided abundantly for my needs during my flight ... showing great ingenuity in deceiving the guards posted by our adversaries ... [Y]ou pronounced the words of the edict in a loud voice, so that it should be known who was the cause of my deadly perils ..." Reading this two millennia later is to sense Lucretius's relief—a palpable, bright yellow relief—at uttering these words. The eulogy has less to do with his wife than with having an audience to whom he can set the record straight about how he has been treated.

One longs for Turia to interrupt her husband: "No, no, you've got it all wrong." But the dead, of course, are speechless. And not listening. Somewhere beneath our sorrow—or other, less congenial emotions—we know this. And so we are graced with such liberties as those found in the "character sketch" written upon the death of Queen Anne by her childhood friend, Sarah, Duchess of Marlboro. It begins: "Queen Anne had a person and appearance not at all ungraceful, till she grew exceeding gross and corpulent." By line four, we encounter her "gloominess of soul" and "cloudiness of disposition."

I am not concerned about turning vicious or political on my dead; my passions lie elsewhere. I sometimes fear weeping before the crowd, as I came close to doing during my grandmother's eulogy, but this is not so bad an event as Hockey's clergy might suppose. Some mourners might take comfort to see they aren't alone with their sniffles and tight cheeks and that welling, that awful, tidal welling in the chest.

What I do fear is inappropriate enjoyment of the audience.

The life of a writer can be simplified as follows: pound keyboard in solitude, struggling over meaning and language, eventually (barely) meeting deadline. Enjoy brief respite, perhaps some praise from editor. Begin again. In between, attempt to convince some family member or casual acquaintance that days are spent in real toil, not lying on the couch sucking candies.

Seldom does this type of writer encounter a person who has read what she's written. Rarely does a writer witness the immediate reactions another may have to her words. She doesn't expect recognition. It was her choice to live this way. Yet she feels the absence of her readers like a black hole in her side.

Enter the eulogy, rare literature of the masses, heard by anyone and everyone, from bankers to bums, lawyers to jocks. Enter attentive listeners, criers, laughers. Here is intoxication, a room of people responding to your voice. Here is your chance to show them what you can do, to prove that you can be more articulate than you appear in real life, to assure them (and yourself) that words do matter. Here are people who may seldom buy books, who have perhaps never seen a literary magazine. Here may be members of your own family, seeing that, yes, Anita does do something with her time. Something useful. At last, it shows.

At last, too, the writer who must make her living at less-than-honourable tasks—for example, composing less-than-illuminating journalism—is thrust into a situation of urgency. She is looked to for wisdom and respite. For compassion and humour. For some glimmer of the ghost of a lost friend, spouse or child. How can she turn away from this naked need? How can she not be proud of her ability to meet it? Disgusted—yes—by her uncanny ability to use the death of a person she loved to make herself feel special, necessary, talented?

Alive.

EULOGY THREE: THE TEACHER

April 19, 2001. I walk through the neighbourhood thinking, in that familiar, dangerous way, of a friend who has until now been spared my morbidity. Her name is Diana Brebner and she is at what increasingly seems like the end of a ten-year relationship with cancer—the wrong end.

She lives nearby, on the eighth floor of an apartment building, with a view of what used to be a hospital and is now a demolition site. I slept at her apartment recently, a companion during a rough night. In the morning, as we sat by the window drinking coffee and eating toast with orange marmalade, she pointed to the half-destroyed building and described the meticulous process she'd been witnessing, of the piecing apart of this structure. Where most would see a godawful mess, Diana saw order and mastery. She liked to be in awe of things.

I met Diana two years ago, when her cancer was in remission. I had enrolled in her poetry workshop at our local bookstore. She became a mentor, then a friend. I could feel her that morning playing teacher again, guiding my gaze to those heaps of rubble.

She was forty-four years old, had written three books and raised two daughters. She gave a first impression of being proper, almost soft, but she was demanding, precise, fearless, unforgiving. Once, in a wild, poetry-inspired act, she left a mangled shopping cart on my lawn. Another time, in a moment I can only describe as transcendent, she sat in her winged-back chair wrapped in a white woolen blanket and told me that, through writing, she'd experienced something like "heaven on earth." How did she describe it? "Wow!"—a statement she used her entire face to pronounce: nose, eyes, lips and cheeks, all layered gracefully around that one syllable.

I "eulogized" my mother on a dusk-walk. Though unsettling, you might put this down to the waning of the day: an imaginative, introspective woman can loosen the hold on herself in fatigue or when the light passes by on an angle, revealing gaps between bricks and foliage, causing odd shadows. But this time it's morning and I'm not walking by the river, giving myself over to the rush of water. I'm on Wellington Street, my busy neighbourhood strip, as I construct Diana's fictional eulogy among buildings, traffic, noise, dust. The sun is not sinking; it blares. I pause at the demolition site, peer through the holes in the fence, try to see what she sees.

Nine days later, I am in a hospital room ringed with people, all of us looking wide-eyed at Diana. She is dead. I am not arrogant enough to think I've brought this on myself. I knew she was dying well before "composing" her eulogy. But I didn't know it the way you know you're hungry or know you've stubbed your toe. I knew it somewhere within that fluffy cloud we create for ourselves when we know death is imminent but are still, as Kubler-Ross stresses about all the dying and their loved ones, holding out for a miracle. Something in me shrinks from what I've done. I can say I was playing at my mother's "eulogy," since, barring a sudden accident, she seems a good, long road from her final days. But to let my mind go at such a delicate time, when a drop of juice, a cracker, a tear, might upset the balance between here and there? This shows a lack of diligence—a failing the high-minded Diana would disdain. What it feels like is betrayal.

Two days later is a meeting with the ministers, for friends and family, in someone's backyard. We are to tell stories, plan the service. The call goes out for participants, and the two Unitarian ministers, a bearded, soft-edged man and quiet, birdlike woman, glance around the table. I avoid their eyes. I have the feeling of pressing down an urge, but my friend's daughter speaks up. Good for her, I think. It's her place to do this, not mine. Besides, I am growing weary of the pattern that seems to be emerging, as though I now must reach this point of decision—to speak or not to speak—every time a person I love dies. I can let this woman depart without my two cents. Without having to consciously tell myself, "No. Keep it zipped."

The choice is not so tough, considering how impressed I am with this little meeting the ministers have called. Here they sit, pens poised over notebooks, scribbling as we talk. For three hours we talk. She was this; she was that. She said this, she said that. She did this and can you believe she did that? Of course, there is laughing and crying. Also, snickers, nose wrinkling, elbowed ribs, meaningful glances, the crunching of chips and carrot sticks. It's a cementing of bonds forged in recent days, as we sat vigil together, many of us having never met before.

People share stories when friends die. It's natural, instinctive. To do so with not only permission but urging from people you'd describe as spiritual leaders—well, that's something. That's grand, top 'o the world. I walk home that night smiling inside, thinking, yes, this is how it's done.

By all of us together. Not just me.

Eulogy Hazards Numbers Three and Four: False Gods and Forever

In her anthology *Readings for Remembrance*, Eleanour Munro writes, "Why human beings come together at all to mourn their dead is a deep unknown."

If you ask me, it's only a mystery most of the time. There are days and moments when such puzzles snap into clarity. In that blessed smidgen of time—before the monster of the cosmos, with a cough of foggy breath, blows the pieces back into a jumble—it all makes quiet sense.

I can point to one such moment in my life, a morning in late May 2000, less than a month after Beat's funeral and one year before Diana's.

I stand among multitudes in the one grand square in Ottawa, at the top of Elgin Street, starting up at the nation's haunting war memorial with its massive archway, beneath which horses gallop and soldiers trudge. The event is the interment of Canada's Unknown Soldier, whose remains have recently been shipped back from France.

Governor General Adrienne Clarkson is, in her regal manner, eulogizing this boy. She begins unremarkably, lamenting his early death, evoking the noble notion of dying for freedom. But she raises the bar, quoting Herodotus: "In peace, sons bury their fathers; in war, fathers bury their sons." There are spirits among us now: ancient writers, slain soldiers, broken fathers. She launches into a list of all the things we can't know about the life that once inhabited this body: "We do not know if he was a MacPherson or a Chartrand. He could have been a Kaminski or a Swiftarrow. We do not know if he was a father. We do not know if his mother or wife received that telegram—" Was he a Prairie boy? Did he have brown eyes? Read poetry? I am nearly swooning. The speech is shamelessly patriotic. She, or more likely her speechwriter, has patched in references to canoes, whales, the Rocky Mountains, even hockey. But underneath the carefully inclusive language thrums a scolding, a bald horror at the disappearance of this life. In itemizing our ignorance so particularly, Clarkson evokes every boy and girl, every thrashing vulnerability and failing of humanity. She breathes life into death, and—spectacularly, chillingly—inserts death into life. It's this perfect marriage of these two eternally opposed truths of our existence that a mourning ritual ought to accomplish. You'd think we'd get it right more often. We've been struggling with it long enough.

More and more, I think getting it right is a matter of honouring—as Clarkson managed to do with this anonymous casualty of war—that one, weird, pimply, bruised, struggling, aquamarine existence; the lone life that has passed. In so doing, we honour them all. But most of the time, this is not what we're trying to do. We are sorry, flailing, creatures; we aim lower. We make the requisite appearance at funerals, share a few hugs and memories, and turn away, back to work, back to "ordinary" life, temporarily shaken: It could have been my mother, my husband, my child. If the death is not too close, we try not to think on it too hard. The life and its end retreats into shadow.

What's worse is when the death is a direct hit. Now we aim higher. We're out for glory.

Neanderthals, as far back as 50,000 BC, buried their dead with provisions: food, weapons and other objects they might "need." The belief that something in us survives death and must continue to have needs also seems intrinsic to humanity. There are doctrines and anti-doctrines that contend death means annihilation but even their proponents follow rituals when a death occurs; even they vow to cultivate in memory something of the life that has passed.

There is narcissism in this, a deep-seated need not just for immortality. We want to live forever, yes, but to be special while we're at it. One of the most heartbreaking books to mess about in this quicksand of desire is American writer Annie Dillard's *For the Time Being*. True to form, Dillard spares us nothing, laying the brute facts across the page like indictments. For example: "There are 1,198,500,000 people alive now in China. To get a feel for what this means, simply take yourself—in all your singularity, importance, complexity, and love—and multiply by 1,198,500,000. See?

Nothing to it." Worse than the lives are the deaths: 164,000 a day, she reports, around the world. "Off they go," writes Dillard, "these many great and beloved people, as death subtracts them one by one ..."

Dillard winds me with magnitude, the crushing honesty of numbers. I take comfort, oddly, in Irion, Mr. Anti-Eulogy himself. It's a thrill to find him describing death, in *Vestige or Value*, as "an intensely personal thing ... as distinctly individual and personal as life." The eulogy may prod our memories, our relationships with fellow mourners, and may even offer insights into our own lives. But what matters is whether the eulogy accomplishes that separation from the crowd of lives and deaths that threatens to suffocate, render insignificant, this one—this one that matters to us.

Does this mean we must make this life out to be better than the other 163,999 that have ended today? One can only become flawless in death. The temptation to cast a glow of saintliness on a dead person is sometimes irresistible, a hold-over of superstition—we don't want no ghosts shaking their mighty fists at us—or our own desire not to be bad-mouthed after we're gone. There may also be an instinctive kindness at play. Is it fair to criticize a person who's beyond encountering any opportunity to improve or change? Once you're dead, as far as the living are concerned you're a finished product. What's the point of complaining about you now? You're not bothering us anymore. But it's more than all of this. We often need to elevate this lost person to something greater than your average human being. We told ourselves incessantly after Joana died that she had crammed more life into two decades than many are capable of in seven. What, other than her untimely death, gave us the right to believe this? But seven years later, I still can't shake the conviction. Nor will I allow that my grandmother was in any way typical. As I reported in my eulogy, she didn't bake cookies, didn't force food down anyone's throats, didn't pinch her grandkids' cheeks. She was different. This was my implication: she was more.

In the face of death, telling ourselves we've had something more matters. Make something bigger, better, and maybe it's easier to hang onto. I have a hardback called *Soldier of Conscience*, a slim, faded, grey volume containing a biography of and funeral addresses for Edward Perkins Clark. Clark died in 1903. His widow had published this vanity memorial within the year. He was a Brooklynite and, if you believe the solemn eulogies preserved here, a highly esteemed editorial writer for the *New York Evening Post*. The Reverend Joseph Dunn Burrell tells us Clark was a man who'd achieved "perfect sincerity" and that "whatever he wrote had upon it the mark of authority." By the time Burrell thanks God for the "privilege of knowing a man so upright, unselfish and loyal," I am looking for the catch. Perhaps he ate like a pig. Patronized his wife. Put too much pressure on his kids—or hardly knew them. I imagine these poor dears huddled in a pew, being force-fed all this praise about an indifferent father.

But I am also tempted to lift some of the quotes, particularly those relating to his prowess as a writer, to pass on to my spouse for possible inclusion in my own eulogy.

No wonder the form is greeted with so much suspicion. The worst can happen when people get up to speak: uncomfortable revelation, bitterness, lies, amateur preaching and long, unbearable speeches that have little to say about the person who's died. To allow it, if you are presiding over a service, is to surrender control. Roman Catholics do so begrudgingly, fearing length, inappropriate content and the eulogy's usurping of the real purpose of the funeral mass: to focus on a hope for resurrection. Muslims don't eulogize their dead; they recite prayers meant to ease the passage of the soul. Romani are not even supposed to utter the name of the person who's died, for fear of summoning the ghost. The book *In Memoriam: A Practical Guide to Planning a Memorial Service*, by Amanda Bennett and Terence Foley, describes various religious services marking death. The Eastern Orthodox priest quoted within is unforgiving regarding any method of personalizing death: "A memorial service isn't simply allowing the bereaved to do whatever they like. The event needs solemnity and mystery." The implication: If people weren't so spiritually lazy, so weak, they wouldn't need to harp on this person's life. They could let the dead go in peace.

French social historian Phillipe Ariès says we once managed exactly this, as a matter of course. He tracks, in the small 1973 volume *Western Attitudes toward Death: From the Middle Ages to the Present*, how we have turned mortality into a personal thing. Before the eleventh-century, he describes, death was "both familiar and near, evoking no great fear or awe." This is Ariès' favourite period. By the later Middle Ages, people were beginning to believe their fate at the Last Judgment would link back to how they had lived their lives. Death has been touched by the singular existence and Ariès' tone has begun to sour. By the sixteenth and seventeenth-centuries, this growing individualism manifests in a resurgence of grave-marking, and by the nineteenth-century, Ariès is aghast at the emergence of what he calls a "cult of memory," which has "conferred upon the dead a sort of immortality." It's a cult, he writes, that grows like gangbusters throughout the twentieth-century: "Those who no longer go to church still go to the cemetery … They meditate there, that is to say they evoke the dead person …"

Ariès emerges through his recounting of this evolution as a plagued soul. I picture him pacing through long nights, fretting over how we've forgotten how to die. I wonder what sort of epilogue he might write today, for, as individualistic baby boomers age and Western society in general takes less comfort in religious notions of afterlife, we have upped the ante on our personalization of death. Funeral homes market themselves on their ability to accommodate whatever quirky wishes people might have. Homemade mourning rituals are almost de rigueur. Nor is it uncommon to hear Elvis and Mick Jagger crooning in funeral parlours. Bristol-board or digital photo essays at wakes are a matter of course. And libraries are stocked with recently published guides on how to stage "creative" services.

These guides inevitably include tips, or entire chapters, on eulogies, for the eulogy is key to the individualization of death. It is "likely the place you want to spend most energy," writes Carolyn Pogue in *Language of the Heart: Rituals, Stories and Information about Death.* As Vancouver Anglican reverend Donald Grayston told the Canadian Press in an article in 1996: "To say someone is resting in Abraham's bosom, you can hear the little voices in people's heads saying 'Oh yeah, does he believe that?' But the common experiences that people share with the departed are something we can all agree on."

Well, maybe not always. As Theroux argues, "If the eulogist is wrong about the deceased, he or she can be quite right about a larger truth." With all respect to Ariès, there is a narrative of growth here. In spooking ourselves so profoundly, we have learned to appreciate every life that touches our own—to distill the moments that create and define who we are; to assert that each of the lives behind that evolution was important.

Of course, the working out of our memory muscles, making them bulge with the lives that have gone before us, can also constitute denial. Which is winning out, growth or fear? There is no place more apt for examining such questions than the Internet, our handy storm sewer for the modern psyche. "Google" the word "eulogy" and pages of links arise, many leading to sites where the texts of eulogies for famous people have been posted, including those for William Shakespeare and William Gilbert (of Gilbert and Sullivan). Mostly, personal homepages appear, where loved ones hardly so famous while living are given tribute. I visit the site memorializing Paul Dean Koontz, created by his daughter, Dianne Evans, which contains the eulogy she read at her father's funeral. Reading it, I learn that this man, an ordinary American who lived in El Dorado, Kansas, fought in World War II, made his living as a geologist, volunteered for the Boy Scouts and bribed his softball-playing daughter with the promise of one silver dollar for each home run she hit.

On other websites I become acquainted with the "elf woman" Margaret Nygard, who died in 1975 and apparently single-handedly saved the Eno River in central North Carolina from unchecked development; Dr. Anthony Dipple, whose son remembers asking him for an explanation of "the Coriolis effect" and receiving a long lesson that somehow connected to Einstein's Theory of Relativity; and Gerry Yablans, who jogged 25 thousand miles over a twenty-year period. I am partial to Bucky Walker, who, orphaned as a teenager, "struggled to make some sense of life," sometimes succeeding and sometimes failing. He "loved to hunt, but didn't have the heart to kill anything." He died at forty-two.

Most of these online eulogies are neither profound nor well written. Many are as empty as a Hallmark card. But I have to force myself to stop clicking. In enough of them to keep me coming back for more, details leap out, wearing the badge of personality, hinting at that fascinating string of events, which can never be duplicated, that make up a life.

Yet I worry. To what extent are these tributes changing the nature of the eulogy? A eulogy, traditionally, is a moment in time. What matters is the speaking of the words aloud at a designated event. On the Internet, this event—and that initial unwillingness to let go—can go on, and on, and on. The sheer number of online souls is unsettling. At the Virtual Memorial Garden (catless.ncl.ac.uk/ VMG/) mourners can, for no cost, post eulogies and messages to dead loved ones. At forevernetwork.com[1], run by the Hollywood Cemetery in California, more elaborate tribute pages can be purchased. The "Diamond Biography," for example, at $995 US, contains twenty-five photos, twenty-five recorded audio descriptions, two videos, an "interactive media scrapbook" and a six-hundred-word biography. The website promises "permanent preservation" (suggesting the company will never fold, change its business plan, or remove your husband from its archives once you are too dead to notice). Speech-writers.com, meanwhile, sells stock eulogies for twenty-five dollars, offering a "selection of suitable" texts for children, mothers, fathers, colleagues, siblings, grandparents, or "friends and neighbours." For $275 and the time it takes to fill out a questionnaire, you can buy a "personalized" eulogy, running about three minutes. "What connection do you have with the deceased and why are you speaking?" "Name a particular habit of the deceased, i.e. he/ she was a great amateur actor/ dancer." Buyers are warned to remember that "it is content rather than length that is important."

I shouldn't wrinkle my nose; we're not all comfortable with our writing skills, particularly in the wake of a death. But this is not fast food or hotel management, where some argument can be made for uniform quality. There's no getting away from the fact that a eulogy is written in haste, by someone in the grip of unfiltered emotions. That is part of its charm and its intrinsic value. Even when it fails, even when it sanctifies. How else can we see who we are, what we must try to overcome?

Not all is lost, for there are also promising changes in the way we eulogize. Along the way, we have begun to learn the power of honest portrayal. Not: he was good or he was bad. Simply: he was like this. A piece in the *L.A. Times* a few years ago concluded that the best eulogies don't shy away from darkness. It quoted sportscaster Bob Costas, who refused to offer praise alone when "eulogizing" Mickey Mantle, who had been a reformed alcoholic. "I felt that if I didn't in some way acknowledge the complexity of his character—the flaws as well as the more appealing parts of him—then the appreciation would sound just like hero worship. The facts of his life did not render untrue what was magnificent about him. If anything, they made it more poignant."

Costas alluded to Mantle's "flaws." He didn't run down the list. He didn't name one. This, to my mind, was enough. It was also a relief. Nobody's perfect and we ought to acknowledge that, or a eulogy may grate. But I rail against the warts-and-all philosophy. Who are we to judge these people, deciding which faults we ought to scrutinize alongside their virtues—indeed, deciding which are faults or virtues? We are well aware we're all imperfect. Must a eulogy drive this home? Why not let a person's few most remarkable or weird or interesting or funny qualities shine, untarnished, just this once?

A friend of mine, Rod Charles, who recently eulogized his father—himself a United Church minister who'd eulogized hundreds—shared with me his philosophy, learned from his dad, of honouring the dead. "You focus on the one attribute this person had that everyone would know, would have felt. Find that one telling thing, the thing they did better than anyone. There is always something to admire and appreciate." Rod compared his eulogy to his father to a practice he had taken of laying blankets over him in the hospital when he was ill. "It's nothing really, I just wanted to do something for the guy. That's what it was. It was the last thing I would say to him; a warm blanket I was putting over him in the church."

His father was dead, gone. He had no more need of blankets. But that's not the point. In *Giving Sorrow Words: How to Cope with Grief and Get on with Your Life*, by Candy Lightner (founder of Mothers Against Drunk Driving) and Nancy Hathaway, a woman explains why she spoke at her niece's funeral. It was a simple eulogy. She shared how they became friends "over a box of crayons," how the girl liked gruesome movies, and she described some time they had spent together. What mattered was saying anything at all. "I was glad I spoke because most of the time nobody wants to hear you talk about someone who's dead. It was a relief to say this is why I loved her; this is why I'm going to miss her so much."

There must be something to respect here. Not all religions are sour on eulogies. Baptists, unless ultra-conservative, allow eulogies, as do Mormons and Methodists. Unitarians build the entire funeral service around memorializing the deceased. Some Buddhists believe proper remembrance aids the soul's rebirth. And Judaism, bless it, doesn't just allow eulogizing; it is a prescribed part of the funeral. If a Jewish funeral took place without a eulogy, one rabbi tells me, "the people attending the service would be amazed."

EULOGY THREE, TAKE TWO

She had short brown hair and rosy cheeks. Grew up in the suburbs; a bookworm, a ballplayer and a clumsy, earnest child. She loved to swim, dreamt of living by the ocean, in dense fog. She thought too much, analyzed her impulses and actions to death. Friends and family counted on her, considered her reliable, steady. The responsible one. She absorbed this impression of herself, tried to live up to it. When she failed, she would lie awake at night, replaying situations in her mind, asking herself why she'd made the decision she did. Why she'd faltered.

Chickened out.

The service for Diana, two nights after our wonderful, uplifting meeting with the ministers, is difficult to sit through. Her daughter has decided she's not able to speak—perfectly understandable. Nobody else volunteered and so the main eulogy is delivered by one of the ministers. She puts forth a valiant effort to relate our sentiments and anecdotes, weaving them around a loose biographical sketch, including all the facets she can of this woman's life and character. But the thing echoes flat and empty. As this is a Unitarian memorial service, containing no mass nor any religious content, we are left with little, certainly nothing with the power to draw us in, rub us against the brutal truth of Diana's death. I leave the church thinking I would have welcomed "Be Not Afraid" or some equally maudlin but appropriately soul-piercing hymn.

Not long after, on a visit to Toronto, I talk with writer Rick Salutin, who has given many eulogies and also dutifully writes about deceased friends in his *Globe and Mail* column. This might seem touching but Salutin is hardly some huggable rag doll. When I ask what he thinks a eulogy should accomplish, he glares from beneath his columnists' slouch. "It's bullshit, really. You try to say something intelligent and insightful. There's no way it can be comprehensive. Anybody who thinks they can sum up the essence of another person … I don't think there is any such thing. It's completely about you. It's what strikes you about this person."

That's what was missing. The kind, thoughtful minister was faithful to everything she was told and that was the problem. What she did, with the best of intentions, was try to sum up—and Salutin is right, this is impossible. I'm reminded of how Theroux describes eulogies as "double portraits." What I begin to think they are, at least the way I do them, is a window onto a relationship. And it's through staring down that relationship that those listening might begin to understand or at least examine their own relationship with the person who's died. For it's not just a person we mourn, it's that particular thing they were to us.

Things crystallize back in Ottawa, when I meet with Susan Brown, a funeral director for Tubman Funeral Homes. Brown wears her brown hair straight and, on her face, a perpetual expression of concern. She folds her hands on the table as we talk. I ask this woman, who's witnessed scores of funerals, what eulogists have in common. I am hoping for characteristics. Perhaps, she will say, eulogists are people who tend to observe more than interact. They are not afraid to talk about death. They are, by definition, witnesses. Storytellers. People seeking answers. I recall a habit I developed in high school of keeping a notebook that contained brief character sketches of all my friends. Just what did this portend?

But Brown is a practical woman in a navy suit who sees a lot of death, doesn't just daydream about it. More important than character traits, she guesses, is a person's relationship to the deceased: "Individuals who are able to get up and speak are very clear on what their emotions and thoughts are toward this individual." Brown is less worried about who says the eulogy than what good ones tend to accomplish. For starters, they give people something to talk about. "We realize nobody wants to be here. It's one of the saddest occasions and one of the most stressful of our lives. And everyone's afraid of saying the wrong thing. It opens that door for people to step forward and say, 'You know, I really appreciate what Bob said about Bill. It was so true and it made me remember a story about …' It opens up those gates." That's no small feat. Brown describes grief as a thing of shifting balance: it begins in overpowering sadness, with emotion that is gradually balanced by pleasant memory. "At the time of the service," she explains, "the weight of grief is physically on everybody's shoulders and heart. The eulogy is like a hook coming out of the sky, hooking into some of that grief and starting to alleviate some of the weight."

That is all a eulogy is. A hook. A hook that you fashion out of your experience. It might be heavy or light or sharp or barbed or rusted or packed with bait. I have been afraid of reducing the people whose lives have affected me deeply to words, forgetting that words are nothing more than a tool. They can't take over a life, merely tattoo it.

And what of these false eulogies I compose for the living? Am I really "practicing" for their deaths? It's not so bald as that. These are pop quizzes I spring on myself, demanding answers: Am I paying enough attention? Am I really seeing this person I care for—appreciating and absorbing her with all the scrutiny and openness she deserves? If she were gone, what might I tell you about her? What could I tell myself?

I open my wine-red journal and read my eulogy to Joana. It is shamelessly enthusiastic but not so bad as I feared: playful and honest, neither sappy nor mean. What strikes me more than the eulogy itself are two comments I wrote outside of it. The first, in glaring red ink and circled amid rough notes for the speech, reads, "Maybe it should be about what I've learned, so everyone can leave thinking about what Joana taught them." The other was written four days after the service, addressed directly to Joana: "I need to thank you for asking me to write something for your memorial. It was a task that kept me up and positive and close to you last week."

So. It's for them. And it's for me. And it's for her. And it seems to work. Why be stingy with any of us at a time like this?

I sit down to write. There will be a second service for Diana, a public memorial, in just a few days. I see this as a second chance. This time I will blast out my admiration and affection for her, scatter it beneath the light for people to examine, to catch in their palms, to consider and question and compare with their own.[2]

EULOGY FOUR: THE LISTENER

I am not the only one who decides to speak at Diana's memorial service. We do it the way it ought to be done, telling tales about her as a teacher, a friend, a mother—sharing the now-precious thoughts and moments she left us with. For that brief hour we feel her among us. We return to our lives rejuvenated, braced for her absence.

About a month later, I receive a devastating phone call. For several moments I stand motionless, saying into the receiver, "Oh my God, I can't believe it. I can't believe it." For a friend is telling me that Diana's younger daughter, Anya, sixteen years old, has been struck by a bolt of lightening. She is dead, leaving her father and sister, a family cut by half in the space of eight weeks—leaving all of us gasping, reeling, unable to voice that unanswerable question: Why?

Again, as in some surreal sitcom, we enact the motions of funeral preparation, meeting with the same ministers, in the same backyard of the same friend. I didn't know Anya well enough to puzzle over my role. I am here to lend what meagre support I can to her father, sister and those close to me who watched her grow up and saw her as one of their own. My job is clear this time: not to bring my own words but to listen to theirs. It's a relief to see that I do know my place—the only relief to be had in these blinding days.

One morning shortly after Anya's funeral I'm on the phone with my younger brother, Matt. He is twenty, bulky and manly, but not so different from the uncommonly wise four-year-old I used to ferry to the park every day after school. He speaks softly. He too is mourning a friend, a victim of one of those crimes we helplessly call a "random act" of violence. Death, I feel, is coming at us from all sides—it will do this; it is ever-present but rarely does it hit the same targets so consistently. Matt and I compare notes on the funerals, the only tangible things we have on which to dwell.

Anya, like her mother, was Unitarian. Her service was bookended with music she liked, involved a vegetable plant exchange (she preferred "practical" plants to flowers) and was packed with tributes and eulogies: one by the minister, who knew her well, one by her father, another by her sister, and many remembrances shared by friends during something of an open-mic session. I listened, entranced, as the pieces of her person, the various translations and interpretations of her life, melded together into a whole being—not exactly her, but pretty darn close. Her wit was biting and inventive. Yes, I had experienced this. Her favourite spot in the house was the back roof over the kitchen. She would absorb any new situation fully, at her leisure, before engaging. This made her appear timid but she was not. She had recently written a precocious note to herself about how to live life as a work of art.

My brother's friend, meanwhile, was sent off with an old-fashioned Catholic mass, containing neither a eulogy nor any other representation of his character. Matt has little to say on the subject except, "It's like they're trying to make them all the same."

Sadly, but also magically, I knew Anya better after her death. This was the power of words, a mystery I was grateful to absorb, for we were superbly fragile that day. Nothing but story, our own narratives, could keep us intact. I was buoyed to see what we are capable of in sorrow, what simple eulogies can achieve: that gentle nudging, massaging—even removal—of the raw, outer layers of grief. How words can keep a soul aloft, hovering above the multitudes, long enough for us all to have that last, blurry, merciful look.

END NOTES

[1]Since this essay was first published the site has changed to hollywoodforever.com/stories, and the trademarked service is called "LifeStories." A basic memorial consisting of a photograph and 100-word text is described as "free," while the charges for more elaborate memorials are no longer outlined on the site.

[2]That eulogy, later published in *The New Quarterly*, is reprinted here, as the opening piece in this collection.

The Last Ka-Ching:

My Dad the Cash Register Man

This summer, Dad sent me and my three siblings a brief email. It began, "Guys, just thought I'd let you all know that the transfer of the business was finalized today." The note did not allude to the preceding months of limbo, nor the decades of labour that had come down to this exchange of paperwork and modest cheque. Dad signed off with characteristic understatement: "I guess it will be a bit of a change."

I was four years old and Dad thirty-two when he quit his job at National Cash Register to open his own business with his friend Wayne Puffer. On Saturdays, they'd go door to door, drumming up clients in towns like Acton and Georgetown. It was a brave move. We lived simply, in a split-level in Burlington. My sister, kid number three, had just been born. Mom had yet to take up one of her many jobs; cash flow was entirely up to Dad. But how could he have known when he signed the incorporation papers for Century Cash Register that the heyday of the sturdy, mathematical machines he could so deftly dismantle and reassemble would run out before the century itself, a demise in lockstep with that of rotary phones and typewriters?

Dad spent his days criss-crossing the GTA, un-sticking cash drawers, delivering receipt paper rolls and loosening seized-up gears. His briefcase was stocked with screwdrivers, rags and carbon-paper sales slips, his fingertips stained purple from untwisting tangled ribbons. He was on call even on Christmas Eve and Boxing Day, the most alarming days of the year for a shopkeeper's sales equipment to break down. Sandy Lahey to the rescue! He sold machines to pizza parlours and libraries, gardening centres and bakeries. CNE vendors. Drug store chains. The legendary Organ Grinder restaurant. A nudist camp near Milton (which caused some marital upset at home after dad sent my brother Sean there on a repair call). I had my own favourite clients, including Chudleigh's apple farm, where we'd go to pick bushels of McIntoshes and then spend a joyful afternoon in the play barn. Other kids partook of these pleasures, but their dads hadn't supplied the machines that would ring up the tally before everyone went home, laden with fruit and pies.

I was the daughter of a cash register man, deeply proud of the role my father played in the workings of local commerce. The perks were all right, too. We took Sunday drives to a pretty country store in Campbellville, where the owner, Dad's client, would scoop extra ice cream into our cones. And at home we got to play "corner store" on a real register. Our 1923 NCR model 852 had a big, round belly lined with accordion-style buttons. I can still feel the pleasure of pressing "total" to enact that ka-ching! The pop and clink of its cash-filled drawer. Life in our house was punctuated by these triumphant, mechanical sounds.

Saturday mornings, Sean, Wayne's son Wes and I were paid piecework for cutting up tiny squares of paper with such words as "pop," "milk" and "candy" typed on them. We'd fit these into key caps, snap the keys into brand new Becker's machines and slap a silver Century Cash sticker on the back. After racing to see who could do the most, we'd walk to a nearby burger joint for lunch and tabletop Pac-Man. Before I got my first retail job, I knew a handy secret: under the machine was a hidden lever that, if flipped, would open a cash drawer when power failed.

Century Cash was never a giant. At its height in the late eighties, the company employed twelve people, my brother included, and afforded us decent family holidays. When computers hit retail full force in the late nineties, business began to shrink. Mom would hint that money was tight. Dad sometimes looked tired, defeated. He'd shrug and say, "Business isn't what it was."

One morning, when I was home from university, I shyly asked if I could tag along on some calls for the first time ever. "Let's go," he said. First stop Lloyd's Variety in Hamilton, due south on Kenilworth from Dofasco. Inside, the ceiling sagged. Stuffed toys swung over shelves stocked with chips, toothpicks, Minute Rice. Lloyd himself seemed part of the jumble, like a box of salt mixed in with the Murphy's Oil. A former steel-plant worker, Lloyd was one of Century Cash's first customers. While Dad opened the register and went at its insides, Lloyd chatted with a succession of tobacco-stained men who'd come in for copies of the *Racing Form*—relics, all. Dad seemed completely at home amid this steady exchange of goods and gossip, yet there was a kind of solitude in the movement of his hands and the concentration of his gaze, a private space occupied by him and the machine.

That is how I see my father: a register dismantled all around him, like a worried scientist in his lab. To imagine him retired is difficult. He's not there yet: so far he's keeping on with the company that bought him out—he's the only guy around who can fix the old-fashioned registers some small-scale clients hang onto. The ink disappeared from his hands years back, when cartridges replaced ribbons. Such changes crept in over decades, some of them minor shifts, others revolutionary.

It's not lost on me that, like him, I've pursued a dicey path. I work for print publications that are beginning to seem as clunky and quaint as old cash registers. It comes to seem reckless. I ask myself how I'll survive if the space I occupy in the world alters so irrevocably as to disappear. But mostly I just do what I do: as with that noisier, more tactile era that we rode with Dad to its very closing, a way of life is never gone until it's gone.

ACKNOWLEDGEMENTS

I am grateful to the editors of the publications where these pieces first appeared, to Dawn Kresan at Palimpsest Press for providing the work this new home, and to Carmine Starnino for encouraging me to collect them here—and for, as ever, his friendship, his patience, his dedication to the cause and his sharp editorial eye. Thank you, also, to Aimée Parent Dunn for a thoughtful and thorough copy edit. Thank you to Matthew Holmes for leading me to Dorothy Roberts and for injecting the necessary gumption into our editorial efforts at *Arc Poetry Magazine.* I am grateful to all the board members, colleagues and readers whose collaboration made the years at *Arc* so rewarding, and to Pauline Conley in particular for more than I can begin to articulate. I feel privileged to include here, among my own, the words of all those who participated in the enclosed interviews and discussions; their ideas and insights enrich the scope of this collection. I owe a weighty debt of gratitude to John Barton for nudging me toward criticism (and *Arc*!) and for ongoing friendship and editorial guidance; and another of equal heft to Moira Farr, for shepherding me through my consideration of the eulogy and for reminding me at the necessary moment, with the warmth and conviction that accompany all her offerings of wisdom, that being a reader matters. I'm grateful to the other staff and participants in the Creative Non-fiction and Cultural Journalism Program at the Banff Centre for the Arts in 2001 (where the piece on eulogies was crafted), to the relatives who welcomed me so unreservedly in Poland in 2005, and to all those whose stories I've attempted to pass on to readers, especially Sandy Lahey, the late Joana Fraser and the late Diana Brebner. Thank you to my fellow poets for forging trails in so many enticing directions, and to all our fellow readers for picking them up.

PUBLICATION ACKNOWLEDGEMENTS

"Diana and the Mystery Shopping Cart" first appeared in *The New Quarterly* vol. XXI (2001), reprinted by permission of the author.

'Her time on earth'

"Dazzling Exile: The Poetry of Dorothy Roberts" first appeared in *Arc Poetry Magazine* vol. 58 (2007), reprinted by permission of the author.

"Hide and Seek: Looking for the Real Gwendolyn MacEwen" first appeared in *Canadian Notes and Queries* (2009), reprinted by permission of the author.

"'An intelligent search': On Three Late Collections by P. K. Page" first appeared in *The Malahat Review* 173 (2010), reprinted by permission of the author.

'Things we hardly feel we own'

"Poets on the Mat" first appeared in *The New Quarterly* 126 (2013), reprinted by permission of the author.

"Nothing too small to say: In Conversation with M. Travis Lane" first appeared in *The Malahat Review* 180 (2012), reprinted by permission of the author.

"All the bounty of the Lord made manifest" first appeared in *QuArc*, a joint issue of *The New Quarterly* and *Arc Poetry Magazine* (2011), reprinted by permission of the author.

"On the Probability of Happiness: with Kim Jernigan and Alice Munro" first appeared in *QuArc*, a joint issue of *The New Quarterly* and *Arc Poetry Magazine* (2011), reprinted by permission of the author.

"The Lure of the Gallery Wall: with Stephanie Bolster and John Barton" first appeared in *Arc Poetry Annual* 2011, reprinted by permission of the author.

A Little Nibble Before Writing: Reviews, 2001-2006

"Anne Simpson's *The Marram Grass: Poetry & Otherness*" first appeared in *The Malahat Review* 169 (2009), reprinted by permission of the author.

"Robin Skelton's Last Poems" first appeared in *The Malahat Review* 160 (2007), reprinted by permission of the author.

"Oana Avasilichioaei, *Abandon*, and her translation of Nichita Stănescu's Occupational Sickness" first appeared in *The Malahat Review* 158 (2007), reprinted by permission of the author.

"Lynn Davies, *Where Sound Pools*" first appeared in *The Malahat Review* 155 (2006), reprinted by permission of the author.

"Catherine Owen, *The Wrecks of Eden*" first appeared in *The Malahat Review* 146 (2004), reprinted by permission of the author.

"Susan Glickman, *Running in Prospect Cemetery*" first appeared in *The Malahat Review* 149 (2004), reprinted by permission of the author.

Short Reviews and Notes from Arc Poetry Magazine

Review of Triny Finlays first appeared in *Arc* 53 (2004), reprinted by permission of the author.

Review of Alison Pick first appeared in *Arc* 52 (2004), reprinted by permission of the author.

Review of Carla Funk first appeared in *Arc* 51 (2003), reprinted by permission of the author.

Review of Susan Gillis first appeared in *Arc* 49 (2002), reprinted by permission of the author.

Review of Sue Sinclair first appeared in *Arc* 48 (2002), reprinted by permission of the author.

Review of S. D. Johnson first appeared in *Arc* 47 (2001), reprinted by permission of the author.

Sharon McCartney first appeared in Arc 46 (2001), reprinted by permission of the author.

Shawna Lemay first appeared in Arc 46 (2001), reprinted by permission of the author.

Notes from *Arc Poetry Magazine* (2004-2011), reprinted by permission of the author.

The real ones are more expensive

"Poland's Hereafter" first appeared in *Maisonneuve* No. 19 (2006), reprinted by permission of the author.

"How to Be Friends With a Redhead" first appeared in *Maisonneuve* No. 22 (2007), reprinted by permission of the author.

"Confessions of a Eulogist" was completed at the Banff Centre for the Arts, 2001, Literary and Cultural Journalism. Published in the anthology *Word Carving: The Craft of Literary Journalism* (Banff, AB: Banff Centre Press 2003), reprinted by permission of the author.

"The Last Ka-Ching: My Dad the Cash Register Man" first appeared in *Toronto Life* (December 2010), reprinted by permission of the author.